William Strachey
1572-1621

WILLIAM STRACHEY
1572-1621

S. G. CULLIFORD
Victoria University of
Wellington

The University Press of Virginia
Charlottesville

Foreword

William Strachey, 1572–1621 was first written as a dissertation for the degree of Doctor of Philosophy of the University of London. The work was made possible by the award of a postgraduate scholarship by the University of New Zealand and was carried out under the supervision of Professor C. J. Sisson, at the time Lord Northcliffe Professor of English at University College, London.

In its present form the biography omits three very detailed genealogical appendixes dealing with the Strachey family, the Cooke family, and the Forster and Bowyer families and a further appendix analyzing in detail the contents of the Strachey commonplace book in the Alderman Library, University of Virginia. Copies of the thesis containing these appendixes are available at the University of London Library and the Folger Shakespeare Library.

S. G. C.

Victoria University of Wellington
March 1965

Contents

William Strachey
1572-1621

1. Introduction

IN THE crowded and turbulent literary world of Elizabeth and James I, in an age unrivaled in the stature of the writers it produced, the figure of Shakespeare towers above his fellows; but among his contemporaries, along with those well known to posterity by the excellence of their works, are some who, obscure and minor figures, have had fame thrust upon them by a coincidence of time and place that brought them to the notice of the playwright himself—Christopher Mountjoy the Huguenot tiremaker, with whom Shakespeare lodged in his house in Silver Street; William Johnson the vintner, proprietor of the Mermaid Tavern in Bread Street; the actors, Heminges and Condell, editors of the First Folio, and the Burbages; Leonard Digges and Francis Willobie—to name only a few who have, each in his own way, increased our knowledge of the poet and of the background against which he worked. Obscure and forgotten works of little or no literary merit have been resurrected from dusty shelves, and their authors' names rescued from oblivion, because in this book or that tract Shakespeare found a hint or a story, transmuted by his genius into an immortal play.

Such was the case with *The tempest*, last and considered by many the greatest of all his plays, which to the scholars of the early nineteenth century became as

vexed as the Bermudas to which it made incidental
reference. Edmund Malone, casting about for Shakespeare's source, decided that the poet had made use
of an account of the shipwreck and remarkable survival
in 1609 of the governor-elect of the newly established
colony in Virginia, written by one Silvester Jourdan,
a member of the party, and published in haste in 1610
to coincide with the wave of interest sweeping the
country at the news.[1] Jourdan's fame was secure until
1892, when H. H. Furness discovered another and more
detailed account—*A true reportory of the wracke, and
redemption of Sir Thomas Gates Knight; upon, and
from the ilands of the Bermudas: his comming to Virginia, and the estate of that colonie then, and after,
under the government of the Lord La Warre, July 15,
1610, written by William Strachey, Esquire.*[2]—a narrative originally in the form of a letter addressed to an
unnamed "Excellent Lady." Although this account was
not published until 1625, Shakespeare had obviously
made more use of it than he had of Jourdan's. Furness
noted further that this William Strachey had been lodging in the Blackfriars after his return from Virginia
and concluded that *"it is not improbable* that Shakespeare and Strachey were intimate friends and *it is not
improbable* that of all men it was Strachey whom, full
of adventures, of shipwrecks, of tempests, of travellers'
stories, Shakespeare 'got quietly in the corner and
"milked." ' "[3]

Twenty-five years later C. M. Gayley analyzed
Shakespeare's debt to Jourdan, to Strachey, and also to
a tract—*A true declaration of the estate of the colonie*

[1] *The plays & poems of William Shakespeare,* ed. E. Malone
(London, 1821), XV, 380–434, in which Malone quotes a paper
privately published in 1808.

[2] Published in *Hakluytus posthumus; or, Purchas his pilgrimes*
(London, 1625).

[3] *The tempest,* ed. H. H. Furness (London, 1892), p. 313.

in Virginia—published by the Virginia Company in 1610 and based on Strachey's account, and found that while Shakespeare had made use of all three, he had leaned most heavily on Strachey's *True reportory*.[4] Finally Dr. Leslie Hotson demonstrated how Shakespeare, through friends on the Council of the Virginia Company, could have gained access to the letter, still in manuscript.[5]

William Strachey, Esquire, then, was entitled also to his own little niche in the hall of fame as author of a vivid narrative of a storm at sea that had suggested to the greatest of playwrights an immortal play.

The name of Strachey had also cropped up in connection with another of Shakespeare's plays. In *Twelfth night*, Malvolio, musing on the possibility of an advantageous marriage, decided, "There is example for't: The Lady of the Strachy, married the yeoman of the wardrobe."[6] Editors, having first conjectured "the Strachy" as a remote district in Asia Minor, came to consider it perhaps a domestic office (a corruption of the *starchery*, presided over by a superior kind of laundress), and finally Halliwell suggested "Strachy was and is an English family surname. William Strachey published Lawes, &c., for Virginia, 1612, and there are verses by him preserved in MS Ashmol. 781." The next commentator, Colonel Henry Strachey, an explorer of Tibet, defended the interpretation "starchery" so vehemently that one senses an uneasy suspicion that perhaps some sixteenth-century ancestress had actually been so tactless as to marry beneath her; and there the matter rested.[7]

Little was known about William Strachey beyond

[4] *Shakespeare and the founders of liberty in America* (New York, 1917), pp. 40–76.

[5] *I, William Shakespeare* (London, 1937), pp. 224–26.

[6] *Twelfth night*, Act II, sc. 5, line 40.

[7] *Ibid.*, ed. H. H. Furness (London, 1902), pp. 156–161.

his own account of his adventures in the Bermudas and in Virginia. American historians had come, however, to take an interest in this man who had played an important part in the affairs of their country when it was yet in embryo. Not only had he written an account of the wreck and on his return to England in 1612 edited a collection of the laws of the new colony,[8] but there also existed in manuscript a history of the colonization and exploration of Virginia,[9] which was rescued from its comparative obscurity in 1849 by the Hakluyt Society and published as Volume VI in their series of early travels and explorations.[10]

The editor, contemplating a biographical introduction to the work, could find nothing about its author. He had, however, been permitted to inspect the pedigree of the Strachey family of Sutton Court in Somersetshire and discovered one William Strachey of Saffron Walden, married in 1588 and alive in 1620; but he could in no way identify him with the writer on Virginia.[11] Alexander Brown, in his monumental *Genesis of the United States*,[12] incorporated this suggestion, which was accepted, but with reserve, by the *Dictionary of national biography*, which stated also that a William Strachey had written prefatory verses to the quarto of Ben Jonson's *Sejanus*, published in 1605.[13]

Odd references to William Strachey continued to emerge. Discovering an epigram "Ad Gulielmum

[8] *For the colony in Virginea Britannia. Lawes divine, morall and martiall*, (London, 1612).

[9] B. M. Sloane 1622; Ashmole MS 1758; Percy MS.

[10] *The historie of travaile into Virginia Britannia; expressing the cosmographie and comodities of the country, togither with the manners and customes of the people*, ed. R. H. Major.

[11] *Ibid.*, Introd., pp. i–ii.

[12] Published in London and in Boston and New York in 1890; see II, 1024.

[13] *D.N.B.*, "Strachey, William."

Strachaeum" among the works of Thomas Campion, in which Campion describes him as an old boon companion, his editor noted cautiously:

There was a William Strachey known as a writer on Virginia and a colonist, who was shipwrecked in the Sea Venture on the Bermudas in the great storm of 1609, and who wrote an account of it to a lady of rank in London which was published in Purchas his Pilgrimes. There was a William Strachey who wrote commendatory verses prefixed to Ben Jonson's *Sejanus*, and from the epigram it would seem likely that this was Campion's friend. There was also a William Strachey of Saffron Walden who was married in 1583 and alive in 1620.[14]

By a comparison of signatures William Strachey, the secretary to the Virginia Colony, was proved to have acted as secretary to Sir Thomas Glover, ambassador to Constantinople in 1606, and to have been dismissed by him after a quarrel;[15] a letter was found written by John Donne in which the bearer, William Strachey, was stated to be "allways my good frend";[16] and a commonplace book containing Strachey's signature was held to prove conclusively that he was alive in 1628.[17] Finally Professor C. J. Sisson discovered a Chancery deposition signed by William Strachey the secretary which proved that he had been, in 1606, a shareholder in the Blackfriars Theatre company.[18] It seemed almost certain that the secretary to the Virginia Colony was the friend of three of the leading writers of the day, each of whom had his own circle of intimate friends:

[14] Percival Vivian (ed.), *Campion's works* (Oxford, 1909), pp. 269, 373.

[15] *Times literary supplement* (cited as *T.L.S.*), July 3, 1930, letter signed William Foster.

[16] *Ibid.*, July 24, 1930, letter signed Charles Strachey.

[17] *Ibid.*, August 7, 1930, letter signed Rupert Croft-Cooke.

[18] Public Record Office (P.R.O.) C24/327, *Evans* v. *Rastell*.

although Jonson and Donne were themselves friendly, they had little to do with Campion, apart from Jonson's literary collaboration in court masques.

All three were well known, and their lives had been thoroughly investigated—biographers detailed the dates of their births and their deaths, the families from which they had sprung, their activities and their associates— yet of their mutual friend the only fact that was known was that he had spent some five years abroad, either in the Levant or in Virginia. Nothing was known of his family background, nor had he been positively identified. Beyond his connection with the theatre, no light had been cast on his activities in England. And inevitably other questions arose. Why should he have been friendly with the great of his day? And if he was an intimate of Jonson, Donne, and Campion, might he not also have been on the same terms with Shakespeare himself? Could he have been a member of the Mermaid Club? Did he have any other friends in the literary world? Why did he go to Turkey and to Virginia— because he was a lover of adventure in an adventurous age; because he found it prudent, just at that date, to remain for a while beyond the seas; or because he had money troubles and hoped in this way to recoup them? Was he rich or poor; of yeoman, country gentry, or merchant stock; from one of the universities, from the Inns of Court, or relatively uneducated? In sum, what sort of a man was he, and how far was he typical of his age? Who were his other friends, how did he fare in life, and what was his role on the Elizabethan scene?

The following chapters are an attempt to answer these questions and to provide a picture of one member of the vivid throng crowding the most vigorous era of English history. Inevitably there are gaps, periods of his life when he vanishes from our sight and we can only surmise what he was doing; and many of the above questions must remain unanswered, for, in the words of a contemporary and possibly an acquaintance of Strachey himself, "who is so skilful as in this dark ocean of antiquity to struggle with time without splitting on the rocks?"[19]

The first problem was that of identification. Who was William Strachey and what was his family? There was no reference to any William Strachey among the various calendared state papers of the reigns of Elizabeth and James I or among the collections of the Historical Manuscripts Commission, and other published material served only to confuse. Historians had come to agree that William Strachey the secretary hailed from Saffron Walden, but there agreement ended, and three rival candidates had made their appearance: one William Strachey, who died in 1634 and whose son by his first wife came to settle in Virginia;[20] his father, who was known to be living in 1620;[21] and another William, the son of John Strachey of Saffron Walden, whose birth in March 1568 was recorded in the Saffron Walden Parish Register.[22]

A published pedigree of the Strachey family,[23] however, stated that William Strachey of Saffron Walden and Wandsworth married, in 1595, Frances, the daughter of William Forster of Crowhurst in Surrey. Unless,

[19] William Camden, *Britannia,* ed. R. Gough (London, 1806), Introd., p. 37.

[20] *Atlantic mo.,* LXXI (May, 1893), 626–34; *William and Mary quarterly,* Ser. 1, IV (1896), 192; *Va. mag. hist. biog.,* XVIII (1949), 81; J. St. Loe Strachey, *The adventure of living* (London, 1922), pp. 58–59.

[21] Brown, *Genesis,* II, 1024; *Va. mag. hist. biog.,* XVIII (1949), 116.

[22] *T.L.S.,* July 24, 1930, letter of Sir Charles Strachey; *D.A.B.*

[23] *Burke's peerage* (London, 1931). But in William Betham, *The baronetage of England* (London, 1801–5), V, 431, it is stated that William Strachey married Frances Bowyer of Camberwell, no date being given for the wedding.

of course, an earlier marriage had passed unrecorded, his son William Strachey, who died in 1634, could at the very outside have attained the ripe age of fourteen when the *Sea Venture* was cast away on the Bermudas and would have been contributing a sonnet to *Sejanus* at the age of ten. Moreover, William Strachey the secretary was described in 1606 as "of Crowhurst" and aged "34 yeeres or thereaboutes."[24] He must then have been born in 1572; and William the son of John Strachey, born in 1568, was also eliminated.

Despite the inherent probability of the identification —the secretary "of Crowhurst" and William Strachey of Saffron Walden taking a bride from the same parish —positive confirmation was still needed. Strachey of Walden could be identified by the will of his father,[25] also William Strachey of Saffron Walden, who died in 1598. Was there then any record of his birth in 1572?

Here appeared the first rock. Although the name of Strachey occurred frequently in the Saffron Walden Parish Register and there was record of his marriage to Frances Forster, there was no mention of his birth among those of a large family of brothers and sisters[26] nor any record of his death. More disconcerting was the fact that he had left no will, although those of his father and of his son were readily available, nor was there any record that letters of administration had been taken out regarding his property after his death. It appeared, moreover, that little or no mention had been made of Strachey by any of his contemporaries.

There remained, however, the vast mass of legal documents covering almost every phase of sixteenth- and seventeenth-century life, and here sidelights on the activities and relationships of William Strachey,

---

[24] In his deposition, P.R.O. C24/327, *Evans* v. *Rastell*.
[25] Prerogative Court of Canterbury (P.C.C.) 9 Kidd.
[26] Identified by his father's will.

late of Saffron Walden, began to appear. Deeds, recording the transfer of property and enrolled for safety at Westminster, showed him living variously at Crowhurst, Camberwell, and Wandsworth, and at "Graies Inne in the Countie of Midd:"—and the secretary had been a member of the Gray's Inn Society.[27] Two original deeds in the Essex Record Office[28] signed by William Strachey of Saffron Walden provided final proof that William Strachey the secretary was the son of William Strachey of Saffron Walden, who had died in 1598.

The problem of his identity solved, there still remained the greater question: What sort of a man was he? Failing any direct allusion to him by contemporaries, three lines of investigation remained: his actions, his friends, and his early life. The details of his life in Turkey were readily accessible, consisting of the letters of two ambassadors, one his friend and one his enemy; for Virginia there were his own account, disappointingly reticent about himself, and the many contemporary works published.

Cases in the Courts of Chancery, Requests, King's Bench and Common Pleas cast light on his circumstances and gave some indication of the people with whom he was connected, as well as providing further dates and activities. Detailed records were available both in the Public Record Office and at Saffron Walden itself from which to build up a picture of the family at Saffron Walden and his early environment.

But for the most important portion of his life disappointingly little information came to light. It was in London that he met Ben Jonson, Thomas Campion, and John Donne; and it was in London that he lived after his return from Virginia. But London, aloof then

[27] Strachey, *Historie of travaile,* dedicatory letter to Bacon.
[28] DDB/772 and D/DGn/174.

as now, did not note his presence. The corporation of
the City of London, drawn from the wealthy merchant
class, concerned itself first with prosperity, either the
prosperity of the City or the prosperity of the individual, and this concern is reflected in its records. Had
Strachey been a member of a City company, served his
apprenticeship, and become a merchant and a property
owner in the City, we could expect frequent mention
of him; had he studied law seriously at the Inns of
Court, been called to the bar, and perhaps ultimately
to the bench, the City would have noted the fact. But
he was merely a transient, a lodger in the Blackfriars—
like his great contemporary unnoticed not only by the
City but even by the parish in which he lived.[29] Indeed
there is no record even of his entry to the Inns of
Court.

Other evidence appeared, however, connecting him
with the literary world of London—a prefatory sonnet
to the posthumous edition of Overbury's *Wife,* a piece
of minor book piracy in which he participated, even
some of his own poems. Record of his death in 1621 was
found at Camberwell, and the commonplace book
proved to be by two hands, one Strachey's, and to contain an original sermon. But again questions arose that
remain unanswered. Was the sermon delivered? Why
was the sermon written? Who was the second wife
mentioned in a deed a year before his death? When did
his first wife die, and when did he remarry?

"But howsoever it be done, & whatsoever I have done,
I have had an especiall eye unto the truth of things,
and for the rest, I hope that this foule frizeled Treatise
of mine will proove a spur to others better learned,
more skilfull . . . and of greater iudgement." So wrote

[29] Either St. Anne's Blackfriars or St. Andrew by the Wardrobe.
Neither has any record of Strachey or of Shakespeare in the
parish register or in the churchwardens' accounts.

Raphael Holinshed,[30] another minor character raised to prominence by the association of his name with that of Shakespeare. Here then is William Strachey, first secretary to the Colony in Virginia, shareholder in the Blackfriars Theatre, member of the Gray's Inn Society, intimate of some of the greater poets of his age, and poet and author in his own right, and yet withal merely an ordinary gentleman in an age when every man was a man of many parts.

[30] *Chronicle* (London, 1807), I, vii.

2. The Stracheys of
Saffron Walden

WILLIAM STRACHEY, secretary to the Colony in Virginia, came of a family that had been settled in Essex for at least a century before his birth. Throughout the sixteenth century the name of Strachey keeps appearing in the records of the county: William Strachey, head of the Abbey at Pleshey in 1524;[1] William Strachey of Rye Hill, yeoman;[2] William Strachey, bailiff of Colchester in the fifties;[3] John Strachey of Little Canfield, an alehouse keeper;[4] and many others. But by far the greatest number of references are to a Strachey family living in Saffron Walden, market town of Uttlesford Hundred, in the northwestern corner of the county. The records of the town abound in Williams, Johns, and Thomases, family names that in their persistence and recurrence make it difficult to establish the relation of one branch of the family to the other within the town and to distinguish one cousin from another.[5] This constant overlapping of contemporaries of the same

[1] *Transactions of the Essex Archaeological Society,* New Ser. XI, 51.
[2] Essex Record Office, Essex Sessions Records, April 30, 1587.
[3] W. Gurney Benham (ed.), *The oath book or red parchment book of Colchester* (Colchester, England, 1907), pp. 166, 174.
[4] Essex Sess. Rec., April 11, 1583.
[5] John Strachey had sons William (b.1568) and John (b.1577), while his nephew William Strachey also had sons William (b. 1572) and John (b.1573?); and prior to 1589 all were living in Walden.

name, while perfectly clear to the compilers of the early records, presents a tricky problem to the twentieth-century student trying to disentangle them.

One clear fact does, however, immediately stand out in such records as are available. The Strachey family of Saffron Walden belonged to that large and important class of Elizabethan society, the yeomen, and the sixteenth century saw the steady development of the family's prosperity and importance within the town and its members' progress toward the status of gentry. In every way they were typical of the yeomen of the day, and so intimately were the Stracheys connected with the affairs of the town in which they lived that it is impossible to relate William Strachey the secretary to his family background without making some reference to the history and development of Saffron Walden.

In the year 1500 the town consisted of a compact collection of some two hundred to three hundred dwellings.[6] On the higher ground above the market place, grouped around the parish church of St. Mary the Virgin, were the houses of the wealthier members of the community, while to the south, on Gold Street and Cucking Stool End, the landless farm laborers lived crowded together in their cottages.[7] Drapers, tanners, butchers, and fishmongers had their shops in the streets just off the market place,[8] while on market days stalls

[6] Public Record Office (P.R.O.) E179/108/155, Lay Subsidy Assessment, 15 Henry VIII, gives the names of 282 householders as "all and synguler persons enhabited" within the town. Lord Braybrooke, *History of Audley End* (London, 1836), attempts to estimate the population of the town in the seventeenth century and arrives at the figure of 3,000. He appears, however, to have based his figures on the mortality rate prevailing in the nineteenth century.

[7] P.R.O. E179/108/155, Assessment 15 Henry VIII. Of 118 residents of the town assessed at £1 for wages, 90 lived in these two streets.

[8] Saffron Walden MSS, Treasurer's Account Book, lists the fines in 1546 of the "bochers and Fyshers." A "Shopp in the bochery" was given to the almshouse (Almshouse Ordinances). John

were set up and a brisk trade was carried on in local produce, particularly malting barley, wool, and saffron.[9]

By this date the town was in a prosperous state. There had been a settlement on the site since Roman times, but the grant by William the Conqueror of the manor of Walden to Geoffrey de Magnaville "gave life to the place." Geoffrey commenced to build his castle there, and his famous son, Geoffrey de Mandeville, first Earl of Essex, had the market removed to Saffron Walden from the neighboring village of Newport;[10] but after his disgrace the manor, descending through a female line, came into the hands of King Henry V.[11] The task of the Manorial Court became solely that of land conveyance, and the residents were left undisturbed by the absentee lords of the manor.

Throughout England were hundreds of small rural communities of the type of Saffron Walden. Relatively isolated, in an age when communications were far from good, their prosperity depended on the fertility of the surrounding countryside and on the market which enabled the residents to sell their produce and to buy what they needed; and in their isolation their interests turned more and more inward to the affairs of the town, and in particular to the parish church and to the market. Left to themselves the residents managed their own affairs and had achieved a system of internal corporate control. In the larger towns this assumption of power had been the prerogative of the large craft guilds. Here, where there were not sufficient representatives of any one craft to form a guild, their place was taken

Strachey owned a shop in "Tanners Row" (Corporation Muniments, I, 111). William Strachey, draper, in his will of 1598, bequeathed a bedstead standing "over the shop."

[9] Treasurer's Account Book, p. 3, names 24 residents renting stalls in the market.

[10] Philip Morant, *The history and antiquities of Essex* (London, 1768), II, 545.

[11] *Ibid.*, pp. 545–47.

by religious guilds, which provided a corporate body with a constitution and clearly defined powers. The religious guild could be, and generally was, the counterpart of the modern benefit society or fraternal organization, with regular payments by members and a central fund to draw on to assist such as were sick or otherwise in distress; the corporate life manifested itself in meetings and regular formal attendances at the parish church.[12] In 1388 there were at least three guilds in existence in Walden,[13] and in 1400, when an almshouse was founded and endowed "in sokowr and sustynaunce of XIII poure men, in a stret clepyd Danelys lane,"[14] the Guild of Our Lady of Pity was founded to administer it. The endowments of the almshouse were the property of the guild, and the trustees, whose names had to appear on every deed relating to the property of the almshouse, had to be "XXIIII of the most worschypful pareschenys (parishioners) of Waldene." From the twenty-four were annually elected the master of the almshouse, and two assistants, who closely supervised the affairs of the house and the welfare of the occupants and could let or sell the lands, answering to the guild at each annual meeting. The ordinances of the Guild of Our Lady of Pity, dating from 1400, show quite clearly that it was primarily a business organization and that the church services, compulsory for both members of the guild and the poor in the almshouse, were in many ways of secondary importance.

The founding and endowment of the almshouse show also the interest taken by residents in the affairs of the town, even at so early a date. Deeds of charity were common, and many a yeoman's will contained a be-

[12] See L. Toulmin Smith (ed.), *English gilds* (London, 1892), Introd.

[13] *Trans. Essex Arch. Soc.*, New Ser. XII, 280–90.

[14] Almshouse Ordinances.

quest of money to be distributed among the poor; but a major undertaking like the foundation of a house of charity had generally to be carried out by an endowed abbey or a wealthy lord of a manor.[15] In this case it was the residents of Walden who founded the alms-house and the residents who endowed it—with an acre of land here, a shop or a tenement there, or a gift of money, generally bequeathed in a will. And so also it was the residents who administered these endowments.

In exactly the same way the affairs of the town were controlled by a religious guild. There is no record of the guild before 1514, but in that year, as a result of the imposition of certain fines on merchants in Walden and the consequent removal of the market to Newport again,[16] a license was granted to the residents of the town to form a Guild of the Holy Trinity.[17] The word-ing of this license would suggest that the sole purpose of the guild was to endow a chaplain to preach in the Church of St. Mary and to meet for communal prayers,[18]

[15] See for instance the Ordinances of the Ewelne Almshouse, Historical Manuscripts Commission, *8th report* (London, 1881), App. 1, p. 624.

[16] Saffron Walden MSS, Memorandum of Accounts: "It appears by a very old Memorandum, That in the 9th of Henry 7th certain Commission[ers] satt in the Town of Walden to Inquire after things & Rents due to the King who among others found, That every person shod. pay for every Quarter of Malt ground to sell— One farthing. For every Quarter of Do. bought or sold—Do. Every man who kept markett & opened a Shop window—Do. That all Brewers and Bakers were compelled to have their corn ground at the Kings Mills & other things & Impositions. . . . Whereupon Chapmen forsook the Town—and then began the Markett at Newport, to the Detriment of this Town. Whereupon John Leach, Vicar of the Town—Dame Joan Bradbury & many others—by the advice of Lord Broke, Mr Roy & other great men in 5 Henry 8th petitioned & gott the Corporation & Gylde." The memorandum referred to is no longer extant.

[17] R. H. Brodie (ed.), *Letters and papers, foreign and domestic, of the reign of Henry VIII*, I, pt. 2 (London, 1920), p. 2772.

[18] *Ibid*.: "License . . . to found a guild in honour of the Trinity . . . to acquire lands to the annual value of 20 marks for a

but in the following year, when the residents of Walden gained control of the market, as well as of the windmill and malt mill in or near the town, it was to the Guild of the Holy Trinity that the license was granted.[19] When in 1523 Dame Joan Bradbury decided to endow a boys' school in Walden, "to teach freely the children that were born in Walden, Little Chesterford, Newport, and Widdington,"[20] the deed of endowment was made with, and the license granted by the king to, the Guild of the Holy Trinity.[21] In 1542 the guild was granted a Court of Pie Powder, enabling it to deal summarily with offenses in the market,[22] and sometime during the reign of Henry VIII it was granted permission to erect "in the markett place of the sayd town off Walden a cage wyth a pillory and a lytyll Close hows Therunto annexid,"[23] which it did, outside the door of one Nicholas Smith who, objecting to its presence, by main force removed it bodily to another corner of the market place.

Not only did the guild control the life of the town, but the Guild of Our Lady of Pity, controlling the affairs of the almshouse, had the same members as the Guild of the Holy Trinity.[24]

In 1548, however, Edward VI, profiting by the

chaplain to pray daily for the King and Queen Katharine."

[19] R. H. Brodie (ed.), *Calendar of patent rolls, Edward VI* (London 1924–29), II, 211.

[20] John Strype, *The life of the learned Sir Thomas Smith, Kt., D.C.L.* (Oxford, 1820), p. 6.

[21] J. S. Brewer and others (ed.), *Letters and papers, foreign and domestic, of the reign of Henry VIII* (London, 1862–1932), III, pt. 2, 1264, No. 2993, entry for 1523.

[22] *Ibid.*, XVII, 259, No. 443/36, June, 1542.

[23] P.R.O. DL1/19/W3, Proceedings in the Court of the Duchy of Lancaster, *The Treasurer and Chamberlains of the Guild* v. *Nicholas Smith.* Undated, but addressed to the Earl of Southampton, who was created Earl in 1537 and died in 1542.

[24] Cf., for instance, Corp. Mun., I, 207, entry for 1511, and Treas. Acc. Book, p. 3, entry for 1546.

example of his father, decided to abolish religious guilds throughout the country and to seize their endowments. Fortunately there was a former resident of Saffron Walden occupying a prominent position at court, Sir Thomas Smith, brother to the then treasurer of the town, and within six months a new charter was granted to the town, and all endowments, save those that were used solely for religious purposes, were given back.[25] In place of the guild the town now had a corporation, consisting of a treasurer, two chamberlains, and twenty-four assistants, reflecting very closely the previous organization of the guild. The office of the twenty-four assistants was for life, and when any one of them died, his successor was to be elected by the remaining twenty-three. The treasurer and chamberlains were to be elected annually from among the assistants, who, freemen of the town, were to be "of most honest behavyor, wyse, sobre, & dyscreate & meete to be Cownsellers to a common wealthe."[26] The administration of the almshouse was to be carried out by the new corporation, so that the twenty-four now controlled all the activities of the town.

A copy of this charter appears among the corporation ordinances of Saffron Walden, along with the names of the first treasurer, chamberlains, and assistants.

A few months later a taxation return was made out for Saffron Walden, and from this it is clear that the members of the corporation were among the wealthier residents.[27] Sixty-two householders of the town were assessed for taxation, of whom twenty-five were rated at twenty shillings or more. Of these twenty-five, no less than seventeen appear as members of the corporation—

[25] Brodie (ed.), *Cal. pat. rolls, Edward VI*, II, 211, February 18, 1549.

[26] Saffron Walden MSS, Corporation Ordinances.

[27] P.R.O. E179/110/342, Assessment, Relief, Uttlesford, Freshwell, and Clavering Hundreds, April 26, 1549.

yet of the assistants only one, John Cotton, has the designation of "gentleman." The rest were yeomen, men of substance, farming land around Walden and living in the town, their prosperity deriving directly from the fertility of the countryside.

Not only did the district produce the finest saffron in Europe, a drug regarded as a cure for most of the ills flesh was heir to, commanding a good price, and ensuring a more than adequate return for the saffron farmer, or "croker";[28] but also the soil was ideally suited to the finest kind of malting barley, hides were tanned and sold in the market, and sheep grazed on the enclosed pastures of the manor. Many of the residents combined other activities with their farming and carried on the trades of woolen drapers, tanners, maltsters, and the like at their premises in the town.

The members of the corporation, as of the guild before it, were in every way typical of the well-to-do yeomen of their day, interested above all in the stability of their existence and in the ordered life of the town in which they lived and of which they were quietly proud.[29] Their sons might leave Walden and make a name for themselves in London,[30] but throughout the sixteenth century the same names appear in the records of the town, as son succeeded father among the assistants of the corporation and continued to control the education of the residents, the affairs of the market,

[28] See Raphael Holinshed, *Chronicles of England, Scotland, and Ireland* (London, 1807–8), I, 393, for an account of the cultivation of saffron, its medicinal properties, and its price.

[29] P.R.O. DL1/8/S3, Proceedings in the Court of the Duchy of Lancaster, 22 Henry VIII, *Strachey and Byrde* v. *Smith*. The plaintiffs, members of the guild, mention that Walden is an important town and that Smith's defiance of them (in a matter of business) does not make for good order in the town.

[30] E.g., Sir Thomas Smith, Gabriel Harvey, and Sir William Bird, M.P. and judge of the Prerogative Court of Canterbury, were all sons of members of the corporation.

the almshouse, and the general running of the town.[31]

Prominent among the members of the corporation, and in every way representative of them, were the Stracheys. Thomas Strachey had been one of the five residents of Walden who petitioned in 1514 for the formation of the Guild of the Holy Trinity, and when the corporation was formed in 1549, one of his sons and two of his grandsons, the only representatives of the family at that time living in Walden, were to be found among the twenty-four assistants. One Strachey or another held the office of treasurer in 1553, 1554, 1567, 1568, and 1581, and in like manner they filled the position of chamberlain. The earliest records of the town show members of the Strachey family acting as trustees for almshouse lands, and this was a task undertaken by every member of the family throughout the whole of the century.

The life of the town centered not only in the market but also in the parish church of St. Mary the Virgin. During the fifteenth century the residents of Saffron Walden had carried out extensive repairs to the church, amounting to a virtual rebuilding, at their own expense;[32] and, when the guild was formed, one of the prime movers was the vicar. The guild, in addition to its control of things temporal, also exercised some control over the affairs of the church, and most of the churchwardens were members of the Guild of the Holy Trinity, and later of the corporation. Unfortunately the records of the church are not as complete as those of

---

[31] See Mildred Campbell, *The English yeoman* (New Haven, 1942), for a full discussion of the role of yeomen, especially pp. 361–88.

[32] Braybrooke, *op. cit.*, p. 150, mentions the rebuilding, and the Royal Commission on Historical Monuments, *An inventory of the historical monuments in Essex* (London, 1916–23), N-W Essex, pp. 228–33, details additions and restorations and when these were made.

the town for the earlier years,[33] but in 1552 we find one member of the Strachey family among the church-wardens.[34] William Strachey who died in 1564, great-grandfather of William Strachey the secretary, had a "seat or a stool" erected in the chapel on the south side of the church and stated in his will that he wished to be buried there beside it and that his executors were to erect over his grave a marble slab bearing his name and the date of his burial. His son Thomas, fourteen years later, desired to be buried "by my father in the Chapell yf yt may be."

Although the residents of Walden were interested first and foremost in the affairs of their town and were closely connected with the land and its produce, they were in no way ignorant country yokels. The object of the founders of the school had been to provide a priest who should be "a profound gramarion to the intent that he may teche gramar within the towne after the fourme of Wynchestre or of Eton,"[35] and copies of the curriculums and timetables of these schools were obtained to serve as a model for the school at Saffron Walden.[36] Twenty years after its foundation the school had a roll of sixty pupils,[37] and at a later date had apparently sufficient reputation to attract pupils even

[33] Churchwardens' accounts survive only from the seventeenth century.

[34] *Trans. Essex Arch. Soc.*, New Ser. III, 61; an inventory of church goods, taken in 1552.

[35] Indenture tripartite of 1525. Further detail is given in A. F. Leach, *The schools of mediaeval England* (London, 1915), p. 287.

[36] These are published in *Archaeologia*, XXXIV (1852), 37, as of the school at Saffron Walden, but this is refuted in *Notes and queries*, Ser. 9, XI (1903), 294.

[37] *The Victoria history of the county of Essex* (London, 1907), II, 521, Chantry Certificate XX, No. 31: "The said Scole house is Foundid by sides the Church Yarde in Walden Aforesaid, and ther is taught in yt abought the nomber of 60 childryn & Aboue."

from beyond the parish. In 1568 two former pupils of Walden School were admitted to Caius College, Cambridge, one from Harling in Norfolk and one from Thriplow in Cambridgeshire;[38] and, according to one authority, "the boys of Walden would receive precisely the same kind and degree of instruction as those of Winchester and Eton, tempered only by the facts that a larger proportion left school at an earlier age, and a smaller number went to the University."[39]

In fact, quite a respectable number of the sons of the more prosperous residents of Walden went on from the grammar school either to the universities or to the Inns of Court. Some then continued with a professional career, while others returned to Walden. The records of the Middle Temple, for instance, show that at least six sons of residents of the town attended there in the course of the sixteenth century, and of them five returned to Walden to live, the sixth, George Nicholls, remaining in London and, in 1560, acting as treasurer of the Temple.[40] So also we find members of the Strachey family not only at the Inns of Court, but also at Cambridge.[41]

Active in the affairs of the town, the Stracheys also prospered in business. In 1528 William Strachey was described as a draper, and later his three sons came to

[38] John Venn, *Biographical history of Gonville and Caius College, 1349–1897* (Cambridge, 1897), p. 63.

[39] *Victoria history, Essex*, II, 521.

[40] C. T. Martin (ed.), *Middle Temple records; minutes of Parliament, 1501–1703* (London, 1904–5), I, 112 (Nicholas Kent, 1557); 128 (John Harrydane, nephew of George Nicholls, treasurer, 1560); 268 (William Adam, 1584); 307 (Robert Nicholls, 1589); 410 (Thomas Cole, 1596); 152 (William Strachey, 1565).

[41] John and J. A. Venn, *Alumni Cantabrigienses* (Cambridge, 1922–27). The members referred to cannot be positively identified but are William, B.A. 1509; Ralph, matriculated 1564, entered Gray's Inn 1566; Elias, matriculated 1565; and another Elias, matriculated 1571.

be associated with him in what must by then have come to be a thriving trade, and one which was to provide the main source of the family's income for the rest of the century.[42] The woolen draper of Saffron Walden, as of any other small rural community, was a different being from his London counterpart. Where the London draper was a member of the Drapers' Company, buying his fleeces in the open market and interested only in the processing of the wool, the draper of Saffron Walden was primarily a farmer. His sheep grazed on his own land, and it was this wool that he dyed, spun, and wove, his workshop being merely one room in his house set aside for the purpose. In addition, one member at least of the Strachey family ventured into malting, and others may have tried their hand at other trades within the town, but it was the drapery business that was the most imporant.

Subsidy returns throughout the century show the family always well to the fore among the wealthier residents of the town, and, as might be expected, it was among the more prominent residents of Walden that the Stracheys married. Various members of the Strachey family married into the families of Pumfret, Thorow-good, Bird, Martin, Pyrke, Semar, Raymond, Godding, Croft, and Lowndes—all names that are to be found among the assistants of the corporation, as members of the guild, or as trustees of the almshouse and all prom-inent in the subsidy returns. Indeed in the latter half of the century most of the wealthier residents of Walden must have been related to one another by marriage. The only marriages in the earlier part of the century that took place between a member of the Strachey family and anyone outside Walden were those of Wil-

[42] E.g., Corp. Mun., IV, 255. Thomas Strachey Jun. and William Strachey Jun. are both referred to as drapers (1557). In P.R.O. C54/1127 their brother John Strachey is also referred to as a draper (1582).

liam and Thomas Strachey to two of the daughters of Ralph Bickerdicke, alderman of Cambridge, some twenty miles away.

Most prominent of all the members of the Strachey family in Walden was William Strachey, grandfather to William Strachey the secretary. The younger son of a younger son, he was especially active in the affairs of the town and managed at the same time to amass a comfortable fortune, so that by 1571 he was far and away the wealthiest resident of Saffron Walden and a man of considerable influence within the town. In the ordinances of the newly formed corporation of 1549 there was a marked emphasis on seniority, and by this date he must have been among the most experienced of the assistants. He had been one of the prime movers in obtaining the corporation, had twice been treasurer, and had shown that he was possessed of considerable business ability and acumen. From 1572 on he played something of the role of an elder statesman, and entries in the treasurer's Account Book note him as present at various municipal dealings. In 1572 William Adam, the treasurer, notes: "Itm layd owt the xxth daye of aprill by Mr Strachie, Mr .Woodhall & me as yt appearthe in a byll for Dyvers thinges towardes the Charter . . . . . viij li. xvj s. ij d."[43] Strachey and Woodhall were both past treasurers, but neither of them was at that time chamberlain, so it is obvious that the negotiations for a modified charter, which was granted the following year, were carried out by the senior and most experienced of the assistants. Likewise an indenture of the same year leasing a portion of the almshouse lands to George Nicholls mentions William Strachey Senior alone by name among the trustees;[44] and the following year his presence is noted when John Harvey,[45] the treas-

---

[43] Treas. Acc. Book, p. 78.   [44] Corp. Mun., I, 338.
[45] Ropemaker of Walden and father of Gabriel Harvey.

urer for that year, pays 20*s.* to Mr. Byngham, the undersheriff.[46]

In 1579, when he was elected treasurer for a third time, he refused the office, choosing instead to pay a fine of ten pounds, which excused him from the office for the rest of his life.[47] This is the first refusal recorded, but refusal may not have been unusual as it is only as a result of an ordinance passed at the time that Strachey's fine appears in the Treasurer's Account Book.[48] By 1579 Strachey must have been feeling the effects of his age, and he apparently chose to live quietly in retirement in Walden and leave the management of his business to his son William, who in 1574 had returned finally to Walden.

With the retirement of William Strachey the grandfather from active participation in the affairs of the town, the role of the Strachey family within Saffron Walden underwent a considerable change. Certainly his son, William Strachey, father to the secretary, had returned to Walden to live, but for the first time a prominent member of the Strachey family played no part in municipal affairs. Also for the first time, a member of the family had married as far afield as London, and it is probable that his interests coincided with those

[46] Treas. Acc. Book, p. 83: "gyven to mr byngam vndersheryfe in presens of Mr Strachey Mr Addam & others . . . xx s."

[47] Treas. Acc. Book, p. 98. "Itm of Mr William Strachie thelder for his fyne for refusall of Thresorershipp after his eleccon, and for a fyne to be discharged of the sayd offyce duringe his lyfe, and that this fyne shall remayne to the vse of the Chamber of Walden . . . x li."

[48] Corp. Ordinances, August 16, 1579, state that according to an order of 1557 "if any of the Companye should be frome thenceforth elected and chosen Thresorer of this Towne, and after such eleccon should refuse to serue in the sayde office: should then vpon euerye suche refusall forfeyte to the vse of him that should next be chosen Thresorer to persiste in the sayde office fyve poundes"; but now the money was to be paid instead into the corporation accounts.

of his wife and were not in Saffron Walden. It may indeed have been parental pressure that induced him to return to Walden.

Educated at the Inns of Court, he had met and married in London Mary Cooke, whose family, wealthy London merchants, had, by the purchase of manors in Kent, become prominent among the Kentish gentry, at the same time retaining connections by marriage with the more wealthy and prominent members of the merchant community in London. Although he had returned to Walden for the birth of his first child, he had then left again and was almost certainly living with the Cookes at Lesness when his sons William and John were born.

Although he lived in Walden from his return in 1574 until his death in 1598, the last decade of the century was to see the complete disappearance of the Strachey family from Walden. The death of his cousin Elias in 1591 meant the extinction of the line of his uncle Thomas Strachey; and when his other uncle John Strachey died in 1589, this branch of the family departed for London, never to return. Finally his own sons left Walden either for London or Cambridge, and at the turn of the century the name of Strachey in Saffron Walden was only a memory which was in its turn to fade as piece by piece the Strachey lands were disposed of by the absent members of the family.

3. Saffron Walden and London

It was in the somewhat narrow and self-sufficient environment of the typical sixteenth-century country town of Saffron Walden that William Strachey passed his childhood. When his father returned finally to Walden in 1574, bringing with him a wife who was a stranger to the town and three small children, Marie, William, and John, the Strachey family was at the peak of its importance and prosperity. The three brothers, John, Thomas, and William the grandfather, were all men of substance and members of the corporation, and all had already held the office either of chamberlain or treasurer. The grandfather had been among the most active of the residents in the affairs of the town and in the development of its government and was assessed as the wealthiest of the burgesses. In addition, the multitude of cousins and relatives by marriage were all persons of importance in the small world of Saffron Walden.

William Strachey the father may have returned to Walden with some reluctance. It had been usual for members of the family, their education completed in London or at one of the universities, to resume the normal life of the town: to carry on the family business, to become members of the corporation and trustees of the almshouse, and to marry within Saffron Walden and settle there. The grandfather, after an active life, was ready to retire from public affairs and to entrust the management of the business to his son, who, from the life of London and the Inns of Court, was summoned to play his part in Walden. During his absence he had been chosen one of the almshouse trustees, a position he filled until his death,[1] but it was only in this comparatively minor role that he followed the normal career of a member of the Strachey family. By his marriage as far away as London he had already made one break with tradition, and now came the second: for the first time one of the senior members and the prospective head of the family within the town failed to take any further part in municipal affairs. Although the corporation expended, in 1590, the sum of sixteen pence to provide a "pottell of wine" when the visiting magistrate dined with the Stracheys,[2] in the corporation's records, at a date when they are fairly complete, there is no mention of William Strachey as a member.[3]

His wife must have found the life of Walden in every way different from that she had previously known in London, where, as a daughter in a well-connected family, she had been welcome in many of the houses of the wealthy merchants of London and where her brother's wedding could attract not only the aldermen of the city, but the Lord Mayor himself, and keep them all feasting and dancing until the small hours of the morning.[4] She may have looked back with some regret to those days and must have had tales to tell of a

[1] Corp. Mun., V, 155 (1572) ; III, 172–73 (1573) ; I, 229 (1577) ; I, 231 (1578) ; V, 175 (1581) ; II, 258, I, 124, II, 309 (1582) ; I, 128 (1584) ; I, 130 (1592) ; II, 138 (1593) ; I, 132 (1594) ; III, 414 (1596) ; II, 144 (1598).

[2] Treas. Acc. Book, p. 137.

[3] Corp. Ordinances include a signed ordinance of 1597, and his name does not appear among those of the members.

[4] Henry Machyn, *The diary of Henry Machyn*, ed. J. G. Nichols (London, 1848), p. 288.

life fuller and more exciting than that of the country town where she now lived, and it is probably to his mother that we have to look to explain Strachey's subsequent break with the town where his family had lived for so long.

Although some fourteen years of his life were spent in Walden, no record has survived. We can be reasonably sure that he received his early education in the schoolhouse "sett on the N. syde of Castell streate, against a little lane there, called Vicar's lane, ledyng . . . into the churche yarde,"[5] under John Disborough, Master of Arts of Trinity College, Cambridge,[6] "a profound gramarion" selected for the corporation by the master of Queens College and paid a stipend of ten pounds a year.[7] He came to know the countryside and at a later date showed himself familiar with the saffron fields that surrounded the town,[8] but of the rest of his childhood we know nothing.

More brothers and sisters were born: Thomas in 1574, Howard in 1576, Anne, who died in infancy, in 1578, and Frances in 1581. The senior members of the family died, and his father came to take more and more control of the family business. Then on April 30, 1587, when he was fifteen years old, Mary Strachey, his mother, was buried in the parish church of St. Mary the Virgin.

A month later his grandfather died, and William Strachey the father, only son and heir, administered the estate and took possession of thirteen houses and more than 200 acres of freehold arable land and pas-

---

[5] *Victoria history, Essex*, II, 519.
[6] Venn, *Alumni Cantabrigienses*, pt. I, Vol. II, "Disborough."
[7] Treas. Acc. Book records the annual payments to him.
[8] Samuel Purchas, *Hakluytus posthumus; or, Purchas his pilgrimes* (Glasgow, 1905–7), XIX, 19. Strachey compares the leaves of a palm tree to an "overblowne Rose, or Saffron flower not early gathered."

ture in Walden and the neighboring parish of Wimbish;[9] a further 100 acres of copyhold land, three houses, and a cottage, held of the manor of Walden;[10] and a brewhouse in the parish of St. Margaret, Westminster—a property consisting in all of five dwellings, three stables, a garden, and a wharf, which had been purchased by William Strachey the grandfather twenty years earlier.[11]

It was in the course of the month immediately after the grandfather's death that his son was granted a coat of arms. There is no record of the date of his application to the College of Heralds, nor is there any indication whether it was made with the sanction of William Strachey the grandfather as head of the family. The conjunction of dates may be mere coincidence, but nevertheless upstart gentry were a frequent subject of derision among the more forthright Elizabethans,[12] and it may well have been that the grandfather set his mind against what might be regarded as ostentation by the independent yeomanry of Walden. On July 4, 1587, however, William Strachey of Rutlands in Saffron Walden, gentleman, became lawfully entitled to bear as his arms "Argent on a cross ingrayled betweene foure Eagles Gules a flowredeluce & foure cinquefoyles Gould and to his Creast or Cognisince vpon ye healme a wreath of his Colours Argent & Gules a lyon rampant ermyn crowned & susteyning a Crosse formy fitched Gould Mantler Gules doubled Argent."[13]

Five weeks later, a little over three months after his wife's death, the father married again. We do not know

[9] Detailed in his inquisition post-mortem, P.R.O. C142/214/211.
[10] Essex R.O., D/DBy/M26.
[11] Described in P.R.O. CP43/96, Recovery, 4 James I, *Clarke* v. *Draper.*
[12] Louis B. Wright, *Middle-class culture in Elizabethan England* (Chapel Hill, 1935), pp. 458–59.
[13] British Museum (B.M.), Harleian MS 1441, f. 8b.

how his eldest son behaved toward his new stepmother, Elizabeth Brocket, of a substantial and well-connected family from the neighboring county of Hertfordshire. He could hardly have welcomed his mother's successor, appearing so soon after her death, but there is no evidence that he was ever antagonistic toward her. He seems, however, from this date to have turned to the Cooke family more than to his own, and later in his life he was to show himself familiar with the part of Kent in which the Cookes lived.[14] Moreover, when he married, he took a wife who was distantly related to his mother's family.

He had only a few months of the new household, however, and then on February 14, 1588, he was admitted as a pensioner to the recently established Emmanuel College.[15] Beyond the record of his admission there is no information available about his life at Cambridge. He took no degree, and there is no record of his leaving the university, nor any evidence of friendships he made while a student there. From Cambridge he proceeded to Gray's Inn. Neither the Admission Register[16] nor the Pension Books[17] of the Inn make any mention of him, but his presence there is attested by a deed of 1605, in which he is referred to as "William Strachey of Grayes Inne in the countie of Midd: gent,"[18]

[14] See Chapter 7, p. 153.   [15] Venn, *op. cit.*, pt. I, IV, 172.

[16] Joseph Foster (ed.), *The register of admission to Gray's Inn, 1521–1889* (London, 1889). This work was compiled from a transcript and verified by comparison with the existing registers. It was also amplified from B. M. Harl. MS 1912, a list of members of the Inns of Court compiled in the seventeenth century by Simon Segar, Garter King of Arms. This MS, which was apparently based on the admission registers, contains no reference to Strachey.

[17] R. J. Fletcher (ed.), *The pension book of Gray's Inn, 1569–1800* ((London, 1901–10), contains a record of various activities relating to the internal organization of the Inn and the names of members called to the bar.

[18] P.R.O. C54/1818, Indenture between Strachey and Bowyer.

and by his dedication to Bacon in *The historie of travaile*, where he states that he is "Bound to your observaunce, by being one of the Graies-Inne Societe,"[19] a claim he would not have dared venture without justification.

Gray's Inn was at this time at the height of its importance. Not only was it the largest of the Inns of Court, but among its members were some of the most influential men in the land. It appears that Strachey was not called to the bar,[20] but that he lived the life of a young man of the wealthier classes of the day, finishing his education at the Inns of Court, mixing with a society of intelligent and cultured gentlemen, and enjoying the many delights that London had to offer. We know that he tried his hand at verses and was friendly with various writers of the day and interested in the theatre, and although these facts emerge at a later stage in his life, there is no doubt that these were also his interests when first he came to Gray's Inn.

On June 9, 1595, Strachey married Frances Forster[21] and for a time quitted London to take up his residence at Crowhurst in Surrey, where his father-in-law, William Forster, was lord of the substantial manor of Chellows. Here he was received into Surrey society. Not only was William Forster a prosperous landowner, but he was also related to the important family of Gainsford of Crowhurst, long established in the county; and, furthermore, Edmund Bowyer, half-brother to Frances, was already a justice of the peace, a member of Parliament, and lord of the large and valuable manor of Camberwell. From this date Strachey allied himself

[19] *Historie* (ed. Major), dedication.
[20] Otherwise there would have been a mention in the pension book. There is no indication that he ever practiced or had any interest in the law.
[21] Recorded in both Crowhurst and Saffron Walden parish registers.

very closely with his wife's family; he appears in legal documents as living either at Crowhurst, Camberwell, or Wandsworth, where John Bowyer, another half-brother, owned the manor of Allfarthing. Nevertheless, wherever he might be regarded officially as living, his connection with London remained close, and it is certain that wherever his wife, and later his children, might be, Strachey had his lodgings in the city and spent much of his time there.

On March 30, 1596, his first son William was baptized at Crowhurst.[22] Meanwhile, at Saffron Walden five daughters, Elizabeth, Anne, Margaret, Abigail, and Martha, had been born to William Strachey the father in his second marriage. Marie had married; Howard was also in London, apprenticed to Francis Allen, a member of the Clothworkers' Company;[23] and Thomas had left Walden and was living in Cambridge.[24] In November 1598 William Strachey the father died and was buried in the parish church at Saffron Walden.[25]

If Strachey had entertained any hopes of benefiting immediately from his inheritance, he was doomed to disappointment. His father's will,[26] which contained detailed instructions regarding the disposal of his estate, bequeathed the entire property, both in Saffron Walden and in Westminster, to his widow Elizabeth for the term of her life, and only after her death was it to pass to his son and heir William. Forty acres of copyhold land in Walden were to be sold to pay his debts, of some £240, and minor bequests of bedsteads were made to his daughter Frances and his sons John and Thomas.

[22] Crowhurst parish register.
[23] According to information supplied by the clerk of the Clothworkers' Company.
[24] Essex R.O. DDB/772 refers to him in 1599 as "Thomas Strachey of Cambridge."
[25] Saffron Walden parish register.
[26] Prerogative Court of Canterbury (P.C.C.) 9 Kidd.

After the brewhouse property in Westminster came into the possession of William, he was to pay, in successive two-year periods, the sum of 200 marks to each of the daughters in turn, and any default in payment on his part entitled the daughters to take possession of the premises and accept the rents until they had received the money due to them. The usual stipulations were made that if William were to die without heirs, the property was to pass to John, and so to the other sons in order of age. Elizabeth was appointed sole executrix.

At first sight the omission of three of his children by his first wife—William, Howard, and Marie—as immediate beneficiaries under this will, seems somewhat surprising; and it may well have been that some quarrel had taken place which led the father not even to leave them some article of personal property—a second-best doublet, the fur-lined cloak hanging in the closet, or even a pewter candlestick—to remember him by. However the general scope of the will was to make long-term financial provision for the whole of his family, and, apart from the beds, there were no specific bequests. Furthermore, provision had already been made for at least two of his sons. John Strachey, writing in 1624, stated that he had been granted by his father an annuity of twenty pounds from lands in Walden some thirty years earlier;[27] and a document in the Saffron Walden Museum states that William Strachey was in receipt of thirty pounds a year from lands during his father's lifetime.[28] It seems likely that the other two sons had been provided for in a similar manner, and the omission of Marie, married in 1596, can possibly be accounted for on the grounds that she had already

[27] B.M. Add. MS 34,730, Letter dated February 12, 1624.

[28] Cabinet 28, Envelope marked "Strachey." It contains information provided by descendants, the Stracheys of Somersetshire. Most of the information provided by this family is of dubious worth, but this item at least has the virtue of probability.

received a substantial marriage portion, although it may have been that her marriage did not find favor with her father.[29]

The family property had somewhat diminished since it had been in the hands of William Strachey the father. It is true that, unlike the grandfather before him, he had a large family to provide for, and annuities and a marriage portion could be a severe drain on capital. Nevertheless, earlier Stracheys had raised families as large, or even larger, and had prospered at the same time. Not only did Strachey leave debts of £240, but, of the thirteen dwellings in Walden bequeathed to him, three had already been sold,[30] and the copyhold lands had been reduced by a few acres.[31] Where William Strachey the grandfather had throughout his life shown the greatest ability both in the affairs of the town and in his own business, his son, inheriting a flourishing drapery business, achieved relatively little, and it may well have been that in addition to the debts he detailed in his will there were others for his heirs to settle.

At the time of his death Strachey had been living in a substantial house in the "middleward" of Walden, with, as neighbors, some of the more wealthy residents of the town, including three members of the corporation, George Nicholls, Thomas Adam, and Anthony Penistone.[32] His widow, however, moved to the other

[29] Her husband, in need of money while William Strachey the father was still alive, was forced to borrow it from Strachey's usurious neighbor, Anthony Penistone. See p. 39.

[30] P.R.O. CP25 (2)/124, Essex Fines, Michaelmas Term, 35–36 Elizabeth, records the sale of two messuages, one barn, and two gardens to Thomas and John Pamfling; and P.R.O. CP25 (2)/124, Essex Fines, Trinity Term, 38 Elizabeth, one messuage and two tofts to William Woodhall.

[31] Essex R.O. D/DBy/M26 shows that William Strachey the father received $101\frac{1}{4}$ acres of land, three houses, and a cottage, whereas his widow took possession of $88\frac{1}{4}$ acres, one house, and one cottage, all copyhold of the manor of Walden.

[32] According to P.R.O. E179/111/500, Assessment, 40 Elizabeth.

end of the town,[33] and Strachey himself came also to live in Walden, taking up his residence in a large house, part of the estate, at the corner of High and Castle Streets.[34]

The will was not proved immediately—only after judgment had been given in the Prerogative Court of Canterbury in a suit brought by Elizabeth, widow and executrix of William Strachey, deceased, against William, his son and heir. The sentence appended to the registered copy of the will gives no indication of the basis of this suit and merely states that both parties would receive justice; but subsequent events would suggest that it was not so much the outcome of a quarrel between the heirs as a legal maneuver, amicably agreed upon, whereby certain provisions of the will might be set aside. If Elizabeth were already contemplating the remarriage that soon took place, the bulk of the property that she would bring as a marriage portion could not be touched by her or her second husband and could be let only for the indefinite term of her life, after which it would revert absolutely to William. Strachey himself, living the life of a young gentleman of means in London, undoubtedly had need of more money than his annuity of thirty pounds, and while he could have borrowed against his expectations, the realization of these depended also on the length of Elizabeth's life and made for uncertainty in his affairs. It would appear therefore that Elizabeth and the

[33] According to P.R.O. E179/111/513, Assessment, 41 Elizabeth.
[34] Essex R.O. DDB/772, Deed of January 6, 1600. The house is referred to as being "now in the tenure and occupation of William Strachey." That this is not merely a legal term denoting ownership is borne out by the fact that the occupants of two other houses mentioned in the deed and owned by Strachey are also named. P.R.O. E179/111/513, Assessment, 41 Elizabeth, shows him living in High St. For a description of the house, which was standing as late as 1920, see Historical Monuments Commission, *N-W Essex,* p. 247.

other heirs agreed between them that part of the Saffron Walden property should be sold, to provide her
with a marriage portion in cash, and that the rest of
the property, with the exception of the somewhat en-
cumbered brewhouse, should come directly into William's hands.

Once probate was granted, on February 13, 1599, the
heirs were free to dismember the estate. In July, Elizabeth took possession of the copyhold land,[35] and presumably the forty acres were then sold. In October,
William Strachey gentleman, Frances his wife, Elizabeth Strachey widow, and John Strachey, all described
as residents of Walden, sold 6 acres of arable freehold
land to Anthony Penistone,[36] neighbor of the late
William Strachey the father; and 26 acres to William
Adam and Thomas Rowley, also of Walden.[37] Fines
levied in the Michaelmas Term, 1599, record also the
sale of 15 acres to William Woodhall and Giles Barker
and a further 11 acres to Penistone and John Fenning.[38]
Two months later William, Frances, Elizabeth, and John
all of Walden, Howard of London, and Thomas
Strachey of Cambridge sold, for the sum of £510, not
only the large house in which Strachey was then living,
but also two smaller houses, "with a gardyne and Dove-
house," to Thomas Adam the younger of Walden.[39] A
month later they sold a further 21 acres of freehold for
an unspecified sum.[40] In this period, of the ten dwellings

[35] Essex R.O. D/DBy/M26.

[36] H. R. Moulton, *Palaeography, genealogy and topography*
(London, 1930), p. 138, No. 521.

[37] Essex R.O. DDB/771; P.R.O. CP25 (2) 125, Essex Fines, Michaelmas Term, 41–42 Elizabeth.

[38] P.R.O. CP25 (2) /125, Essex Fines, Michaelmas Term, 41–42
Elizabeth.

[39] Essex R.O. DDB/772; P.R.O. CP25 (2) /125, Essex Fines, Michaelmas Term, 42–43 Elizabeth.

[40] P.R.O. C54/1665, Indenture, Strachey and Adam, February
12, 1600.

and 218 acres of freehold land received from William Strachey the father, at least three dwellings and 79 acres of land had been sold by his heirs, and there may have been other sales of which we have no record.

These transactions completed, Strachey left Walden, and Elizabeth, on May 8, 1600, married Thomas Wolrich, head of a substantial family resident at Cowley in Suffolk.[41] Wolrich's widowed mother, Honor, came to live in Walden after her son's remarriage, but Elizabeth disappears from the Essex scene and probably lived, with her daughters, in Suffolk.[42]

A subsidy assessment made later in the year provides evidence that, in spite of the land already sold, a substantial area in Walden was still in Strachey's possession.[43] Of the thirty-seven residents of the town assessed for taxation on the value of their lands rather than of their goods, only one is rated higher than Strachey. Although this return would seem to indicate that he was living in Walden as late as September 22, 1600, it is clear that this was merely his address for taxation purposes. Before the next subsidy was granted to Queen Elizabeth by Parliament in 1602, Strachey, through the assessors for the Crowhurst area, notified the Exchequer that he had been resident there for some time and that in future he would be liable for taxation on his holdings in Surrey.[44]

Not only had Strachey taken possession of the lands in Walden, but he had also assumed the responsibilities of head of the family. The earlier sales of land had

[41] Saffron Walden parish register. Wolrich pedigrees appear in G. W. Marshall (ed.), *Le Neve's Pedigrees of the knights* (London, 1873), p. 142, and in G. Grazebrook and J. P. Rylands (eds.), *The visitation of Shropshire, taken in the year 1623* (London, 1889), II, 508.

[42] P.R.O. E179/111/519, Assessment, 42 Elizabeth, shows Honor Worledge, widow, living in Walden but contains no mention of Elizabeth.

[43] *Ibid.*   [44] P.R.O. E115/380/76.

rendered void his brother John's annuity, "so that," said John, "then he made me a new annuitie from him selfe,"[45] a statement borne out by Strachey in 1605, when, selling land in Walden, he noted specifically that an annuity of twenty pounds to his brother John must still be paid.[46] So too Howard, early in 1601, by now free of the Clothworkers' Company and in need of the sum of £200, borrowed it of his brother William.[47] This must have been repaid, since there is no further mention of it, but another act of assistance to a member of his family had considerable repercussions.

On April 4, 1596, five days after Strachey's first son William had been baptized at Crowhurst, his elder sister Marie had married Clement Turner, of Wratting Parish in Suffolk, a captain in the queen's service.[48] As in the case of a more famous contemporary, the bride was some years older than the groom,[49] and their first child was born five months after the wedding. They may have lived for a time in Walden, where the births of two of their children are recorded in the parish register,[50] but by September 1598 they were living in Wratting, where Turner "hadd newlye taken certeyne groundes into his occupation and wanted monye to stocke them with." In urgent need of forty pounds he approached Anthony Penistone, his father-in-law's neighbor, "a man of lardge conscience and to take holde of all advauntages," and after some argument succeeded in borrowing the sum at the usual 10 per

[45] B.M. Add. MS 34,730, f. 2.

[46] P.R.O. C54/1818, Indenture, Strachey and the Bowyer brothers.

[47] P.R.O. LC4/194/369, March 6, 1601.

[48] Saffron Walden parish register.

[49] P.R.O. Req2/391/188. Clement Turner is stated to be the same age as Howard Strachey, i.e., some six years younger than Marie.

[50] A "man childe" buried on September 30, 1596, and a daughter, Martha, christened on November 29, 1597.

cent interest, provided also that he board two of Penistone's daughters and his wife "trayne them uppe in
sewinge."[51]

Turner, forced to yield to these "unconscionable de-
maundes," signed the usual bond acknowledging his
debt and undertaking to pay double the sum should
he fail to repay the loan on the appointed date. Twelve
months later he sent Penistone a "waigh of Suffolk
cheese and two Fyrkins of Butter," worth four pounds,
but, reasoning that the moneylender, satisfied with his
rate of interest, would make no difficulty about extend-
ing the loan, omitted to repay the principal. Penistone,
known for his "extreme and hard usage of men in taking of Forfaytures when they were in his daunger,"
promptly commenced a suit against Turner in the
Court of Common Pleas and, toward the end of 1600,
was awarded judgment for the whole eighty pounds
and costs. Turner, now faced with a debtors' prison,
was summoned by his creditor to the London house of
his brother, Michael Penistone, with a promise of
some friendly arrangement regarding payment; then
Penistone, his victim safely in his hands, informed him
that the sheriff's men had been called and were waiting
at the door. One thing only could save Turner from
immediate arrest—that his brother-in-law should offer
some of the Strachey lands in Walden as security for
the debt and sign a joint bond with Turner acknowledging the debt of eighty pounds to Penistone. Strachey,

---

[51] These transactions are detailed in P.R.O. C3/289/13, *Strachey
v. Penistone*. Penistone, a member of the corporation and one of
the more prosperous residents of Walden, came of a family prominent in Oxfordshire, various members of which were fairly
prominent in London commercial circles. See Harleian Society,
The visitations of Essex, 1552, 1558, 1570, 1612 and 1634 (London, 1878–79) ; J. J. Howard and G. J. Armytage (eds.) , *The
visitation of London in the year 1568* (London, 1869) ; and W.
H. Turner (ed.) , *The visitation of the county of Oxford, taken in
the years 1566, 1574 and in 1634* (London, 1871) .

summoned in haste from his lodgings and seeing that nothing else could save Turner from prison, signed the bond. If between them they failed to pay the sum of eighty pounds by June 24, 1601, they stood to forfeit £160 to Penistone.

This was a simple and profitable transaction. For the outlay of forty pounds and certain recoverable legal costs, the Saffron Walden usurer stood to increase his holdings by double, or if all went well, four times that amount. Before the bond fell due, however, Turner was ordered to the garrison at Berwick on Tweed, where, Strachey gleefully told Penistone, as one of Her Majesty's serving officers, he could not be sued for debt. Penistone thereupon "laid secrett wayte to attache and arest" Strachey and at the same time commenced another suit in the Court of Common Pleas. Strachey, knowing full well that his signed bond was all the evidence this court required and that he must inevitably lose the case, commenced counteraction in Chancery to gain a stay of proceedings.

Turner, in Berwick, took no part in the case, so we have no confirmation of Penistone's counteraccusations:[52] that Turner had entrusted the money to Strachey, who had used it for his own ends, and that Turner was very "discontented" at such an action on Strachey's part. Strachey of course denied it.

The case however lapsed, and the only further record we have states that on June 21, 1602, Strachey appeared in court and paid 25 shillings costs.[53] By commencing his action in Chancery, Strachey had secured an injunction preventing Penistone from proceeding with his suit in Common Pleas; and it seems certain that Penistone, faced with further and costly litigation and the inevitable delay in payment, was prepared to settle out of

[52] In his answer in this same suit.
[53] P.R.O. C33/102, f. 707.

court. It was probably for this reason that Clement Turner, gentleman, of Berwick on Tweed, borrowed the sum of £120 from one Robert Turner, gentleman, possibly his brother, on February 27, 1602.[54]

Strachey himself appears to have been in need of ready money, and at this time was forced to borrow the sum of £100 from Josias Bull, of London,[55] but any financial troubles he may have had were solved, temporarily at least, by the death of Elizabeth his stepmother, in 1602.[56] The brewhouse property was now unconditionally his, and it was probably to provide for the first of the payments out of the rents, and to assign a marriage portion to his sister Frances, that on June 27, 1603, he signed a recognizance, acknowledging that he owed John Lancaster, of Westacre in Norfolk, the sum of £200.[57]

These activities, however, while casting some light on Strachey's relations with his family and on his financial affairs, tell us nothing of his life in London, and it is not until 1604 that we find evidence of a friendship that could have been made only in London and that seems

---

[54] The bond he signed on this date is referred to in P.R.O. KB27/1412, f.470, *Turner* v. *Turner*. He was sued for this sum in 1608, had judgment awarded against him, and languished in Marshalsea prison for some two years until, his debt paid, he was released on March 17, 1610.

[55] P.R.O. LC4/194/407, Recognizance dated June 20, 1600.

[56] P.R.O. C2 Jas.I/S10/51, *Shiers* v. *Strachey*. Strachey in April 1619 states that Elizabeth died "aboute seventeene yeares nowe last past."

[57] P.R.O. LC4/195/224. The only record of this marriage is a statement in a printed pedigree that John Lancaster married an unnamed daughter of Strachey of Saffron Walden. See Walter C. Metcalfe (ed.), *The visitations of Suffolk, 1561, 1577, and 1612* (Exeter, 1882), p. 201. If this recognizance was made in connection with this marriage, Frances is the only one of the daughters of William Strachey that it could have been. The Lancaster family was, moreover, related to Clement Turner, Strachey's unfortunate brother-in-law. Lancaster's father in his will, P.C.C. 43 Stafforde, mentions lands owned in Wratting Parish.

to stem directly from his presence at the Inns of Court. In this year there issued from the busy press of Simon Stafford a work entitled *The view of Fraunce*,[58] containing a dedicatory letter signed by Francis Michell and one set only of commendatory verses:

To his worthy friend Fraunces Michell.

Svch as would trauaile without•charge or paine,
And here in England take a view of France,
Read but this booke, and reape true english gaine,
By others labors. What in due obseruance
You find in your contentments and loud-ease,[59]
Giue to his worthie paines: And worthiest friend
With your owne worth your owne indeuors please;
"Vertue hath alwaies in her selfe her end.
    The fortune of the presse then nere respect.
    Sale and prophane applause, meere fooles affect.

William Strachey.

Michell in his preface states that his "worthie paines" were confined to translating marginal notes from French to English, and that, as former secretary to the Archbishop of Canterbury, John Whitgift, he found himself idle after his master's death on February 29, 1604, so proceeded to sort and assemble a multitude of loose papers in the archbishop's collection. Among these was an account of France, written on his return to England in 1598 by Robert Dallington, then secretary to the Earl of Rutland. Michell had wasted no time in placing this account in the bookseller's hands, and he and Strachey had shared between them in the production of a stolen, if not a surreptitious, copy of another's work.[60] The preface makes clear the reason for publica-

---

[58] Entered to J. Bailey, an obscure bookseller in Chancery Lane, on March 27, 1604, but not published until after May 9, the date of Michell's prefatory letter.

[59] I.e., "lov'd-ease"?

[60] Stafford, the printer, had himself been in trouble in 1598 for

tion. After telling the reader, "I promise not to per-
fourme any further or better seruice of this kinde, for
I purpose (if I can) to bestowe my time more profit-
ably then in the bookmaking trade," he goes on to hope
"what testimonie of his favour to the deceased Lord, his
maiestie will be pleased to affoord to his Lordships
dependants that are left alive, yet are some of them
vndone by his Lordships death"—a theme that he de-
velops at some length in the succeeding paragraphs.
It is clear that he did not subscribe to Strachey's view
that "Vertue hath alwaies in her selfe her end," but
chose rather to intimate in this discreet manner to
prospective patrons that he was now in a position to
offer his services.[61]

Strachey's "worthy friend" was not a writer, but first
and foremost a member of the legal fraternity. The
eldest son of Humphrey Michell of Old Windsor,[62]
steward of Windsor Castle[63] and member of Parliament,[64] Francis Michell was admitted to Emmanuel

---

printing an unauthorized copy of the *Accidence* and had had his
press confiscated, but by 1604 he was reestablished and flourishing
in his trade. See R. B. McKerrow (ed.), *A dictionary of printers
and booksellers* (London, 1910), and C. B. Judge, *Elizabethan
book pirates* (Cambridge, Mass., 1934), pp. 115–33.

[61] Dallington, however, recognizing the work, was quick to pre-
vent its unauthorized sale, and though we have no record of the
steps he took, one copy only exists with Michell's preface and
Strachey's verses, in the Cambridge University Library. Several
other copies, reprinted in a Shakespeare Association Facsimile in
1936, are to be found with the same title page, but nothing other
than the text. The following year Dallington reissued the work
as *A method for travell. Shewed by taking the view of France.
As it stoode in the yeare of our Lord 1598.* A comparison of the
two works shows that Dallington had taken possession of all
Stafford's printed sheets and added to them a new title page and
a somewhat irate twelve-page preface, printed by Thomas Creede.

[62] B.M. Add. MS 19,819, ff. 1–2, gives a detailed pedigree.

[63] W. H. Rylands (ed.), *The four visitations of Berkshire* (London, 1907–8), II, 179.

[64] See *Return of members of Parliament, Part I* (London, 1888).

College in 1584[65] and to Gray's Inn on August 13, 1590.[66] From 1594 to 1597 he had acted as secretary to Sir William Russell, Lord Deputy of Ireland,[67] and, after his death, both as secretary and commissary of musters under his successor, Lord Burgh.[68] The latter held office for only a few months, and, amid the disorder following his death, Michell was dismissed from his post, allegedly for misconduct.[69] He returned in some haste to England early in 1598 but did not immediately sever his connection with Ireland, since in 1600 he was granted the wardship of an orphaned Irish youth from one of the outlying provinces.[70]

After his return to England he resumed his studies at Cambridge and graduated Bachelor of Laws from the newly established Sydney-Sussex College in 1603.[71] It may have been through the influence of James Montague, first master of this college and by this date Dean of Lichfield,[72] to whom he later dedicated his pirated copy of *The view of Fraunce*, that Michell obtained his post as secretary to Whitgift. Here he came in contact with some of the most learned men of the day, among them John Stow, William Camden, Sir Henry Wotton, Izaak Walton, and the archbishop's protégé Richard Hooker. Whitgift's first biographer, Sir George Paule, controller of his household, tells us that "his home, for the lectures and scolastic exercise therin performed, might justly be accounted a little academy, and in some

---

[65] Venn, *op. cit.*, part I, III, 181.   [66] Foster, *op. cit.*, p. 77.
[67] See *D.N.B.* under "Michell," which, however, identifies him as an Oxford-educated native of Essex. See also H. C. Hamilton and others (eds.), *Calendar of state papers, Ireland* (London, 1860–1912), and J. S. Brewer and William Buller (eds.), *Calendar of the Carew MSS* (London, 1867–73) for this period.
[68] *Cal. S. P. Ireland*, 1597–98.   [69] Foster, *op. cit.*, p. 77.
[70] J. Morrin (ed.), *Calendar of the patent and close rolls of Chancery in Ireland* (Dublin, 1861), II, 561.
[71] Venn, *op. cit.*, part I, III, 181.
[72] See *D.N.B.*, under "Montague."

respects superior and more profitable"; [73] and Michell
in his preface gives his late master his full meed of
praise, noting further that Whitgift could convert even
those "brainsick sectaries" the Puritans. Humphrey
Michell was a Puritan, and his son implies that as a
result of a quarrel with his father over religion he was
himself "undone."[74]

Any setback had, however, been only temporary. A
man of considerable ambition and ability, Michell had
already held responsible positions under three admin-
istrators, had acted on Whitgift's behalf in the negotiations prior to the accession of James I to the throne of
England,[75] and was destined to fill positions of still
more importance: to spend six years beyond the seas
and suffer imprisonment by the Inquisition in Rome
in the service of Salisbury;[76] to become, on his return
to England, a bencher of Gray's Inn[77] and a justice of
the peace for Middlesex;[78] to be appointed a commis-
sioner for enforcing the monopoly of gold and silver
thread and to be knighted in 1620; a year later, after
a public outcry at his abuse of his position, to endure a
state trial, to suffer degradation from his knighthood,
expulsion from the Inns of Court,[79] and imprisonment
in Finsbury jail;[80] and then to live in poverty and ob-

[73] *D.N.B.*, under "Whitgift," quoting Paule's *Life*.

[74] Although heir, he received from his father only a gown and a
signet ring, according to his father's will (P.C.C. 58 Kidd). He
unsuccessfully challenged the administration of the estate in
1606 (P.C.C. 36 Stafforde).

[75] Various editors, *Calendar of state papers, domestic series*
(London, 1856–), 1625–26, p. 267; *D.N.B.*, "Michell."

[76] *Cal. S.P. Dom.*, 1603–10, pp. 176, 399; *D.N.B.* "Michell."

[77] Fletcher, *Pension book*, I, 202; February 3, 1613.

[78] W. le Hardy (ed.), *County of Middlesex; calendar to the
sessions records* (London, 1935–37), I, 240. He first appears as a
justice in September 1613.

[79] Foster, *op. cit.*, p. 77. His expulsion is noted against the
record of his entry.

[80] *D.N.B.*, "Michell"; T. B. Howell (ed.), *A complete collection*

scurity until his death in the reign of Charles I.[81]

We do not know whether Strachey was still friendly with Michell during the latter years preceding his disgrace, but in 1604 he had as a friend a man to whom a considerable future was assured. It may have been that Strachey himself was present at the "lectures and scholastic exercises" of Whitgift's "little academy," but it is not until the following year, 1605, that we find positive evidence of a larger circle of his friends, again in London.

Sejanus, first acted in 1603 by Shakespeare and his company, appeared on sale from the press of Thomas Thorpe,[82] and in addition to Jonson's brief Epistle to the Reader the quarto contained prefatory verses by his friends: George Chapman, his collaborator in *Eastward ho* and fellow prisoner during the turmoil caused by its presentation in 1605; John Marston, the other collaborator in the same play; Hugh Holland, fellow of Trinity College, best remembered for his sonnet contributed to Shakespeare's First Folio; PHILOS, conjectured to be Richard Martin, prince of revels at the Middle Temple;[83] Cygnus, Th. R., and Ev. B.; and William Strachey.

Strachey's contribution, although described as "one of the most cryptic things in Elizabethan literature,"[84] is a conventional sonnet, pointing the moral of the play, and gives no indication of his relations with the playwright.

of state trials . . . to 1783 (London, 1816–28), II, 1131–35; W. Notestein, F. H. Relf, and H. Simpson (eds.), *Commons debates, 1621* (New Haven, 1935), *passim*.

[81] *D.N.B.*, "Michell."

[82] Entered for publication November 2, 1604, but not printed until 1605.

[83] Leslie Hotson, *Shakespeare's sonnets dated* (London, 1949), p. 50.

[84] John St. Loe Strachey, *The adventure of living* (London, 1922), p. 57.

Upon SEJANUS.

How high a poor man showes in low estate
Whose base is firme, and whole frame competent,
That sees this Cedar, made the shrub of fate,
Th'on's little, lasting; Th'other's confluence spent.
And as lightning comes behind the thunder
From the torn cloud, yet first invades our sense,
So every violent fortune, that to wonder
Hoists men aloft, is a cleere evidence
Of a vaunt-curring blow the fates have given
To his forst state: swift lightning blindes his eyes,
While thunder from comparison-hating heaven
Dischargeth on his height, and there it lies:
If men will shun swolne Fortunes ruinous blastes,
Let them use Temperance. Nothing violent lastes.

                                                          William Strachey.

Nevertheless Jonson, comfortably established as one
of the leading playwrights of the day, was not including
prefatory verses merely to give weight to the printed
version of an already successful play but rather to express the cordial relations existing between Jonson
himself and certain of his friends or collaborators, to
whom he acknowledges his debt: "The following, and
voluntary Labours of my Friends, prefixt to my Booke,
have releived me in much, whereat (without them) I
should necessarilie have touchd."[85]

In a society where the perpetually busy presses
catered to a public with an avid taste for reading,
writers came to associate in many ways. Playwrights
collaborated; poets contributed prefatory verses to one
another's works and in their own commended or crit-
icized their friends or their rivals; sides were taken in
wordy battles by the pamphleteers; and quarrels were
begun and concluded, friendships made and broken,
because of the printed word. Nevertheless, in this form-
less and somewhat chaotic literary society there sprang
up groups whose friendships were to endure.

[85] *Sejanus*, Epistle to the Reader.

Legend associates the most famous of these with the Mermaid Tavern in Bread Street, where, on the first Friday in every month, there used to meet a company of "Right generous, jovial and mercurial Sireniacks,"[86] according to Thomas Coryate, who, having left England on his voyage to India in October 1612, ensured the widest possible circulation of his burlesque letters by addressing them to what has come to be known as the Mermaid Club. Moreover, he gives us the names of some of the members, among them Ben Jonson, John Donne, Richard Martin, and Hugh Holland, as well as others we know to have been their intimate friends: Christopher Brooke, witness at Donne's secret wedding and an old friend from his earliest days at Lincoln's Inn; Jonson's friend Inigo Jones, architect and designer of the scenery for his masques; and John Hoskins of the Middle Temple, for many years an intimate of Richard Martin.

There has been some argument about the nature of this Mermaid Club: whether it was a gathering of writers or whether it was more political; whether Shakespeare was ever a member and whether it was at the Mermaid that the reputed wit combats took place with Ben Jonson; and for what length of time the Mermaid was the center of these meetings.[87] One thing does stand out however. In 1612 these members were friends, and we have evidence that certain of them were friendly at an earlier date.

Hugh Holland contributed a prefatory sonnet to *Sejanus* in 1605, and when, in 1607, *Volpone* was first printed, among the prefatory verses was a poem by John Donne.[88] Whether or not the PHILOS who also

---

[86] Thomas Coryate, *Coryat's Crudities* (London, 1776), III, sigs. M2-M4.

[87] See I. A. Shapiro, "The 'Mermaid Club,'" *Mod. lang. rev.*, XLV (1950), 6–17; and Hotson, *op. cit.*, pp. 76–88.

[88] E. K. Chambers, *The Elizabethan stage* (Oxford, 1923), III, 367.

contributed verses to *Sejanus* was Richard Martin, there
is ample other evidence of his lifelong friendship with
the playwright.[89] There is, moreover, evidence that each
of these friends of Jonson was also friendly with
Strachey.

John Donne, writing in 1608, commended him to
Sir Henry Wotton as "Mr William Strachey allwayes
my good friend";[90] Richard Martin, writing to Strachey
in 1610 mentioned "our aunciant acquaintance & good
intentions";[91] and later, in Turkey, Strachey was to
show how much he preferred the company of Hugh
Holland to that of his master, the ambassador.[92] Finally
we find Strachey writing in friendly terms to Peter
Ferryman,[93] who appears not only as an intimate of
Jonson but also of Chapman's close friend, Matthew
Roydon,[94] regarded in his day as "a poetical light . . .
which shines not in this world as it is wisht, but yet the
worth of its lustre is known."

There can be no doubt that Jonson in 1605 had
his circle of friends, who may or may not have met
together in the Mermaid Tavern, but among whom
were some of its later habitués; and among these friends
was Strachey, himself on a friendly footing with some
of the leading writers of the day—Hugh Holland,
"thought worthy by some to be mentioned with Spen-
ser, Sidney, and other the chief of English poets";[95]
John Marston, considered by Meres one of the leading
satirists and by 1605 a coming dramatist; George Chapman, as early as 1598 reckoned along with Shakespeare
as one of "our best for Tragedie" and among "the best
for Comedy";[96] John Donne, of Lincoln's Inn, former
secretary to Lord Keeper Egerton, whose verses, highly

[89] Hotson, *op. cit.,* p. 47.   [90] See p. 93.   [91] See p. 125.
[92] See p. 80.   [93] See p. 94.   [94] See *D.N.B.,* "Roydon."
[95] *D.N.B.,* "Holland," referring to a contemporary comment.
[96] Francis Meres, *Palladis Tamia* (London, 1598).

thought of, still circulated among his private friends—
and, as well as the writers, Richard Martin of the Middle
Temple, member of Parliament and prominent lawyer,
to whom Jonson was to dedicate *The poetaster* in his
1616 folio.

And as the verses of Holland, of Donne, or even of
Matthew Roydon were circulated in manuscript, or as
the poets themselves at some convivial gathering de-
claimed them, so Strachey himself was ready with his
sonnet or his epigram. Only one of his manuscript
verses has survived, and that from a much later period
of his life,[97] but we have the word of another poet
ranked with the greatest of his day that his old boon
companion William Strachey was the maker of many
elegant little verses and an energetic champion of the
Muses.

Among the poets of the Inns of Court was Thomas
Campion, of Gray's Inn, who, in an epigram addressed
"Ad Gulielmum Strachaeum" tells us:

> Paucos iam veteri meo sodali
> Versus ludere, musa, ne graueris,
> Te nec taedeat his adesse nugis,
> Semper nam mihi charus ille comptis
> Gaudet versiculis facitque multos,
> Summus Pieridum vnicusque cultor.
> Hoc ergo breue, musa, solue carmen
> Strachaeo veteri meo sodali.[98]

This epigram serves moreover as added confirmation
of Strachey's presence at Gray's Inn. Campion made
few friends at Cambridge, and of the names mentioned
in his works in greater or less terms of intimacy the

[97] "Penitential verses," see p. 140.
[98] Vivian, *Campion's works*, p. 269. The epigram appeared only
in Campion's 1619 volume, but there is no indication when it
was written. It shows, however, that Campion and Strachey had
been friends for some time.

majority are connected with the Inn.[99] Many of the
young men of the Inns of Court, moreover, tried their
hand at verses and were also interested in the theatre
and friendly with writers. A suit commenced in Chancery in April, 1605, shows that Strachey's friendship
with Jonson was not merely that of an amateur of the
theatre with one of the leading playwrights, but that
Strachey himself was in close contact with theatrical
affairs.[100]

In 1600 Henry Evans, former manager of one of the
companies of boy players, the Children of the Chapel,
which had been inactive for some fifteen years, leased
from Richard Burbage his reconstructed playhouse in
the Blackfriars, intending to "erect or sett vp a companye of boyes . . . to playe playes and interludes."[101]
The revived company had from the start the services of
Ben Jonson as playwright, and by the time it had produced in 1601, among other plays, both *Cynthia's revels*
and *The poetaster,* the players were sufficiently popular
to merit Shakespeare's reference to "an eyrie of children, little eyases, that cry out on the top of question,
and are most tyrannically clapped for it." Trouble in
1601 over the alleged abduction of boys for service
with the company had led to a decree in the Court of
Star Chamber censuring Evans and ordering that all
assurances made to him regarding the playhouse should
be delivered up and canceled. Evans had prudently
anticipated this decree by assigning his interest in the
theatre to his son-in-law, Alexander Hawkins, and,

[99] *Ibid.,* p. xxviii.

[100] P.R.O. C33/107, f. 600, *Kendall* v. *Evans.*

[101] For the history of the Blackfriars Theatre and the Children of
the Chapel or, as they were later called, the Children of the
Revels, see Chambers. *Eliz. stage,* II, 23–61 and 475–517; E. K.
Chambers, *William Shakespeare* (Oxford, 1930), II, 52–71; F. G.
Fleay, *A chronicle history of the London stage, 1599–1642* (Lon-
don, 1890), *passim;* and C. W. Wallace, *The Children of the
Chapel at Blackfriars, 1597–1603* (Lincoln, Neb., 1908), *passim.*

furthermore, in need of capital to place his venture on a sound footing, had sold a half-share to three partners, Edward Kirkham, William Rastall, and Thomas Kendall.

Nevertheless Evans had decided it might be wise to leave the country for a while, and on his return in 1603, finding the theatres closed as a result of the plague, resolved to surrender his lease, but, the plague waning, changed his mind. Toward the end of the year, having spent some twenty pounds on repairs and redecorating, he obtained a new patent from Queen Anne, naming the company the Children of the Queen's Revels. When the theatres reopened the children immediately re-gained their former popularity. But although the com-pany was successful, and Middleton could advise a gallant, "if his humour so serve him, to call in at the Blackfriars, where he should see a nest of boys able to ravish a man," the affairs of the partners were not running smoothly.

Evans, the repairs to the theatre completed, called on Kirkham, Rastall, and Kendall to pay their share of the expenses, according to the terms of their agreement; and, when they refused to do so, proceeded against them for debt. They, in their turn, began a counter-action against Evans and Hawkins in Chancery,[102] and when, finally, in July 1606, witnesses appeared to give evidence on behalf of the defendants, among them was William Strachey of Crowhurst, gentleman, aged thirty-four years or thereabouts.

In his deposition[103] Strachey makes it clear that he was also a shareholder in the company, and we have

---

[102] The progress of this case is recorded in P.R.O. C33/107, ff. 597v and 600r; C33/109, f. 385v; C24/327; C33/111, ff. 483v and 542r; and C33/113, f. 79r. Depositions on behalf of the plaintiffs should, according to the index, be found in C24/327, but these have apparently been lost.

[103] P.R.O. C24/327.

evidence that another share was held by Jonson's collaborator and friend, John Marston, who also wrote for
the Children of the Revels. We do not know when these
shares were taken up, but apparently at some date after
the agreement had been made with the other three
partners Evans, still in need of capital, divided up his
own half-share in the company and allowed the two
young gentlemen from the Inns of Court to enter into
partnership with him. For an outlay of between £150
and £200, and a further payment of eight shillings a
week to provide "the dieting and ordering of the boys
used about the plaies there," each partner received
one-sixth of the profits, amounting, during the period
of success and popularity of the Children of the Revels,
to some £100 or £150 a year.[104] Each partner was
bound, however, to pay his share of any expenses in-
curred in repairs to the playhouse, in the purchasing
of stage properties, and the like.[105]

Although the suit commenced at common law was
merely a matter of debt, by the time action was under
way in Chancery it had come to include allegations of
nonpayment of the weekly eight shillings on the part of
Rastall, Kendall, and Kirkham; and it is clear, moreover, that the partnership was on the verge of dissolu-
tion, with Evans' opponents having the various stage
properties valued with a view to their disposal.

Strachey tells us that he "having some interest in the
busynes belonging to the said howse[106] hath payd a
sixthe part of such reparacons to the said Evans abowte
some two yeres now past[107] . . . the same amounting to
the sume of three pounds thirtene shillings and fower

[104] Chambers, *Eliz. stage*, II, 52. This was Kirkham's estimate of
the value of his share.
[105] *Ibid.*, II, 45–46. This was according to the agreement of 1601.
[106] I.e., the Blackfriars Theatre.
[107] I.e., in 1604. However, since the repairs were carried out in
1603, Strachey must have been associated with the theatre earlier
than that.

pence"; that he had heard Evans demand "of the said playntifes or their assignes according to his vsuall custom euery saturdy his said sume of viij.s." and that he had heard them refuse to pay; that, "at such tymes as [he] hath come and receiued his part, which hath bene sometymes once, twyce, and thrice in a week," Rastall, Kendall, and Evans had also received their share of the "beneffitt proffitt and commodity and gayn that haue risen and growen by reason of the said plaies"; and that, on Evans' behalf, he had often offered "the plaie bookes goods aparel and properties belonging to the said playes and exercise" to the other partners that they might be valued.

It is clear then that by the time we find Strachey as a friend of Ben Jonson he had been actively associated with the stage in London for some years. Furthermore, repairing to the theatre "once, twyce, and thrice in a weeke," he must have met many of the writers who were associated with it, including Samuel Daniel, who had been appointed by Queen Anne official censor of the plays to be acted by the Children of the Revels, and Marston, Chapman, and Day, all of whom, as well as Jonson, had written plays for the company. Further there were close ties between Jonson and his circle of friends and Shakespeare and his company. Not only was Richard Burbage the owner of the Blackfriars Theatre, but *Sejanus* itself had first been acted by the King's Men at the Globe in 1603, and we may be sure that Strachey, both as a shareholder in the company and as a friend of Jonson, came into contact from time to time with the most famous of all the companies of players and with their leading actor-writer.

This same case in Chancery gives us a partial answer to the mystery of the "Lady of the Strachey" who married the "Yeoman of the Wardrobe."[108] Among the

[108] Francis Peck, *Desiderata curiosa* (London, 1732–35), II, 12, listing the officials of Elizabeth's household, makes it clear that

deponents on Evans' behalf was also "David Yeomans
dwelling in the Blackfriars London Tailor of thage of
33 yeres or thereabouts," who, in his evidence, mentions that he is "tyreman" of the Blackfriars Theatre.
An obscure figure, there is no record of his marriage,
and we are left to speculate on the identity of this wife
who increased his fortunes or his position and on her
connection with Strachey. If this marriage took place
around this time, when we know that Yeomans was
connected with the Blackfriars Theatre, the "Lady"
could not have been one of Strachey's sisters, and the
most probable guess would appear to be a maidservant.

Along with the internal quarrels of the shareholders,
the company found themselves in trouble with the
authorities. The serious affair of *Eastward ho* in 1605
cost them the patronage of the Queen, and in 1606
Day's *Isle of gulls* led to those responsible for it being
cast into Bridewell, with a further loss of favor for the
company. The suit between the partners was finally
decided in Evans' favor,[109] but it was clear that some
reorganization was necessary, so Robert Keysar, a London goldsmith, having purchased Marston's share, assumed the management of the company. Of Strachey's
share we hear no more. He may have reassigned it to
Evans or to one of the other partners, and there is no
mention of him as a shareholder when the lease was
finally surrendered to Burbage and the King's Men in
1608.

The country gentleman come to the Inns of Court,

---

there was no such post as "Yeoman of the Wardrobe," but that
the staff consisted of the master, 2 clerks, a porter, a rent gatherer,
4 tailors, 3 embroiderers, and a skinner. That this is a detailed list
is borne out by the fact that in other departments the relevant
yeomen are listed, including the Yeoman of the Revels, the Yeoman of the Hunting Harriers, the Yeoman of the Stirrup, and
even the Yeoman of the Close Cart.
[109] P.R.O. C33/113, f. 79.

typical of the young gallant of the day, might be found in his idle moments at the playhouses, in the taverns, at the bearbaiting, cockfighting, or gaming—in general sharing the pleasures of the fashionable world or of the dubious society that clustered on its fringes. Jonson and his friends were in no way pale models of restraint and virtue, and we may be sure that Strachey, in addition to his support of the Muses, participated fully in their leisure activities. Penitent before his death he tells us

> Harke!   I have sinnd against Earth & heaven
> Early by date late in the even
> All manner sinnes all manner wayes
> I have committed in my daies[110]

and, even making allowance for some exaggeration due to remorse, we may well see him as one of the roaring boys, prototype of a young gallant, sowing his youthful wild oats within the city. But all this cost money, and many were the snares set for the unwary and many the impecunious gallants ready to assist in the mulcting.[111]

By 1605 Strachey was beginning to encounter money troubles. On June 23 he mortgaged all his property in Saffron Walden to his brothers-in-law, John and Sir Edmund Bowyer, for the sum of £510[112]—a much safer procedure than proffering it as security to a money-lender of the Penistone type, though it may well have been that they had been forced to come to his rescue because of debts falling due.

The brewhouse property, moreover, instead of being

[110] "Penitential Verses," Ashmole MS 781, f. 135.

[111] Sir William Fennor, *The counters commonwealth* (London, 1617), *passim*; reprinted in A. V. Judges, *The Elizabethan underworld* (London, 1930).

[112] P.R.O. C54/1818. Though this is a normal indenture of bargain and sale, no fines are recorded conveying the property to the Bowyers, and, moreover, when the property was finally sold in 1617, Strachey appeared as a vendor along with the two brothers.

a clear source of income, had become something of an
embarrassment, with Matthew Clayton, husband of one
of a pair of litigious daughters of Edward Taylor, from
whom Strachey's grandfather had bought the premises
in 1569, contesting his title in a series of suits in the
Courts of Requests and King's Bench[113]—suits which
Clayton and the sisters lost, but which, since they were
presented *in forma pauperis*,[114] meant that Strachey,
unable to recover his costs, was forced to bear the expense of his defense himself. This represented a considerable financial outlay in actions from which only
the lawyers benefited and in the course of which
Strachey found himself in imminent danger of arrest
for contempt of court.[115] As a final blow, the court, while
recognizing the validity of Strachey's title to the premises, took into account the plaintiffs' poverty and
awarded them the sum of forty shillings per annum for

[113] No proceedings are available for the cases in Requests, but
we have Strachey's word in P.R.O. C2 James I/C21/83, *Clayton* v.
Bowyer, that they took place and that the plaintiffs were dis-
missed every time. He is borne out by P.R.O. Req 1/50, and P.R.
O. Req 1/22, Entry Books of Decrees and Orders; and by P.R.O.
Req 1/199, Witness Book, which records also a suit between
Clayton and Strachey as early as 1604 and another suit between
Clayton and Elizabeth Dodd in which Strachey gave evidence.
Since Elizabeth Dodd appears as a codefendant with Strachey
and the Bowyers in the Chancery case above, it is certain that this
was also connected with the brewhouse. In King's Bench, Clayton
brought "severall eiectione firmes . . . in forma pauperis . . . in
bothe which suits it passed agaynst the title of the Complaynants
by nonsuite."
[114] G. Jacob, *A new law-dictionary* (London, 1772) : *"Forma
Pauperis,* Is where any person has just cause of suit, and is so
poor, that he cannot bear the usual charges of suing at law . . . in
which case . . . the judge admits him . . . without paying any
fees to any councellor, attorney, or clerk.
"If a cause goes against a *pauper,* or a plaintiff *in forma pauperis* be nonsuit; he shall not pay costs to the defendant, but
shall suffer such punishment in his person as the court shall
award. (23 H.8. c.15.)"
[115] P.R.O. Req 1/50, October 17, 1605.

ten years, payable out of the rents of the property.[116]

His capital diminished, and with it his income, Strachey faced a prospect familiar to many a young gentleman of the day: inability to live the life he was accustomed to without the assistance of the money-lenders, with their extortionate rates of interest and their bonds for double the sum advanced; failure to meet the debt and the alternative of flight and out-lawry or arrest by the sheriff's men; suit for debt in the Courts of King's Bench or Common Pleas and the attachment and loss of his property; and always the specter of the debtors' prison, where the unfortunate gallant might languish "two, three, four or five year, nay a dozen or twenty years together, before he can get himself released; or if he can chance to prevail so much with his creditors as to enfranchize him, it must be on some unreasonable, unconscionable condition."[117]

"Thus," adds William Fennor with feeling,

do many gentlemen perish under the hands of cruel creditors! . . . his lands extended on, his woods felled down before his face, those legacies and portions he should pay to his brothers and sisters, paid away to satisfy his debts . . . and so beggars a whole worshipful family, who before that cursed time had lived a hundred years or more in grace and favour in his country.[118]

Not only had Strachey obligations to his sisters as head of the family, but another son had been born to him, Edmund, baptized at Crowhurst on February 26, 1604.[119] The time had come for him to make a break with his life in London and seek some way of re-establishing his steadily dwindling fortune, if for no other reason than that his sons, when they came to man-

---

[116] P.R.O. Req 1/22, October 30, 1605.
[117] Judges, *op. cit.*, p. 446.   [118] *Ibid.*, p. 447.
[119] Crowhurst parish register.

hood, might have the start in life to which they were entitled as the sons of a gentleman. Unqualified in law and not experienced in trade, the only post he could fill was that of a secretary or, like his friend Marston, he could take holy orders. One other way existed out of his difficulties. He could seek his fortune beyond the seas in the service of one of the powerful trading companies of merchants. As we shall see, Strachey took the post of a secretary, but combined it with travel out of the country, and was to be, moreover, in the service of two of the large trading companies in the course of the next seven years of his life.

4. Turkey

WILLIAM STRACHEY, country gentleman and erstwhile gallant, while not yet reduced to the straits his friend Ben Jonson was later to envisage for another young man from the Inns of Court—

it shall be sued for its fees for execution, and not be redeemed; it shall cheat at the twelvepenny ordinary . . . for its diet all the term time, and tell tales for it in the vacation, to the hostess. . . . It shall fright all its friends with borrowing letters; . . . it shall not have money to discharge one tavern reckoning; . . . it shall want clothes, and by reason of that, wit, to fool the lawyers—[1]

was nevertheless forced to adopt the remedies suggested: "to repair itself by *Constantinople, Ireland,* or *Virginia.*" He was to visit all three, and it may well be that Jonson had the fate of his friend Strachey in mind when he penned the lines.

First on Jonson's list was Constantinople, and the means were at hand. Thomas Glover, secretary to Henry Lello, ambassador to the Grand Signior at Constantinople and representative of the Levant Company, had returned to England in 1605; and, finding considerable rivalry at home, with numerous ambitious gentlemen trying to oust Lello from his post, Glover

---

[1] *Epicoene,* Act II, sc. v.

decided to sue for it himself.[2] Although he attributed
his success to divine guidance,[3] he was able to present
a number of sound reasons why he should supplant his
former master: his long service with the Levant Company,[4] the risks he had run on their behalf, and his
knowledge of the Turkish tongue;[5] and by April 10,
1606, Thomas Glover had been chosen as the new
English ambassador to Constantinople.[6]

The company no doubt considered that a change of
ambassador could do no harm. A year earlier, finding
trade with Turkey at too low an ebb to justify the expense of maintaining a representative there, it had
prepared to wind up the business; but the King, provided with an ambassador at no cost to himself, had the
directors summoned before the Privy Council and
briefly instructed that "in concert they were to study
how to keep the business alive and to maintain an
Ambassador at Constantinople, as that was his Majesty's
firm resolve."[7] Lello himself, dissatisfied with his post,
hoped to be recalled,[8] and we may be sure that Glover
was not slow both in suggesting to the merchants how
he could bring about an increase in trade and in
criticizing the ineffectiveness of his master.

Certainly, if any improvement were to be effected in
conditions at Constantinople, Glover might be expected
to bring it about. The son of an English father and a

[2] P.R.O. S.P.97/5, f. 85, Glover to Lello, November, 1606.
[3] *Ibid.*, f. 85b.
[4] Alfred C. Wood, *A history of the Levant Company* (Oxford,
1935), p. 80. He had acted as secretary, first to Barton, then to
his successor Lello, since 1597.
[5] P.R.O. S.P.97/5, f. 85b.
[6] P.R.O. S.P. 105/143, f. 4, Letter of April 10, 1606, notifying
Lello of his replacement. It was acknowledged by Lello on June
12 (B.M. Cotton MS Nero, B.XI., f. 147b).
[7] H. F. Brown and A. B. Hind (eds.), *Calendar of state papers,
Venice* (London, 1900–25), 1603–7, p. 237.
[8] *Ibid.*, p. 318.

Polish mother, born at sea while his parents were sailing to London, he had spent most of his life in the Levant; and, in addition to the Polish tongue, which he spoke fluently, he had a "perfect understanding" of the Turkish language and a profound knowledge of Turkish law.[9] Furthermore, he was an irascible, flamboyant character, convinced of his own ability and prepared to yield to no one when he considered himself, as he invariably did, in the right.

In this he was in complete contrast to Lello, "a learned, wise, and religious English gentleman,"[10] whose enemies, Glover among them, accused him of damaging English influence by his timidity.[11] When first he assumed office in 1599 Lello had, indeed, allowed himself to be outwitted by the French ambassador, and he had not, during the seven years that he had held office, accomplished any major feats of diplomacy—but neither had he antagonized any of the other European ambassadors living in Constantinople and in most matters could count on their support, and as a body of Christians contemptuously allowed in a Moslem land, where the abortive Crusades were still remembered, their strength lay only in their apparent unity.[12] Turkish diplomacy, when bargaining with a Christian ambassador, consisted in flying into a passion, hurling the coarsest abuse, and soon passing from invective to threats, or even blows. To this the ambassador could remain unperturbed and eventually proffer a bribe, or, generally with less effect, try to give as good as he got.[13]

[9] Wood, *op. cit.,* p. 80.

[10] William Biddulph, *The travels of certaine Englishmen* (London, 1609), p. 40.

[11] John Sanderson, *The travels of John Sanderson in the Levant,* ed. W. Foster (London, 1931), p. 225.

[12] G. F. Abbott, *Turkey, Greece and the great powers* (London, 1916), pp. 1–2.

[13] *Ibid.,* p. 14.

If Lello were an exponent of the former method, Glover was to shine at the latter, and to the thrifty merchants of the company it was clear that this must help to reduce one of the normal overheads of the Levant trade —the gilding of the ever-open Turkish palm.

It is as well at this stage to mention the manner in which the French ambassador outwitted Lello, and the events leading up to it, for the aftermath of this quarrel was to assume some importance during Strachey's brief stay in Turkey and indirectly lead to his dismissal from Glover's service.

The various European colonies in Turkey lived under the protection of special treaties, known as capitulations, which enabled them to retain their nationality as long as they chose, to be governed by their own ambassadors and consuls without any interference from the Ottoman judicial authorities, and to conduct their business on clearly defined terms.[14] Traders whose countries had made no special treaty with the Turks had no personal safety or liberty of traffic, and therefore used to put themselves under the protection of one of the recognized nations, paying in return a percentage of the value of the merchandise protected. This was known as "consulage." The earliest English merchants in the Levant traded under the French flag, but once established they began to vie with their former protectors for the consulage of unattached foreigners, or *forestiers*. Barton, the second English ambassador, was granted the consulage of these *merchants forestiers*, but while he was away from Constantinople in 1596, campaigning with the Grand Signior, the French ambassador had Barton's consul at Alexandria denounced as a spy and summarily executed. Another English consul was installed at Alexandria on

¹⁴ *Ibid.*, p. 3.

Barton's return, but with his death in 1597 the French ambassador, by means of a substantial bribe to the Grand Vizier, secured again for his country the consulage of the foreign merchants.[15] Lello, Barton's former secretary and now his successor, very wisely decided to let the matter rest there, seeing clearly that the only ones to benefit from the altercation would be the Turks —the Grand Signior and his hierarchy of viziers—who were prepared to accept bribes from all and sundry. De Breves, the French ambassador, was rewarded for the blow that he had struck for French prestige by being allowed to retain for himself the consulage of the *merchants forestiers*.[16]

It was against this background of events that Thomas Glover was appointed the new representative, both of his king and of the Levant Company, and was, by April 1606, seeking to provide himself with a staff that would adequately indicate his importance in this post. He expected that Lello, although anxious to return home, would regard his supplanting as an act of treachery and that the embassy servants at Constantinople would tend to be loyal rather to their former master than to his successor; hence he appointed an entirely new staff, considerably greater in size than Lello's had been. In a post which involved carrying on a voluminous correspondence both in affairs of state and in matters of business, it was vital that he should have an efficient secretary.

Strachey had every opportunity to encounter Glover, and to offer his services in this capacity. His cousin John Strachey knew the new ambassador and had spent some four or five years in the Levant in the service of Sir John Spencer, former Lord Mayor of London, an immensely wealthy member of the Levant Company;

---

[15] *Ibid.*, pp. 84–85.   [16] P.R.O. S.P.97/5, f. 111.

and this cousin, moreover, made a free man of the Clothworkers' Company after his return to England in 1604, was now trading with Turkey on his own account and maintaining his own representatives at Tripoli, Zante, and Constantinople. John Strachey's tales, and his example, must have made it clear that money was there to be gained; and moreover, if it was prestige that was sought, the post of secretary to the ambassador gave every chance of advancement. Harborne, the first ambassador, had been succeeded by his secretary Barton; Lello, sent out as secretary to Barton, had stepped into his shoes a few months later; and now Glover, Lello's secretary, was in his turn to replace his master.[17]

Strachey could, however, bring a greater influence to bear than his cousin's acquaintance, or even friendship, with Glover. In December 1605 James I had granted a new charter to the Levant Company, and in the re-organization of the company following this grant Sir Thomas Lowe, Lord Mayor of London, was elected governor.[18] His elder brother, Sir Timothy Lowe, had married one of Strachey's cousins, Christiana Cooke; Sir Timothy's daughter Anna had married yet another of the Cookes, Christiana's brother George; and Strachey's mother-in-law, Elizabeth Forster, was a cousin of the Lowe family.[19] It seems probable that he was able to call on this important relation by marriage for assistance, and at a general court of the Levant Company, held sometime in 1606, Strachey was presented by Glover, recommended for the post of secretary, and accepted by the company. He was now not only Glover's

[17] Wood, *op. cit.*, p. 80.

[18] M. Epstein, *The English Levant Company* (London, 1908), pp. 68–69, 153–211.

[19] R. Hovenden (ed.), *The visitation of Kent, taken in the years 1619–1621* (London, 1898), p. 116; G. E. Cockayne, *Some account of the lord mayors and sheriffs of the city of London . . . 1601 to 1625* (London, 1897), p. 20.

personal servant, but also an officer of the company, and responsible to both.[20]

Nothing remained but to set his affairs in order and to prepare for an absence from England of indefinite length. We have no record of the date of his appointment, which probably coincided with that of Glover as ambassador;[21] but on May 4, 1606, Strachey assigned the brewhouse property in trust to his brothers-in-law Sir Edmund, John, and Benjamin Bowyer, partly to make some provision in the form of a jointure for his wife Frances and partly to end the entail on the property in order to sell portion of it.[22] July 7 saw him deposing in Chancery as to his interest in the Blackfriars Theatre, and August 17 his appearance before King James at Hampton Court as a member of Glover's retinue, when the new ambassador received his credentials in the form of a letter to Sultan Achmed.[23]

[20] P.R.O. S.P.105/110, f. 12: Company writing to Glover, "your Secretary Mr. Strachey whome you likewise comended for that place And was entertayned at your Request And albeit your seruant yet he was chosen our Officer."

[21] The court books of the company do not go back to this date, but the fact that he was obviously winding up his affairs would argue that he was expecting to leave England as early as May 4.

[22] P.R.O. C54/2425, a deed of 1620, refers to this transaction and to an indenture made at the same time which is no longer extant. It is borne out by P.R.O. Ind. 17184, f. 2, making over the title to the Bowyers on May 8, and P.R.O. C2 Jas. I/C21/83, *Clayton v. Bowyer*.

[23] W. A. Shaw, *The knights of England* (London, 1906), II, 140, indicates that Glover was at court on this date and suggests that it was also the occasion of the conferring of his knighthood. *Calendar of state papers, domestic series, James I, 1603–10*, however, refers to him as Sir Thomas Glover in April of that year. The King's letter to the Grand Signior (P.R.O. S.P.97/5, f. 76) is dated August 16. It is not specifically stated that Strachey was present, but Glover later mentions "thirty of my men in lyveryes of redd cloathe, as I shewed myself before his Majesty in England" (P.R.O. S.P.97/5, f.102b.) ; in view of Glover's love of show, it is unlikely that he would have let slip any chance of parading his whole staff.

Glover, his retinue assembled, was now ready to sail in one of the company's ships, the *Royal Exchange*, of some 300 tons burden, at the moment taking on cargo in the Thames.[24] His friend John Sanderson considered Glover's followers a jolly band. Writing to a Constantinople merchant, Robert Barton, in August 1606, he tells him, "I have a very good lute by me, which I wishe with you; but Sir Thomas carieth with him all sorts of instruments and excelent men in musique, as I am tould."[25] The Levant Company, thrifty always, was prepared to pay only for a retinue of fifteen men, so that the rest of his followers were gentlemen traveling at their own expense or servants for whom Glover paid.[26] This in no way deterred him, however, and he sailed with thirty servants, as well as "half a dozen of voluntary gents," a train that he confessed was "somewhat extraordinary."[27] His wife and her three personal servants completed the party.[28]

About the middle of September 1606 the *Royal Exchange*, her loading completed, weighed anchor and set sail for Constantinople by way of Algiers, Zante, and Chios, the normal route; and on the eve of his sailing Glover received final instructions from the company.[29]

[24] Epstein, *op. cit.*, p. 225.

[25] Sanderson, *op. cit.*, p. 233, Letter of August 28, 1606.

[26] P.R.O. S.P.105/143, f. 7b: "Item according to the order of Courte Wee haue taken order with the Owners of the Royall Exchange to paie them here for the Victualles of the 15 men which goe vpon their charges, and for anie more that goeth in the Shippe they are to satisfie the Owners themselves."

[27] P.R.O. S.P.97/5, f. 85b.

[28] *Ibid.* Lady Glover died of the plague two years after her arrival in Constantinople. Sanderson thought very highly of her and described her as "a most discreete, wise, milde, a very gentill gentillwoman; a lamb by her father [i.e., her maiden name] and no lesse in hir owne nature; a lady wourthy to be ever most beloved" (*op. cit.*, pp. 233–34).

[29] P.R.O. S.P. 105/143, f. 7b, dated September 15, 1606.

He was to stay in Algiers two days only, and there to "treate with the King and Duana for our future quiett Trade"; the stay at Zante was limited to four days, and at Chios, a Mediterranean paradise, to six. Glover was to make an inventory of all plate and household furnishings provided by the company for the use of the ambassador and to take possession of them from Lello for his own use, and he was to endeavor to recover the consulage of the *merchants forestiers*. Among instructions regarding the multifarious details of trade, there cropped up also the inevitable favor for a friend of the owner: "Wee Doe deliver vnto you Bookes in Eubrewe Greeke and Latten sent by Mr Broughton to you which bookes he Desireth you to dispose of at Constantinople vppon severall learned Jewes at your Discreation which doe prove out of the Prophits that the Messias is alreadie come."[30]

At the same time the company sent instructions to Anthony Abdy,[31] its chief representative among the merchants in Constantinople, regarding Glover's salary, which had been fixed at 3,000 chequins a year, with the addition of certain consulage dependent on trade.[32] The chequin, or Venetian *zecchino*, was a favorite

---

[30] See *D.N.B.*, "Broughton, Hugh. (1549–1612)." According to this authority he was not in England but in Middleburgh at this date, so the volumes may have been sent to the company by a friend or relation. There is no evidence that he was in any way connected with the Levant Company. A. W. Pollard and G. R. Redgrave's *A short-title catalogue of books printed in England, Scotland and Ireland, 1475–1640* (London, 1946) lists 49 works by him, not one of which, from the title alone, appears to fit the description given. Nevertheless his hobby was arguing with Jewish scholars.

[31] Sanderson, *op. cit.*, p. 205, n. 1. On his return to England he married a daughter of the Lord Mayor and later became an alderman. Prior to his death in 1640 he was prominent in both the Levant Company and the East India Company.

[32] P.R.O. S.P.105/143, f. 6b.

medium of exchange owing to its constant weight and purity, fluctuating in value between 6*s.* 8*d.* and 9*s.* At this date it was probably worth nearly 9*s.*; the ambassador's salary was quite substantial.[33]

The voyage passed without incident. Glover was successful in his negotiations with the ruler of Algiers,[34] and it may have been after leaving this port that they encountered the storm to which Strachey later made reference: "I had beene in some stormes before . . . upon the coast of Barbary and Algeere."[35] Zante was safely passed, however, and on November 10 the party arrived at Chios,[36] which "for the pleasantnesse is called the Great Turkes Garden."[37] From here Glover wrote to Lello, announcing that he was on his way and demanding that Lello immediately vacate the house he was occupying and have it ready for Glover and his retinue to move into on their arrival.[38] The new ambassador had never been noted for his tact, and this letter, a curious mixture of arrogance and piety, could hardly have predisposed Lello toward his former secretary. Lello moreover had no cause to think highly of the company, which Glover now represented. After the letter of April announcing his replacement he had heard nothing further, and his pleas for financial assistance had gone unheeded.[39] Consulage due to him from Aleppo had not arrived, and he had been forced to seize and pawn cloth belonging to the merchants.[40] He had written to Robert Cecil, Earl of Salisbury,

[33] See Sanderson, *op. cit.*, p. 295, for a discussion of the currencies used.
[34] P.R.O. S.P.105/110, f. 1.   [35] *Purchas his pilgrimes*, XIX, 8.
[36] P.R.O. S.P.97/5, f. 85.
[37] Sanderson, *op. cit.*, p. 37, n. 7. For a fuller description see Thomas Dallam, *The diary of Master Thomas Dallam, 1599–1600*, ed. J. T. Bent (London, 1893), pp. 443–46.
[38] P.R.O. S.P.97/5, f. 85.
[39] B.M. Cotton MS, Nero B.XI, f. 148b.   [40] *Ibid.*

begging him to intercede with the company on his behalf,[41] but by the time Glover's letter arrived he had reached the stage of casting around to see what personal belongings he might reasonably sell.[42]

Glover, vaguely expecting possible antagonism on the part of his former master, pointed out further in his letter that since he was inferior to no man among his countrymen and eminently suited by natural endowments to fill the post of ambassador, there was no reason whatsoever why Lello should envy or malign him. Later he was to quote this letter to show that he had extended a hand of friendship to Lello, but it would be hard to imagine a more provoking letter for a retiring ambassador to receive after he had served his country with honor for nearly ten years and was now cast off by his employers, in desperate financial straits, and patronized by his successor, his former secretary who had supplanted him. He appears not to have felt his replacement keenly, but the slight came in the niggardly treatment of him, the representative not only of the company but also of the King.

At Chios Sir Thomas Glover's jolly band of lutists received the addition of a further member, and, whatever Strachey may have thought of his master and of his companions on the voyage, there can be no doubt of his pleasure at encountering again one of the old friends of his London days. Glover tells us himself, and in some detail, of the meeting:

[41] P.R.O. S.P.97/5, f. 74b, August 3, 1606: "well I am sure I have found little love and favour from them, for all my paines & troubles in there affayres. but I hope your honor will patronize your poore servant in all his honest actions and suffer them not to wronge me" (*ibid.*, f. 80, October 22, 1606).

[42] *Ibid.*, f. 84b, November 8, 1606: "my poore estate, which is dryven so lowe, that I am forced to see what I have about me, and doe expect little regard from them, vnles by your honors recommendacons . . ."

Nowe concerninge . . . Mr Hugh Holland your Lordship shall vnderstande, that in my voyadge to Constantinople touchinge at an Ilande within the Arches of Pellagho, some 400 mille distant from Constantinople by name Sio, I founde the same man vested in longe robbes after the Greeks order, but some what bare, and vnderstandinge him by proffetion a Scoller, and an Englishe Gentleman of 500 li lande a yeare, I fell to examine him from whence he came, and for what place he was bounde, he repplied, that vppon suche a tyme he came out of Englande, (beinge litle after the execution of the late Traytors) went for Italie, and soe to Roome and thence as a Pillgrime he came to Naples, and being there (sayeth he) vnderstandinge of my cominge for Constantinople with the presente, deliberated to goe to Constantinople to see the same delliuered; and afterwards determined to take his iorney or pillgrimadge for Gierusalem, and soe for Englande; I perciuinge of his beinge at Roome, by his sayed reporte, as allsoe his cominge out of Englande in soe dangerous a tyme, I begune to suspecte him not to be loyall to his Prince: and further inquiringe of what relligion he was and whether he had a passe or a licence, as ordinarie gentlemen of his sorte usuallie have from the honorable Counsayle: he repplied that he was a Papiste, which relligion he will never denie, and for the pasporte allsoe (he sayed) to have it vnder the kings Maiesties owne hande, but (queathe he) I have lefte the same in Venice, and had not it about him, and that Sir Harrie Wotton his Majesties Ambassador in Venice, could testiffie boath the same, and of his loyaltie towards his highnes and the contrie, for that at his beinge in Venice, he hath shewed it him, yet bycause I thought it was noe reasone to giue credit to his bare words, I willed him to have patience, and that he should not goe from me, vntill I had sufficient certifficat from the sayed Sir Harrie Wotton, of that pasporte and his loyaltie towards his soveraigne, and soe in deede I stayed him, and in the meane tyme vsed him not as a prysoner, but rather as my Companion, with all gentlenes possible; . . . he is a subtile disputer, and like a Romishe malcontente in all his

argumentts (as far as he dares) contynewally malign-
ethe our contries religion, and gouerment.[43]

One can perhaps feel some sympathy with Glover if
he tried by argument to gain ascendancy over Holland,
who, no cloistered scholar, was the friend of greater
men than Glover and had sharpened his wits in the
irreverent company of the dramatists. Indicted for
recusancy early in 1604,[44] he had nevertheless managed
to satisfy the authorities of his loyalty to his king and
had obtained permission to travel abroad;[45] and, after
visiting Venice and Rome he had, as Glover tells us,
decided to visit Constantinople to see the pageantry
that was to accompany the installation of the new ambassador and the delivery of the present that he was
bearing from King James to the Grand Signior.

In 1599 Elizabeth had sent the Turkish ruler "a great
and curious present,"[46] a pipe organ, designed to "scan-
dalise other nations, especially the Germans." James,
to ensure the maintenance of good relations with the
Turks, took the opportunity to send a further present
with Glover—this time apparently a large quantity of
fabrics and brocades.[47] And although the thrifty king
made some token payment of his share in the venture,
the bulk of the cost had to be borne by the Levant
Company.[48]

[43] P.R.O. S.P.97/5, f. 116.

[44] H. Bowler (ed.), *London sessions records, 1605–1685* (London, 1934), p. 3.

[45] Logan Pearsall Smith (ed.), *The life and letters of Sir Henry
Wotton* (Oxford, 1907), I, 408. There is no record of the date
when this permission was granted.

[46] *Cal. S. P. Dom.*, 1598–1601, p. 156; Dallam, author of *Travels*,
accompanied this present from England to Constantinople.

[47] P.R.O. S.P.97/5, f. 102b.

[48] *Cal. S. P. Dom.*, 1603–1610, p. 270. James may have contributed £5000 toward the present, but the merchants' complaints
about the expenses to which they were put in this connection suggest that he found some way of recovering the money (P.R.O. S.P.
105/110, ff. 1 and 3).

Although they were now near Constantinople, difficulties of navigation in the landlocked Aegean cost the *Royal Exchange* a further month before the Dardanelles were reached.[49] An advance party arrived in Constantinople on December 17, 1606;[50] and on December 23 the *Royal Exchange*, accompanied by one of the company's smaller vessels, the *Allethia*,[51] which had overtaken them in the straits, anchored in the port.[52] The party remained on board for five days, and on December 28, the Grand Signior and his women having come down to the waterside, the two ships engaged in a mock skirmish, discharging their guns and maneuvering within the narrow confines of the harbor. The display so pleased the Turk that he sent two of his officers to thank and welcome them and presented Glover with two vests of cloth of gold and the captains of the ships each with a vest of cloth of silver. When the party landed they were received with the greatest acclamation and, escorted by a large body of troops, made their way through the crowded streets to the ambassador's house[53]—to find that Lello, according to instructions, had moved out, but into the house next door; and, in defiance both of Glover and of the company, had taken with him every stick of furniture, every hanging, and every piece of plate, leaving the house as bare as the day it was built.[54] Glover tried ineffectually to recover the property and wrote indignantly to the company of Lello's enormities.[55] Lello in his turn maintained stoutly that it was his own property,[56] apparently forgetting that once thwarted, in however minor a degree,

---

[49] *Cal. S. P. Ven.*, 1603–7, p. 449.   [50] P.R.O. S.P.105/110, f. 1.

[51] Of 160 tons burden (Epstein, *op. cit.*, p. 226).

[52] P.R.O. S.P.97/5, f. 89.   [53] *Ibid.*

[54] P.R.O. S.P.105/110, f. 3.

[55] *Ibid.*, The company is replying to a letter from Glover dated January 14, 1607.

[56] B.M. Cotton MS, Nero B.XI, f. 149b.

Glover would go to any lengths to reestablish himself— as later events were only too clearly to prove.

On January 8, 1607, Glover, accompanied by Lello and Strachey, presented the first of his credentials to Hassan Pasha, lieutenant to the Viceroy, and delivered to him a portion of the present. The Turk, to Glover's great disgust, cast aside his letter unread once the servants entered bearing the present, but "for his heighnes sake graced me, my predicessor Mr Lello, and my secretarye with each of vs a vest of cloth of gould,"[57] according to the custom of the country. While still outwardly maintaining cordial relations with his successor, Lello had found that he was in every way as arrogant as he had feared and soon wrote both to the company, and to Secretary of State Salisbury, complaining that Glover was "a man so blowen bigger with his owne pryde, that they who have sett him vp, as an Idoll against me, & therfore much les myself, are to hope but litle good from him."[58] The same ship had carried also letters from Glover complaining of Lello,[59] but both ambassadors knew that it would be four months before a reply could be expected and that their differences, unless they dragged on that long, must be settled between them there in Constantinople. Lello moreover felt strongly about the niggardly attitude of the company, which would allow him only 600 chequins for his homeward voyage, a sum barely sufficient to pay his debts,[60] and which had ordered him to return as quickly and as cheaply as possible, like a dismissed employee rather than a retiring ambassador.[61]

[57] P.R.O. S.P.97/5, f. 91b.
[58] *Ibid.*, f. 95b; B.M. Cotton MS, Nero B.XI, f. 149b.
[59] Lello's letters were dated January 15, 1607. P.R.O. S.P.105/ 110, f. 3, refers to a letter from Glover, bearing date January 14, 1607, and unfortunately no longer preserved, in which he complains about Lello.
[60] P.R.O. S.P.97/5, f. 95b.   [61] *Ibid.*, f. 99b.

By the end of January Lello's patience with the company was exhausted. He had hoped that the merchants resident in Constantinople would come to his aid, but some of them had demurred; and he found Glover's attitude changing from arrogance to open malice. Perhaps correctly he attributed this to the fact that Glover, having acted against him behind his back, felt uneasy in his mind about having done so, although there remained the fact that Lello, by taking possession of the furniture, had crossed him and so laid the foundation for Glover's enmity. Nevertheless, Lello, in his exasperation, went so far as to threaten that if he received no satisfaction from the company, he was prepared to take the matter to the King and the Privy Council.[62] As yet he was still officially ambassador, and was to remain so until Glover had presented his credentials to the Grand Signior himself—and this, in view of the much more liberal allowance made to Glover by the company and of Glover's greater retinue and obviously more important status, all added to Lello's indignation.

On February 8 Glover and Lello made their last public appearance together, and for the last time hid their open hostility to each other. Glover, at last confirmed in his position, wrote exultantly both to Salisbury and to the Levant Company,[63] detailing his reception at the hands of the Grand Signior, who "hath not only graced me, and some of my gentlemen, contrary to all his former customes & Canons with vests of cloath of gould, but hath graunted me other allowaunces of provicion for my house at my first cominge, as none of my Predicessors, nor any forrayne Ambassador ever had at their entrance." He conjures up in detail the scene,

[62] B. M. Cotton MS, Nero B.XI, f. 150.
[63] P.R.O. S.P.97/5, f. 102b; S.P.105/109, f. 28. These two letters are duplicates.

vivid under the Mediterranean sun: the swarming crowds of sightseers in their brilliant costumes; the multitude of Turkish soldiers drawn up to receive them, *capudgis,* janissaries, *chauses,* and *boltagis* in their thousands lining the route and escorting the party to the palace; Glover and Lello "richly attired, fittinge to this contry fashion," with their servants in liveries of red and blue and their retinue of gentlemen "cloathed in longe gownes of cloath of gould," crossing from Pera to Constantinople by frigate amid a thunder of guns from the ships in the harbor and the wild delight of the crowd; and their reception on shore, when, mounted on the finest Turkish steeds, they rode in procession to the palace, picking their way through the cheering crowds thronging the streets. At the dinner a hundred *capudgis* in cloth of gold bore silver dishes of food to the Christian visitors, where, upon a rich seat, they dined with the viziers. When the banquet was at an end, Glover and Lello were vested in golden robes and their gentlemen in gold and silk, and, accompanied by eighty-two *capudgis* bearing the presents, they came in turn before the Grand Signior, sitting apart on a pearl-studded throne, and made obeisance to him. After this Lello, "by his Interpreter," surrendered his place, and Glover, "by worde of mouth," made his speech and delivered up the King's letter. Glover details how in reply the Grand Signior ordered that he was to be given satisfaction in all things and to be paid as much honor as, or even more than, any other ambassador and how, finally, the audience over, the party were accompanied again to the waterside, and, with a last thunder of ordnance, sailed for Pera, accompanied by various of the *chauses,* for a final banquet.

Lello having surrendered his charge to Glover had no occasion for further dealings with him and turned instead to the French ambassador, not his old adversary De Breves, who had returned to France in 1605,[64] but his successor De Salignac,[65] who was regarded both by Lello and the English merchants in Constantinople as a "wise gentleman & a greate good lover of our Nation."[66]

Dissension had also begun to appear in Glover's own somewhat overcrowded household,[67] and relations with the English merchants were becoming strained. Glover, notwithstanding, proceeded to throw all his energies into obtaining the renewal of the English treaty with the Turks with the object of bringing the foreign merchants again under the English flag. He used as a pretext to open the discussions the fact that in the French treaty their king was described as "King of Kings," or "Emperor," while James was dismissed merely as "King."[68]

On March 18, 1607, he wrote jubilantly to inform Salisbury that he had managed to insert into the treaty, which had been sealed, "that all the Fleminges, and all other marchaunts Forastiers whatsoever should come vnder the kinge of Ingland his banner," justifying his action by pointing out that he dealt with the French only as they had dealt with Lello and that he had acted only in the interest of his king and country.[69] Energy expended in such a worthy cause proclaimed the greatest patriotism, but in the same letter the reason for his enthusiasm was revealed. As the grateful French king

[64] *Nouvelle biographie universelle,* ed. Hoefer (Paris, 1852–77), VII, 354.

[65] I can find no reference to him; and Glover, notoriously free in his spelling of proper names, refers to him as "de Sellamake," which I take to be De Salignac.

[66] P.R.O. S.P.97/5, f. 119.

[67] *Ibid.,* f. 105. Glover, by February 15, "hath carried such a traine & retynue with him, that he is all readie growne wearie of some of them."

[68] *Ibid.,* f. 109.   [69] *Ibid.,* f. 111.

had rewarded De Breves' success, so Glover had no hesitation in suggesting that his efforts merited the like substantial reward, the grant for life of the income gained from the consulage of the foreign merchants.

The French ambassador, needless to say, moved immediately in the matter and made such vigorous representations to the Grand Signior that the treaty was immediately rescinded.[70] This must have taken place by the time Glover wrote to Salisbury, and, although he exulted in his success, he must have seen the golden prize slipping from his grasp. He needed to blame someone else for his failure and chose at once those nearest to hand: Lello, who was on friendly terms with the French ambassador, and Strachey, who had by this time shown clearly that he preferred the company of Lello to that of Glover.

Writing to Salisbury, Glover continued his tale of complaints against Lello, but now Strachey's name appears also as one of Glover's enemies:[71]

Though I am verie sorrie and noe lesse unwillinge (right honorable to complayne of my Prodecessor Mr Lello, yet necessitie doeth soe much vrge me, beinge too too vnsuportable and able to beare noe longer, his ould inueterat enuie nowe breakinge out into open mallice. First at my comminge to Constantinople (notwithstandinge the extraordinarie honors I shewed him, in gracinge him euerie way forthe, and giuinge him the vpper hande untill wee appresented ourselues vnto the Gran signior) he did not onlie maligne me undeseruedlie amongst his common and familliar frends in extenewatinge my credit and authoritie and in perticuler bycause he was not able in his tyme to procur to inserte this article of the merchantes foristiers in our Capitullations, he hath worked vnderhande most shamefullie with the Frenche Ambassador to crosse me herin, and vppon his reporte the sayed Frenche Am-

[70] *Cal. S. P. Ven.*, 1603–7, p. 485.
[71] P.R.O. S.P.97/5, f. 114.

bassador did not stick to tell the Vizeroys here, that I was not the Kings Ambassador but the merchants, and that I had not commission from my Kinge to worke in this bussiness of the merchantts forastiers but it was my owne willfull doeinge soe that he did his best indeuour to crosse my designes herin; yet God whoe is stronger than an enuious man or the Divell, hath furthered my iust cause; yet the ill will of the sayed Mr Lello . . . is to be considered and at his cominge into England worthilie to be checked.

All this obiections of myne against him (besids the reporte of men of sufficient credit) twoe principall causes makethe me to confirme in my consciens to be trewe. the first, after we haue kissed the Gran signiors hande, from the 8 of Februarie vntill this present howre, his howse beinge next adioyninge vnto myne, he never but once or tweys vouchsafed to come to see me, neither to heare the worde of God preached, but contynewally once or tweys a weeke some tymes at night, and some tymes in the daye was in the Frenche Ambassadors howse banketinge and confferinge with him of what matter God he best knowethe. . . .

More ouer I hauinge intertayned a Gentleman in Englande on Mr Stracchi to my Secretarie vppon iust suspition and manifest reporttes that whatsoeuer designe I had pretended against the Frenche, it was presentlie reffered vnto him, which I suspectinge by manie circumstances . . . to proceede from Mr Lello. and seeinge my sayed Secretarie allsoe contynewally frequentinge his howse, gave him chardge to the contrarie; notwithstandinge the sayed Secretarie not onlie allmost euerie night, when I and all my people were abeade by stelthe went in to the sayed Mr Lellos howse, but allsoe his Majesties lettres to the Gran signior I hauinge givne him to translate it into Englishe, he hath not onlie shewed them vnto a notorious Papist on Hugh Hollande whom I have stayed vppon a suspition . . . but alsoe hath givne him the coppie therof which I doe sende your Lordship here inclosed vnder the sayed Hollande his owne hande for a testimonie, which gave me a greate suspition that he dealte vnhonestlie with me, whervppon I could doe noe lesse then to bid him avoyde my howse . . . hauinge fownde him to doe thinges expreslie contrarie to my order, espetially in soe suspitious a tyme and manner.

In effect, Strachey had little choice in the matter. On the one side was Glover, quarrelsome and arrogant, with dissension already among his followers and with a riotous and ribald household;[72] and on the other side were Lello, a cultured gentleman, a scholar, and a fellow member of Gray's Inn,[73] and, naturally allied with Lello, Strachey's old friend Hugh Holland. However he spent his time when on duty and however he felt toward his master, he obviously had far more in common with the residents of the house next door, and it was natural that his leisure moments should have been spent there. It was a far cry from the treachery that Glover was later to allege, but equally it was far from prudence. Glover's demand was for uncompromising and unswerving loyalty to himself alone, and his accusations against Strachey fell naturally from his lips. He knew, however, that it was impossible to keep his designs a secret in the intrigue-ridden city, and in spite of Glover's protestations against both Strachey and Lello it is clear that the French ambassador did not begin to take effectual action until the treaty was sealed and its contents common knowledge.

Glover's proof of Strachey's treachery is of the slightest. He encloses copies of King James's letter to the Grand Signior, in Latin in Strachey's own hand[74] and in translation in Hugh Holland's,[75] but since the contents of the letter were in no wise secret, and since both the copy and the translation were probably made at his order, the enclosures prove nothing. He did not stop at writing to complain of his secretary however.

[72] *Ibid.*, f. 101.
[73] Joseph Foster, *Admission register*, p. 104, March 13, 1603.
[74] P.R.O. S.P.97/5, f. 76.   [75] *Ibid.*, f. 76b.

The same evening, March 17, 1607, he burst into
Strachey's chamber, accompanied by the master of his
house, Nicholas Heath, and, finding Strachey there
alone with James Rollok, his manservant, proceeded to
abuse him for keeping company with Lello, whom he
described as a traitor to his king and his country.[76] He
ended by dismissing his secretary from his post. Strachey
promptly joined Glover's antagonists next door, and
Lello, in his defense, wrote to Salisbury that Strachey's
only crime was that he had seen too clearly what Glover
was up to.[77]

The quarrel between Glover and Lello had come also
to include money matters. The merchants had paid
1,000 dollars to Glover to defray Lello's expenses and
pay his debts, but Lello found that he was unable to
lay hands on the money, which he thought Glover had
probably spent on bribes in prosecuting his suit with
the Turks.[78]

The progress of the quarrel was halted by Bairam,
the Moslem festival, and, with all official business at a
standstill, the two adversaries spent their time composing letters about each other to Salisbury and to the
company—Glover recording with some satisfaction
that Lello had profaned the festival by going with the
French ambassador to a picnic banquet in the fields
outside the city and imputing his "rashnes and im-
prudentie either vnto his pationat mynde . . . or else
to the mallicious dulnes of wit which by natur he ever
hath had."[79] Lello meanwhile complained to the company that Glover was "a man so dronke with pryde
and wantones, that he hath not only forgotten me
sometymes his master, but him self & you & of whose
insolences heere to Complayne it were but lost labor."[80]

Bairam over, the Viceroy demanded the return of

---

[76] *Ibid.*, f. 151.   [77] *Ibid.*, f. 119.   [78] *Ibid.*, f. 119b.
[79] *Ibid.*, f. 123.   [80] B.M. Cotton MS, Nero B.XI, f. 151.

Glover's treaty, since he was clearly in the wrong, and after violent argument Glover restored it.[81] A third ambassador had by now become involved in the affair— Ottavian Bon, the Venetian. Asked by the Grand Vizier to act as a mediator, he had no option but to tell him that the foreigners were covered by the flag of France. "This," added Bon, "somewhat displeased the English Ambassador"; and he went on to detail to his masters how he had tried to smooth things over between the rivals.[82]

Glover, "somewhat displeased," promptly concluded that Bon was hand in glove with the French, and so with Lello. Bon had drawn his attention to the presence in Constantinople of a number of French soldiers of fortune, who might not take kindly to Glover's vilification of their countryman. The ambassador immediately took this to be the revelation of a plot hatched against him by Lello and saw himself murdered, a martyr to his country's cause. Convinced that his days were numbered, his main preoccupation was to ensure that his assassin, Lello, would be brought to justice.[83] At the same time he summoned various influential members of the English community in Constantinople, among them Anthony Abdy, the company's financial agent, William Biddulph, his own preacher,[84] and William Pearche and Edward Long, merchants, and, producing a document purporting to prove that Lello had combined with the French ambassador to murder him, demanded that they sign it. This they refused to do.[85] He then produced another document stating that he had ordered Lello to leave the country,[86]

[81] P.R.O. S.P.97/5, f. 138b.
[82] *Cal. S. P. Ven.*, 1603–7, p. 493.   [83] P.R.O. S.P.97/5, f. 138b.
[84] Author, under a pseudonym, of *The travels of certaine Englishmen*. See Pollard and Redgrave, *S.T.C.*, 3051–52.
[85] P.R.O. S.P.97/5, ff. 135, 150.
[86] *Ibid.*, f. 131. It was signed eventually by his household servants.

but when the merchants indicated that they were prepared to sign this but not the other, Glover disgustedly
sent them away to tell Lello of the steps he was taking.
Lello's reply, which came to Glover's ears, was to smile
and observe "that the man was not well in his witts."[87]
The messengers returned to Glover with word from
Lello that he would not leave the country until he had
received the 1,000 dollars provided by the merchants
for his expenses, which sum, as he feared, had already
been spent by Glover, who tendered the specious excuse that he was thus saving the company exchange that
they would otherwise lose if the money had to come
from Venice.[88]

On the following evening, Good Friday, April 3,
1607, Nicholas Heath, Glover's master of the household,
burst in on Lello, "being at dinner with divers stran-
gers . . . and said openly to his face that his maister
sent him to tell the said Mr Lello, that he was a traitor
to his prince & contrey and so he wold prove him here &
in England."[89]

Strachey, although dismissed from his post as Glover's
secretary, refused to accept his dismissal from the company's employment and as late as April 16, 1607, was
signing himself "William Strachey, gent, Secretarie to
the Levante Companie."[90] It may have been that he was
hoping to see Glover's dismissal and his replacement by
Lello, a possibility that Glover did not find remote
since we find him next writing to Salisbury of a plot
by his adversaries, the Venetian ambassador among
them, to have him imprisoned in his own house or cast
into the Seven Towers, a Turkish bastille on the out-
skirts of the city, and then the Turks "would approve
Mr Lello for his modest and civill behavior" to take

[87] *Ibid.*, f. 150.   [88] P.R.O. S.P.105/109, f. 31.
[89] P.R.O. S.P.97/5, f. 150.
[90] To Lello's list of complaints, see below.

his place. This was to be accomplished by a bribe of 3,000 chequins.[91] Once again this detailed accusation was based on the merest hint, given this time by the Viceroy, and only after a bribe. Glover in his present state of indignant credulity was no match for the wily Turk, who could see golden vistas opening before him if only the quarrel could be kept up.

Lello, meanwhile, taking a leaf from Glover's book, prepared a statement detailing his adversary's outrageous behavior, which was witnessed by a number of the more responsible members of the English community. Even if one discounts the evidence of such supporters of Lello as Hugh Holland, William Strachey, and Biddulph the preacher, with whom Glover had now quarreled and whom he had dismissed from his post,[92] the merchants took Lello's part, and since their one desire was peace and quiet trade it is clear that they found Glover at fault.

Glover promptly listed them among his enemies also[93] and poured forth more invective against Hugh Holland, who, he maintained, had composed the deposition. Certainly the two final copies sent to Salisbury are in his hand, but the draft is by Lello.[94] Probably the three scholars, Holland, Strachey, and Lello, had a share in its compilation, but it seems most likely that the final draft was entrusted to Hugh Holland because of his ability to write an immaculate Italian hand.

Lello now had another grievance against Glover— that behind his back he had called him a fool and to his face a traitor. Fool indeed he might be, albeit an

[91] P.R.O. S.P.97/5, f. 156.
[92] As a result of his refusal to witness Glover's allegation of treachery against Lello (P.R.O. S.P.105/109, f. 31). However, they were later reconciled and Biddulph reinstated.
[93] P.R.O. S.P.97/5, f. 138.
[94] *Ibid.*, f. 135, draft by Lello, dated April 16 and unsigned; ff. 150, 152, signed fair copies dated April 17, in Holland's hand.

honest one, but a traitor, never. This was to his mind Glover's crowning insult.[95] Glover, however, could now see his main difficulties coming to an end. On May 2 he wrote to Salisbury that Lello, finding he could not prevail, had resolved to leave within a fortnight in company with the Ragusan ambassador and proposed to return to England by way of Venice.[96] He changed his mind, however, and sailed on May 24 in a small English ship, the *Triumph*,[97] for Chios, where he was to take another ship and so return to England.[98] His last night in Constantinople was spent with the French ambassador, "banketinge and carowsinge," and Glover records with some disgust that "in theire cuppes . . . boathe him selfe, and the Frenchman vsed manie vnseemly, and ignominious speeches of me."[99] So Lello departed, breathing a final threat of using all the influence at his disposal in London to ensure that Glover received his just deserts.[100] Apparently he was held up in his voyage, but by September 16 he was in Venice, having come by way of Crete, Zante, and Corfu. He spoke before the Doge and Senate,[101] and two days later was given permission to visit the treasury of St. Marks and the Senate armory. He then left, traveling overland,[102] and was back in London by November 17, 1607.[103]

Presumably Strachey accompanied Lello as far as Chios, since by June 1 he had quitted Constantinople and was in the process of composing an extraordinary document to Glover, which the ambassador with due ceremony had copied and dispatched to Salisbury by

---

[95] *Ibid.*, f. 146.   [96] *Ibid.*, f. 156.

[97] Epstein, *op. cit.*, p. 226, gives her displacement as 160 tons, but Glover says she was of 50 tons burden.

[98] P.R.O. S.P.97/5, f. 165b.   [99] *Ibid.*, f. 172.

[100] *Ibid.*, f. 162.   [101] *Cal. S. P. Ven.*, 1607–10, p. 33.

[102] Sanderson, *op. cit.*, p. 64, gives an account of one of the overland routes from Venice to London.

[103] *Cal. S. P. Ven.*, 1607–10, p. 66.

the hand of one Captain Saxey, an Englishman returning home, who Glover hoped would give verbal testimony to Salisbury on his behalf. Among other points for Saxey to bear in mind, he raises the following:

Thirdlie how that most malicious knave my Secretarie, Wm Stracchi, hath not onlie betrayed me, in discoveringe of my bussynesses and secretts unto Mr Lello and the French Ambassador but allsoe (not withstandinge my kinde usadge of him) after his departur hence, rather like a villian, then a Gentleman, made and gave out most slanderous reportts, as if I should cause to poyson the Master of my howse Geordge Coxdon, and accordingly write me his inuective lettre, with a most audatious, impudent, and prosumtious charge in his Majesties name, to sende my Phisition home to answeare such obiections should be layed to his chardge, for ministring poysone vnto the sayed Coxdon, all which you selfe have seene to the contrarie, the man beinge livinge to this present howre.[104]

Coxden's sins are attested by Nathaniel Percival in a document dated April 28, 1607, and consist of vilification of Glover: that he secretly sold part of the present; that if Lello were a traitor, Glover might well be; that Glover was the vilest man that ever came out of England; that he was paying adulterous attentions to a Turkish wench whom he used to visit in his closet, in his nightshirt; and that, in order to enjoy this pastime undisturbed, he had made arrangements to have his wife kidnaped by the Turks.[105]

Such temerity was summarily punished. Coxden was imprisoned by Glover, bastinadoed, and then given a cudgeling by his irate master that left him with two broken toes.[106] After this he was apparently kept in confinement, so that Strachey's accusation at least had some basis of probability. It is impossible to be sure

[104] P.R.O. S.P.97/5, f. 191.
[105] *Ibid.*, f. 186. [106] *Ibid.*, f. 181.

when and how the letter was written. Probably it was composed en route to Chios and there transferred to another ship, arriving in Constantinople on July 12 or 13. Glover's copy runs as follows:

The Coppie of Wm Strachie his presumtious comission, and false calumniation. [Endorsement in Glover's hand].
To Sir Thomas Glover Knight his Majesties Ambassadore ordinarie in Const. with the Gran. Signior alias the great Turke

These are in his Majesties name (with all Reverence to the place which yowe) to require and chardge you that accordinge to the lawes of greate Brittany (of which you are now happily become a member, & muste therefore be pleased to take knowledge of the Justice thereof) you cause to be forth cominge at all tymes (from the Date hereof) one John Kitly your phisition, to answare vnto such things as shalbe in his Majesties name Layd vnto his chardge, especially the Death of one George Cocksden whome (beinge Prisoner in your Lordshippes howse) yt is generally suspected that hee the sayd Kitly hath latly poysoned, yf your Lord shippe shall not cause him to procure good and sufficient bayle and surties to answare this suspition of murder that vppon the calling heare vppon and that accordinge to the Lawes in this Case provided in England, hee maye be forth cominge, your Lord shipe shall therby I asure you incur the heavy peanalty of the Lawe and his Majesties Displeasure, and that your Lord shipes excuse maye not stand good in the Ignorance of the notice hereof (for the loue of Justice, honnor of my Prince and countrie and in the Jennerall nature of pitty to mankinde, in all which three I knowe your Lordshipe, presenttinge that sacred persone which you doe is as sensably tuched as my selfe:) I have caused this writtinge to be deliuered you, and the coppie heareof to be subscrybed vnto by Diuers both gentlemen and marchants: Datted the firste of June, 1607.[107]

[107] *Ibid.*, f. 189.

Coxden, dragged from his cell, subscribed to the document that "I doe witnes with my hand that I am alive the xiiijth of this present July 1607 and that the aboue premisses are most false and sclaunderous."

Glover also enclosed to Salisbury a document, unfortunately no longer preserved, purporting to be in Strachey's own hand.

I haue hertofor certified your honour of the treacherous dealinge of Wm Strachey my Secretarie, whoe first betrayed all my bussinesses vnto Mr Lello, which action beinge cherished by him, and him selfe receyved into his Secrecie, he played the doble traytor, and discouered all his proceedings againe vnto me, as testified his contracte writen with his owne hande, which Mr Lello will not beleaue befor he readeth it, and if it shall please your Lordship to pervse the sam, you shall perceiue there vnconscionable dealinge with me.[108]

Glover, with his English adversaries safely out of the way, could now continue his quarrels with the other ambassadors undisturbed by the complicating presence of Lello. From Chios, Hugh Holland apparently continued his journey to Jerusalem,[109] and it may be that Strachey accompanied him.[110] By the beginning of 1608, however, Holland was again in London,[111] and Strachey's presence is recorded on June 20, 1608, twelve months after he left Constantinople.[112]

[108] *Ibid.*, f. 179b.

[109] Thomas Fuller, *The history of the worthies of England*, ed. P. A. Nuttall (London, 1840), III, 603.

[110] He gives the merest hint that he may have been familiar with the Lebanon in *The historie of travaile* (ed. Major), p. 129, where, referring to the trees in Virginia he says, "The cedars, for savour and cullor, maie compare with those of Lybanon, the clymate of the one and the other differing little." While the cedars were famous, the Lebanese climate was not necessarily common knowledge.

[111] P.R.O. Req 1/199. He gave evidence in Requests in *Warde* v. *Stretton* in Hilary Term, 1608.

[112] P.R.O. C.P.40/1887, f. 903, *Tien* v. *Strachey*.

So far, for the details of the quarrel and the part Strachey played in it, we have had to rely on the accounts of the two principals, and most of the mention of Strachey comes from the indignant Glover. After Lello and his companions had left Constantinople, however, the Levant Company began to receive news of the quarrel, and it is possible to judge, from the company's letters, where the greater fault lay. Its officers, after all, knew both the contending parties, and, while they found both at fault because of their indiscretion in permitting the quarrel to become an open scandal, they were inclined rather to rebuke Glover. They pointed out that Lello was "so honest as wee cannot suspect him either to Compasse your liffe or to be a traitor to his Prince & Countrye," that the ambassador paid too much heed to idle gossip, and that his actions tended to confirm "that which was ever doubted that your place you now hold hath made you forgett your self." As for Strachey, "howsoever he hath failed soe farre as might deserve sequestracion from his place yet we thincke it too hard to turne him out of your house in a strang Country without freinds or meanes." They suggested that Glover become reconciled with the other parties and drew a moral lesson, pointing out the merits of Barton, Lello's predecessor, whose modesty and temperate character had made him a credit to his country, a lesson nevertheless wasted on Glover, who despised Lello for the same qualities.[113]

Nor could Glover gain any credit even for his efforts in the matter of the consulage of the *merchants forestiers*. He had, after all, failed, and so the company wanted the matter brought quietly to an end. Salisbury likewise rebuked him, pointing out that the ambassador had acted with the greatest irresponsibility at a

[113] P.R.O. S.P.105/110, f. 12.

time when the King was particularly anxious to keep
on good terms with the French, and he very pointedly
omitted to reply to Glover's request for the grant of
the consulage as a reward.[114] Salisbury at the same time
wrote to Lello, indicating that he was prepared to dis-
believe Glover's reports of him, but since there was
obviously a quarrel, and so a scandal, it must be ended
in the simplest way, by Lello's departure.[115]

The company had nothing to say to Lello but wrote
to Strachey, who had by this time left the city, as follows:

Mr. Strachey wee have received your Lettres of late
from Constantinople and others from Sir Thomas
Glover importing a breach betweene you in dismissing
you from your place and his house which although wee
could desire had bene carryed in more milder sort, yet
now there is noe remedy. And we must needs tell you
that you much overshott your self, in that knowing
the breach betwixt Sir Tho: Glover & Mr Lello, who
hath much forgott himself in this buysines in seeking
the disgrace of Sir Tho: Glover, you notwithstanding
have daylie conversed with Mr Lello, contrary to all
fidelitye and have not let to assist him in penning his
lettres for England to the disgrace of Sir Tho: Glover,
And now in making a Certificate against him, where
you shold rather have shewed yourself a Newter, then
have intermedled in buysines against him to whome
you ought to have bene most faithfull: wee have wrot-
ten to Sir Thomas Glover that theis Matters maye be
reconsyled, and because wee hold that you have much
fayled therin, wee thinke it fitt that you first make
your submission, which if it cannot be, wee have written Sir Tho: Glover to give you allowaunce for your
coming home in honest and frugall sort
Wheras you make request for your allowaunce of
your chardges in apparell, our agreement with you was
to give you 100 chequins per annum, and wee looke
to be noe farther chardged And so wishing you to take

[114] P.R.O. S.P.97/5, f. 166.   [115] *Ibid.*, f. 168.

such course for your retorne as may be most for our easie chardge, and your speedy retorne with our hartie Comendacions wee bidd you Farewell.[116]

Constantinople—the first of Ben Jonson's alternatives —had ended disastrously, with Strachey further out of pocket as a result of his experiences and the debtors' prison correspondingly closer. Nevertheless, he had not altogether given up hope of repairing his fortunes in the Mediterranean. Lello, on his return, took his quarrel with the Levant Company, as he had threatened, to the Privy Council;[117] so it was apparent that anyone who had been associated with the former ambassador could hope for little from the company. However, Strachey's old friend, John Donne, although living in obscurity and poverty in his house in the Strand,[118] could recommend Strachey to an old and influential friend of his Oxford days, now holding an important post in Italy, Sir Henry Wotton, His Majesty's Ambassador at Venice, scholar and friend of the writers of the day, with whom Hugh Holland had stayed on his way to Constantinople and to whom Glover had written for confirmation of Holland's loyalty.[119] Lello, passing through Venice, had undoubtedly told Wotton of the quarrel and almost certainly had his sympathy. Furthermore, Hugh Holland, on his way home from Jerusalem, had visited Wotton and obtained from him a letter vouching for his loyalty to the King;[120] again Wotton must have had an account of the quarrel from the side favorable to Strachey; so, armed

[116] P.R.O. S.P. 105/110, f. 13.

[117] *Ibid.*, f. 30, Company to Glover, July 13, 1608. Unfortunately the records of the Privy Council for this period have been destroyed, so no details are available.

[118] Evelyn M. Simpson, *A study of the prose works of John Donne* (Oxford, 1924), p. 27.

[119] From Constantinople. See p. 72.

[120] Pearsall Smith, *op. cit.*, I, 408–9.

with a letter of introduction from Donne, he sailed for Venice.

Sr The relacon of occurrences heere I leaue to this gentleman Mr William Strachey allwayes my good frend (who is desirous your Lordship should know so much) and sometymes secretary to Sir T. G: I dare boldly say that the greatest folly he ever committed was to submitt himself and parts to so meane a Master. you may thinke this a preposterous course in steed of comending a gentleman to open his imperfections, but I know your Lordship so wise as out of contraries to draw true and necessarie conclusions: and to say but truth for me to open my mouth in his commendations were but to play the owle or some other bird in a painted cloath in whose mouth some sentence is put which most men know: and so of his vertues. only this I shall intreat that bysyde his merit he may for my sake find himself welcome.[121]

Apparently Wotton was unable to help him, and Strachey returned again to England.

His indignation had not subsided, and his fulminations against his former master at length came to the ears of Glover's friend John Sanderson, who, on December 15, 1608, wrote to the ambassador that "Master Fenton tells me that one Stracie is making a booke against you; which yf it should be so, it peradventure may cost him both ears."[122] Apparently this libellous work remained only a threat. Strachey's connection with the Levant Company had come to an end.

June 20, 1608, saw him borrowing the sum of thirty pounds from one Jasper Tien,[123] a wealthy Dutch gold-

---

[121] Simpson, *op. cit.*, p. 317.

[122] Sanderson, *op. cit.*, pp. 257–58.

[123] P.R.O. C.P. 40/1887. Tien appears as a merchant, a member of the Dutch congregation in London but born in England, in R. E. G. and E. F. Kirk (eds.), *Returns of aliens dwelling in the city and suburbs of London, Henry VIII to James I* (Aberdeen, 1908), III, 153. In 1618 he sold to the king, for £800, "a diamond in the form of a heart, cut with lozenges in a ring of gold . . . sent

smith living in Fenchurch Street. This apparently
earned him only a temporary respite, since early in
1609 we find him writing in response to an appeal by an
arrested debtor, Ben Jonson's friend, Peter Ferryman:

Good Mr Feryman, I am hartely sorrie, that out of
my present estate, I can not tender that true act of my
love, which bothe your fortune requires, & my deere
accompt of you should lead me to. But be Judge your
old frend Mr Royden, whether I stand not in muche
danger to come to that place of dead men, to that Gol-
gotha for want of present money my self. Howbeit, yf
either my creditt, or any frend of myne that you knowe
that can add to make myne better, or any travayle or
whatsoever that you can imagine to be in my power or
at my commaunde or intreatie, I will & stand most
willing to exercise & imploy for you, set me but downe
the meanes, & then if I doe it not, thinke me vnworthy
to be loved of you. Onlie beleve I have not ready one
quarter of so muche money yf it wolde purchase your
delyverie for which I am sorie: for I wolde have you
perswaded I love you and make much of your knowledge: And so wishing your advice & direction for any
thinge that shall lie in my abilitie to worke for you I
letany my english thus: from where you are, good lorde
deliuer us.
Your true unfayned frend, William Strachey.[124]

Ferryman was, according to his own statement,[125] a
gentleman by birth and education, having been a member of the Inner Temple[126] and a courtier under Eliza-

by his Majesty unto his dearest daughter, the Electress Palatine"
(Fredrick Devon, *Issues of the Exchequer* [London, 1836], pp. 221,
237). His will was proved in the Prerogative Court of Canterbury
in 1623.
[124] Folger Shakespeare Library MS 420, 423, f. 30b.
[125] *Ibid.*, ff. 63b–64.
[126] *Ibid.*, f. 64, contains a testimonial that Ferryman's statements
are known or believed to be true, but as this is an unsigned copy
we do not know who the signatories were. There is no mention
of him among the records of the Inner Temple.

beth. He had served under Sir Philip Sidney in the Low Countries and after Sidney's death had been in the service of his father-in-law, Sir Francis Walsingham. In 1596 he had accompanied one Francis Maddison, gentleman, of London, on a visit to Jerusalem,[127] and he claimed to have spent much time, at his own considerable expense, abroad in the service of the King.[128] Prior to his departure for Jerusalem he had apparently retired from London to Childrey in Berkshire,[129] possibly his birthplace, since there is a record of a family named Ferryman in that district.

All this, however, merely reflects another Elizabethan gentleman. The interest of Peter Ferryman is that there appears to be little or no record of him elsewhere and that he was, at the same time, a friend of several writers. The friendship with Matthew Roydon the poet, to which Strachey refers, dates at least from 1589, when, along with Peter Bales the scrivener, they became jointly bound in debt to Edmund Peshall.[130] At the same time Ferryman was writing to Sir Thomas Randolph in an effort to obtain for Bales a permanent post,[131] and ten years later both Ferryman and Bales were involved in the aftermath of Essex' rebellion—in an affair concerning certain of Essex' letters to his Countess which had been copied by Bales at the request of one John Danyell.[132] Roydon was an intimate of George Chapman. When Ferryman in 1612, aged and poor, applied for a post at the newly founded Hospital of King James, Charter House, Ben Jonson wrote to

[127] *Ibid.*, f. 65. [128] *Ibid.*, f. 64b.
[129] P.R.O. E115/148/52, Certificate of Residence dated 1595.
[130] P.R.O. C2 Eliz/F2/49, *Ferryman* v. *Peshall*. It is this same Edmund Peshall with whom John Strachey was engaged in a lengthy series of lawsuits.
[131] *D.N.B.*, "Bales."
[132] *Ibid.*, and *Cal. S. P. Dom.*, 1601–3, pp. 56, 57, 78, 107.

the secretaries of two of the governors, urging them to help in Ferryman's suit.[133]

In Hilary Term, 1609, Peter Ferryman of Childrey in Berkshire appeared in the Court of King's Bench in an action for debt brought against him by William Hobbes.[134] The sum, which amounted to twenty pounds, had been borrowed two years earlier, and Ferryman, unable to pay his debt, lost the case and was faced with the prospect of having his belongings taken and sold.[135] He may have been liable for other debts, which had been paid by the efforts of his friends; but Strachey makes it clear that he, personally, had reached a serious financial state. He may even have been reduced to keeping to his house to avoid his creditors, a common state of affairs at a time when the unfortunate debtor could be arrested the moment he set foot in the street.

Jonson had mentioned Constantinople, Ireland, or Virginia as places where one might repair one's fortunes. Another contemporary reference gives these places an even more pertinent significance: "I dare not walk abroad to see my friends, for fear the serjeants should take acquaintance of me. My refuge is Ireland or Virginia."[136]

We have no definite record that Strachey visited Ireland at this time, but that he was acquainted with the country we may be sure from references and comparisons that he makes in *The historie of travaile*.[137] Whether or not he visited Ireland to escape his creditors or to make some money, at this time or earlier, there still remained the final alternative—Virginia.

[133] Folger MS 420, 423, f. 64b.

[134] P.R.O. K.B.27/1412, f. 758, *Hobbes* v. *Ferryman*.

[135] The verdict of the court is given on the plea roll cited.

[136] John Cooke, *Greenes Tu-quoque; or, the city gallant* (London, 1614), Act I, sc. ii. It was written in 1611.

[137] See Chapter 7, p. 159.

5. Virginia

WOTTON, while unable to help Strachey to find a post either in Venice or elsewhere in the Mediterranean, was nevertheless in close touch with affairs in England, and it may have been at his suggestion that Strachey came to interest himself in the Virginia venture.

Certainly, before Strachey's departure for the Levant a high degree of enthusiasm for the plantation of Virginia had been aroused in England, largely through the efforts of the indefatigable publicist and propagandist Richard Hakluyt, whose *Voyages*,[1] published in their final form by 1600, had been designed not only as a history of English exploration but as a guide to future efforts. This final edition contained a good deal of information about the American continent, including letters written to Hakluyt by many of the explorers themselves, Harriot's description of the country,[2] and Peckham's manifesto regarding the establishment of plantations in America.[3] Hakluyt had subsequently

---

[1] *The principal navigations, voiages, traffiques and discoveries of the English nation* (London, 1598–1600). He had earlier published *Divers voyages, touching the discoverie of America* (London, 1582) and a first and much smaller version of *The principall navigations* in 1589.

[2] Thomas Harriot, *A briefe and true report of the new found land of Virginia* (London, 1588).

[3] Sir George Peckham, *A true reporte of the late discoveries . . . of the newfound landes* (London, 1583). This account, by the

been a prime mover in the foundation of the Virginia Company and appeared in 1606 as one of the four patentees of the first charter granted to the company.[4] He was at this time preacher to the Middle Temple and had succeeded in interesting not only the members of the legal profession, but also the gentlemen and courtiers of the city who, educated at one or the other of the Inns of Court, still remained in close touch with their affairs.[5]

The imagination of the literary world had also been stirred, and alongside a steady stream of broadsides and tracts, some factual but all to a greater or less degree imaginative, appeared such descriptions as that in *Eastward ho,* which Strachey must have seen on the stage at the Blackfriars Theatre in 1605, of a land where gold was more plentiful than copper in England and where rubies and diamonds could be picked up on the seashore "to hang on their children's coats and stick in their caps, as our children wear saffron guilt brooches and groats with hobles on 'em."[6] Michael Drayton, in his "Ode to the Virginian voyage," which appeared the following year, drew also on published accounts of the land and gave some indication of what the venture owed to Hakluyt:

> And cheerfully at sea
> Success you still entice
> To get the pearl and gold

---

chief backer of Sir Humphrey Gilbert's expedition to Newfoundland, contained also a statement of the English claims to the country and the arguments in favor of settling there.

[4] Alexander Brown, *The genesis of the United States* (London, 1890), I, 52.

[5] For accounts of Hakluyt's influence and activities see George Brumer Parks, *Richard Hakluyt and the English voyages* (New York, 1928), and Edward Lynam (ed.), *Richard Hakluyt and his successors* (London, 1946).

[6] Act III, sc.ii.

And ours to hold
Virginia
Earth's only Paradise.

Thy voyages attend
Industrious Hakluyt
    Whose reading shall inflame
    Men to seek fame
And much commend
    To after times thy wit.

In 1605 Captain George Waymouth had returned to
England from a voyage to Virginia, bringing with him
the first American Indians ever seen in England, creatures of an alien world whose mere presence served to
whip up enthusiasm of a more superficial kind; at the
same time, for the more discerning members of the
public, Rosier's *True relation* of this voyage appeared
on the shelves of the booksellers.[7] In 1606 a charter was
granted to the Virginia Company. While ships were
still exploring and mapping the coast, the company had
set things in motion, and on December 20, 1606, three
vessels set sail from England with the first of the colonists for Virginia. By the time Strachey quitted Constantinople to return to England, these colonists had
established themselves in the country, had built a fort
at Jamestown, were industriously exploring the hinterland, and were getting cooperation from the Indians,
who had not yet come to realize the dubious benefits of
white settlement. The vast stores of gold had not yet
been located, but reports steadily trickling back to England made it clear that they were daily expected, and
enthusiasm was at its height.

By 1608, though the venture had not been as successful or as immediately profitable as had been anticipated,

[7] James Rosier, *A true relation of the most prosperous voyage
made . . . in the discovery of . . . Virginia* (London, 1605).
Waymouth arrived in England on July 18, 1605.

there still appeared to the company every hope of success. Some reorganization, however, particularly in the government of the colony, was needed. Plans were already afoot for the grant of a new charter from the king, and, while this was under consideration, the company set out to secure as much financial support as possible.[8] Intending adventurers were urged to join the company, being promised that those who subscribed early should have their names inserted in the charter. The terms were framed to attract both those who would adventure personally and those who would provide capital. An emigrant with a trade was promised 100 acres of land, and persons of condition going to Virginia would receive a proportionately larger division. Further, to attract capital, a large section of land was promised in return for a share of £12 10s. when a survey had been made. All produce for the ensuing seven years would be sold on behalf of the company and was expected to provide as great a profit as the land division. The owner of a single share was to become a full member of the company.

The capital thus raised was not intended to provide a basis for long-term operations, but to finance a single large expedition to reinforce the colonists already there, the company having come to the conclusion that its problems were not to be solved by the dribbling in of colonists to maintain the small settlement at a constant strength, but rather by the consolidation and expansion of the already established plantation.[9]

Enthusiasm in the city was again high, and among the 659 individual patentees of the charter were to be found representatives of all aspects of the commercial life of

[8] Charles M. Andrews, *The colonial period of American history* (New Haven, 1934–38), I, 92–105; William Robert Scott, *The constitution and finance of English, Scottish and Irish joint-stock companies to 1720* (Cambridge, 1910–12), II, 250–52.

[9] Andrews, *op. cit.*, I, 106.

London.[10] Prominent among them were two well-known members of the Middle Temple—Christopher Brooke, John Donne's most intimate friend, appointed by the new charter a member of the Council of the company, and Richard Martin, friend of Ben Jonson and of Strachey, soon also to be appointed to the Council.[11] Donne himself was interested at this time in the affairs of the company and, although he took up no shares in the venture, he apparently saw in it a means of escape from his oppressive poverty. John Chamberlain, writing to Sir Dudley Carleton in February 1609, mentioned that Donne was seeking the post of secretary to the colony in Virginia.[12] It was natural enough that Strachey should have interested himself in the venture and have undertaken to pay the £25 necessary to purchase two shares;[13] but unlike most of the shareholders of the Virginia Company he went a stage further and ventured personally to Virginia.

Here, then, was his last alternative. In 1605 writers, reflecting popular beliefs, had pictured Virginia as a treasure chest, with wealth to be had for the taking; but in 1609, in spite of the company's propaganda, a more cynical view prevailed, and the new colony was regarded

[10] Brown, *op. cit.*, I, 208–37, lists the names of the shareholders as they appear in the charter.

[11] As secretary, before November 8, 1610, when he and other members of the Council entered *A true declaration of the estate of the colonie* for publication.

[12] *Cal. S. P. Dom.*, 1603–10, p. 492. Donne's penury was relieved shortly after this, when his father-in-law decided to pay the dowry and he was able to support himself by his writing (Simpson, *John Donne*, p. 28).

[13] Susan Myra Kingsbury, *The records of the Virginia Company of London* (Washington, 1906–35), III, 88, lists Strachey among the shareholders in 1618. His name appears in the charter, however, making it clear that he had undertaken to pay for the shares allotted to him before May 23, 1609. His brother-in-law, Sir Edmund Bowyer, along with a number of other members of Parliament, became a shareholder in 1610.

more as a refuge from the troubles, and in particular the financial troubles, of England. If Cooke's embarrassed gallant could tell his audience that his chance of escape from his creditors lay in Ireland or Virginia, Middleton could also make the further suggestion that the current opinion was that colonists left for Virginia in haste, saving themselves by precipitate flight.[14]

It is clear that Strachey was not appointed secretary to the colony while in England but traveled solely as a gentleman settler. Although the company had advertised for and endeavored to recruit tradesmen, artisans, and laborers for the colony, each of the contingents that had gone before had contained a large proportion of men of gentle birth and of varying degrees of ability, ranging from the responsible and energetic members who formed the Council of the colony and were in many ways responsible for its survival to those whom John Smith indignantly stigmatized as being of

tender education and small experience in martiall accidents: [who] because they found not English cities, nor such faire houses, nor at their owne wishes any of their accustomed dainties, with feather beds and downe pillowes, Tavernes and Alehouses in every breathing place, neither such plenty of gold and siluer and dissolute liberty as they expected, had little or no care of any thing, but to pamper their bellies, to fly away with our Pinnaces, or procure their meanes to returne to England.[15]

Among the gentlemen of the former class was one Matthew Scrivener, who had taken a place on the Coun-

[14] *The roaring girl*, Act II, sc.ii: "Take deliberation, sir: never choose a wife as if you were going to Virginia." E. H. Sugden, *A topographical dictionary to the works of Shakespeare and his fellow dramatists* (Manchester, 1925), s.v. "Virginia" comments, "the idea being that those who go there go on a sudden impulse to escape the law."

[15] John Smith, *Travels and works of Captain John Smith*, ed. E. Arber and A. G. Bradley (Edinburgh, 1910), I, 83.

cil at his arrival in Virginia in January 1608,[16] and of whom the company, as a result of the work he had done there, thought highly.[17] Instructions to Sir Thomas Gates, who was traveling to Virginia with this new expedition as governor of the colony, included the following passage:

4. Being setled in your governement, you shall call vnto you, for your further advise and graver proceedinge, their principall officers and gentlemen whom we do ordaine and appointe to be of ye councell and who for earliness of their vndertakinges and their greate paines and merits doe well deserue this honour & respect from vs. Sir George Summers knight and Admirall of Virginia, Captaine John Smith nowe President, Captaine John Radclif, Captain Peter winne Seriant maior of the fort, Mr Mathewe Scrivenor whom out of our good experience of his abilities in that kinde we doe name and apointe to be secretary of that Councell . . .[18]

From this it is clear that the position of secretary to the Council in Virginia was regarded by the company as being of considerable importance. In Scrivener they had chosen a man of proven ability, who had already unofficially filled the position and who had been most energetic on the behalf of the settlers there. Unfortunately, however, before Gates had even departed, Scrivener was drowned while trying to cross the James River in an overloaded skiff on a stormy day. Although the accident occurred in January 1609, news of it had not reached England by May, when the company's final instructions were issued to the new governor.[19]

On May 15, 1609, six ships lying in the Thames

[16] *Ibid.*, I, 107.

[17] *Ibid.*, I, 101. Smith describes him as "a very wise understanding gentleman."

[18] Kingsbury, *op. cit.*, III, 13, dated May, 1609.

[19] Smith, *op. cit.*, I, 143, describes the accident, which he attributes to Scrivener's obstinacy in attempting the impossible.

weighed anchor and set sail for Plymouth, there to complete loading and, having been joined by two others,
leave for Virginia. Various estimates, ranging from 500
to 800,[20] are given of the number of colonists with this
fleet, but, even if the lower figure is the correct one, this
was the greatest number of ships and settlers that had
left the shores of England for Virginia up to that time
and represented the most ambitious project yet entertained by the Virginia Company. Pending the arrival in
Virginia of Lord De la Warr, who had been chosen to
act as governor of the colony, Sir Thomas Gates was
traveling with the fleet to act as deputy governor there,
while the fleet itself was to be under the command of an
experienced sailor, Sir George Somers.[21] Both these gentlemen had been associated with the company since its
birth, and both had joined with Hakluyt in petitioning
for the foundation charter of 1606.

At Plymouth the ships spent a fortnight provisioning
and equipping. Here they were joined by Somers, who
embarked on the flagship, the *Sea Venture*, a vessel of
some 300 tons, under the command of Captain Christopher Newport, "a Marriner well practised for the
Westerne parts of *America*."[22] Crew and passengers to-
taled some 150 souls, among whom were both Gates and
Strachey. On June 2 the fleet set sail, but meeting contrary winds, was forced to put into Falmouth, and sailed
again from there on June 8, 1609.

Apart from a minor outbreak of plague aboard one

---

[20] *Ibid.*, I, 161, states there were 500. Sir Stephen Powle, quoted
in Andrews, *op. cit.*, I, 108, says 800.

[21] See *D.N.B.*, "Somers." Samuel Purchas, *Hakluytus posthumus;
or, Purchas his pilgrimes* (Glasgow, 1905–7), XIX, 5, states suc-
cinctly in a marginal note, "Sir G. Summers a good mariner and
tried Souldier." Strachey describes him as "a Gentleman of ap-
proved assurednesse, and ready knowledge in Sea-faring actions."

[22] So he was regarded by Smith, *op. cit.*, II, 386. His life is given
in *D.N.B.* He had commanded the first fleet of three ships taking
colonists to Virginia in 1606.

of the ships, the voyage passed without event until the expedition was only some seven or eight days from Virginia. Then, on July 24, after some six weeks at sea, "there hapned a most terrible and vehement storme, which was a taile of the West Indian Horocano,"[23] sufficiently violent to impress even such an experienced seaman as Captain Gabriel Archer, master of the *Blessing*. The ships were separated, and each captain steered his own course for Virginia. Four met again after the storm—the *Blessing*, the *Lion*, the *Falcon*, and the *Unity*, the latter with only ten of her colonists fit and most of her sailors disabled. Some days after they had arrived safely at Jamestown the *Diamond*, second in command of the fleet, came limping in, her mainmast gone and many of her crew injured; after her came the *Swallow*, likewise dismasted and leaking badly. But of the *Sea Venture* there was no sign.[24]

Strachey's *True reportory of the wracke, and redemption of Sir Thomas Gates Knight*[25] provides the only detailed account of the fate of this ship and of the 150 sailors and colonists aboard her. He tells of the "dreadful storme and hideous" blowing from the northeast, increasing in violence as night drew on; of the numbed and hopeless terror of all on board when first the storm struck the ship, their "clamours dround in the windes, and the windes in thunder," with "nothing heard that

[23] Purchas, *op. cit.*, XIX, 2, Letter written by Captain Gabriel Archer on his arrival in Virginia. Archer had been among the first colonists to come to Virginia in 1606 and since that time had made a number of voyages to the colony from England. At one time he had been on the Council in Virginia as one of the members of the faction opposing John Smith. See Smith, *op. cit.*, *passim*.

[24] Purchas, *op. cit.*, XIX, 2–3.

[25] *Ibid.*, XIX, 5–72. Much more superficial in treatment is Silvester Jourdan, *A discovery of the Barmudas* (London, 1610). Robert Rich, *Newes from Virginia* (London, 1610), consists merely of doggerel verses.

could give comfort, nothing seene that might incourage hope."[26] Bare-masted, the *Sea Venture* wallowed helplessly in the heavy seas, changing course with every gust of wind, eight men at a time having barely the strength to manage the tiller, while to all on board "there was not a moment in which the sodaine splitting, or instant over-setting of the Shippe was not expected."[27]

After a day and night of terror it was discovered early the following morning that the battering of the seas had caused the ship to spring her seams and that there were already five feet of water in the hold, increasing in depth every minute from a multitude of leaks in the ship's hull. The shock of this discovery produced a desperate resolution among the passengers. Sir George Somers took charge, divided the whole company into three parties, and, opening three of the hatches in spite of the danger of a swamping wave, set them to work pumping and baling. Members of the crew, candles in hand, clambered amid the cargo in the holds, seeking with every means in their power to stanch the leaks, but with the calking gone from the seams there was little they could do. Strachey from his own experience sums up the feeling of all on board: "The Lord knoweth, I had as little hope, as desire of life in the storme, & in this, it went beyond my will; because beyond my reason, why we should labour to preserve life; yet we did."[28]

For three days and four nights they labored without respite, one hour at the pumps or baling and one hour off, Gates and Somers themselves taking their turn with the others, and still the storm showed no sign of abating. Cargo and luggage, and even the ship's armament, had been thrown overboard to lighten her, and Strachey records with pride that "there was not a passenger, gentle-

---

[26] Purchas, *op. cit.*, XIX, 7.   [27] *Ibid.*, XIX, 8.
[28] *Ibid.*, XIX, 9.

man, or other, after hee began to stirre and labour, but was able to relieve his fellow, and make good his course: And it is most true, such as in all their life times had never done houres worke before . . . were able twice fortie eight houres together to toile with the best."29

From the moment the first clouds had started to gather until the fourth morning of the storm, it had been impossible to get so much as a glimpse of the sky, and so continually had the ship's heading varied that the navigators had no idea of their position. On Friday morning, four days after the storm had struck, Sir George Somers sighted land, and, maneuvering to the smoother water in the lee of the island, he succeeded in beaching the ship some three-quarters of a mile from the shore. The two remaining boats were launched, and by evening all on board, men, women, and children, were safe on shore on one of the islands of the Bermudas.

In spite of the prodigies they had performed, it is doubtful whether those on board could have survived another day of the storm. Not only had they labored incessantly for some ninety-six hours, under conditions of the greatest discomfort and danger, but "the leakage taking up all the holde, wee could neither come by Beere nor fresh water; fire we could keepe none in the Cooke-Roome to dresse any meate, and carefulness, griefe, and our turne at the Pumpe or Bucket, were sufficient to hold sleepe from our eyes."30 Jourdan indeed goes as far as to say that by this time, utterly spent, they had given up hope and had resolved to close the hatches and leave the rest to the sea; that some of them, "Hauing some good and comfortable waters in the ship," had settled down to drink their farewell toast together; and that it was only the sight of land that revived them and set them again to pumping.31

29 *Ibid.*, XIX, 11.　　30 *Ibid.*, XIX, 12.
31 Jourdan, *op. cit.*, p. 5.

The Bermudas, an archipelago of some five hundred islands, had been avoided by all mariners on this western route because of the difficulty of navigating the shoal-blocked channels and because of the sudden storms that could trap a ship among the islands, giving it no sea way to maneuver. These practical considerations of seamanship had been superseded in the sailors' minds by a conviction that the islands themselves were not only barren and inhospitable but actually evil, and they had come to be known as the Isles of Devils. The castaways, however, found that the islands were fertile and nature generous. There were fruit in abundance, an excellent supply of fish easily caught, birds of all sorts to trap, tortoises, and, thanks to an earlier visit by the Spaniards, many wild hogs. The fresh-water supply was erratic, but wells in carefully chosen spots supplied all needs.

The colonists could hardly have been more fortunate in the leaders they had with them on the island. All three of them, Gates, Somers, and Newport, were men of experience, energy, and resource, and they wasted no time in getting the community settled. As soon as possible, everything that might be of use—foodstuffs, equipment, rigging, tools, and tackle—was brought to the shore from the ship, and preparations were made for what might prove to be a prolonged sojourn on the island. Gates was also mindful of his responsibility toward the colonists in Virginia, and so, without delay, he had the ship's longboat refitted and decked over with timber from the wreck and stepped a mast and sail in it. In this small craft the mate of the *Sea Venture* and six sailors set out to sail the five hundred or more miles to Virginia, bearing with them a detailed letter of instruction from Gates to the settlers there, appointing a council to look after the affairs of the colony until he should arrive. Arrangements were also made that signal fires would burn on the shores of the island to guide into the harbor the craft sent to the rescue of the castaways.

It was thought that the only ship from Virginia available for the rescue would be the pinnace that was based there; consequently, on the day that the longboat left, August 28, 1609, a party under the command of Sir Thomas Gates laid the keel of a pinnace, to be of some eighty tons, that would supplement the vessel they expected. Fortunately, aboard the *Sea Venture* had been one Martin Frobisher, a shipwright from Gravesend, "painefull and well experienced . . . and a skilfull workman."[32] Under his direction the party proceeded to build a vessel some forty feet long and nineteen feet broad, drawing eight feet of water. This project, which was begun a month to the day after the *Sea Venture* had been beached, was carried through to eventual completion only by the efforts of Sir Thomas Gates, who had first conceived the scheme. Dissension and a mutinous spirit had already begun to appear among certain of the colonists.

John Smith mentions the trouble that had been caused in Virginia in the early days of settlement there by those who were "meerely proiecting verbal and idle contemplatours," and "those so deuoted to pure idlenesse that though they had lived two or three yeares in Virginia lordly, necessity itself could not compell them to passe the Peninsula, or Pallisadoes of Iames Towne."[33] Now, "so willing were the major part of the common sort (especially when they found such a plenty of victuals) to settle a foundation of ever inhabiting there; as well appeared by many practises of theirs (and perhaps of some of the better sort) "[34] that it was only with the greatest difficulty that Gates was able to induce them to set about the heavy manual labor in-

[32] Purchas, *op. cit.*, XIX, 27–28.
[33] Smith, *op. cit.*, I, 83.   [34] Purchas, *op. cit.*, XIX, 28

volved in the building of the boat. Although a certain amount of material could be obtained from the wreck, this was mainly tackle and rigging, and for the hull of the pinnace the cedars that grew in abundance on the island had to be felled, sawed, squared, and shaped. Strachey says that Gates was able to draw the reluctant idlers to work only by his personal example and that there was no task, however mean, to which he would not set his hand.

Nevertheless, only three days after the work had begun on the pinnace the first mutiny was discovered. Six of the settlers, led astray by the sailors' tales of the snortage of food in Virginia, had resolved to stay in the Bermudas. Having determined that they would not help with the building of the pinnace but would actively hinder it in whatever way they could, they set out to convince the rest of the workers that they were much better off where they were than they would be in Virginia. When this was discovered, they fled to the woods but soon repented, and after they had pleaded with Gates were allowed back to carry on with the work.

From Strachey's account it is clear that he was a member of Gates's shipbuilding party, and though he is disappointingly reticent about his own part in affairs on the island, it is likewise clear that he showed sufficient energy and ability to gain the good opinion of the three most important men on the island, and also of the commoner sort. In January, when a mutineer was sentenced to death, his entreaties so moved the hearts of "all the better sort of the Company" that they petitioned the governor to pardon him, "as likewise," says Strachey, "did Captain Newport and myselfe, and never left him until wee had got his pardon."[35] Later in their sojourn on the island, two children were born: in February 1610 a girl, to whom Captain Newport and Strachey

[35] *Ibid.,* XIX, 32.

acted as godfathers, and in March a boy, whose godfathers were Newport, Strachey, and Master James
Swift.[36] Strachey had clearly come to assume some importance in the eyes of the community since he was
selected for this honor, associated in this way with Newport, and close to the governor.

While the party under Gates toiled with the construc-
tion of the pinnace, Somers, awaiting the return of the
longboat sent to Virginia, kept watch on the coast; he
sailed among the islands, mapping them and gaining
as much information as possible about their resources.
One of his first actions after landing had been to set
out and plant a garden, with seeds that had been aboard
the *Sea Venture*. In this he had met with no success,
the plants springing up at first but then dying; the few
surviving were subsequently eaten by the wild hogs.

After three months' fruitless wait it became clear
that the boat for Virginia had been lost[37] and that all
rescue must depend solely on their own efforts. Somers
thereupon decided to build another ship to supplement
Gates's pinnace; this would enable all the colonists to be
transported to Virginia at the one time. Accordingly,
on November 27, he borrowed from Gates twenty of
his laborers and two of his four carpenters and, on a
separate island, laid the keel of a smaller ship. In addition to these shipbuilding activities, the colonists had to
perform the communal tasks of gathering food and
building shelters. Every morning and evening public
prayers were held, and each Sunday two sermons were
delivered by the minister. Moreover, much of the settlement was maintained on military lines, guards being

[36] Shown as a shareholder in the 1609 charter and elsewhere
described as Ensign James Swift, he was still in Virginia as late
as 1620.

[37] From accounts he received later Strachey believed that the
boat actually reached the coast of Virginia, but, falling in with
hostile natives, the crew were murdered.

posted to watch over the stores of arms, food, and equipment. There was no danger of trouble with natives, the islands being uninhabited, but there was a very present danger of mutiny.

In January there was another minor outbreak of dissension, this time on the part of the minister's clerk, who found it a matter of conscience to refuse to obey the commands of the governor and who endeavored to get accomplices to help him build a small ship so that they might quit the island on their own. He was sentenced to death, but by the entreaties of Strachey and others pardoned. Each of these outbreaks was, however, merely a symptom of a graver discontent among the colonists, which reached a head in March, when there came to light a plan to break into the storehouses, seize the arms there, and kill the governor. On this occasion it was not the work of a few dissentients but a plot much more widespread, and in its size lay its weakness. The conspiracy was revealed by one of the fainter-hearted members, but the authorities could take no immediate action. General distrust spread among the members of Gates's shipbuilding party, and everyone went armed for the first time on the island, each doubting the loyalty of his neighbor. Effective remedy was made the more difficult by the fact that all of Sir George Somers' party were in the plot and were on another island, away from the main body. The matter was finally brought to a head by the insubordination of one of the gentlemen colonists, Henry Paine, who, refusing to obey an order, was publicly courtmartialed and shot. The rebels in Somers' party, fearing that Paine might have betrayed them, fled in a body to the woods, at the same time petitioning Gates that they might remain there. Finally, after negotiations between Somers and the mutineers, they all returned to work with the exception of two, who were eventually abandoned on the island, and the boat was completed.

On March 30, 1610, Gates's pinnace was launched and anchored in the shelter of a breakwater that had been built, while the work of rigging her went on apace. A further month saw Somers' vessel afloat and lying alongside the other. On May 10 the larger vessel, the *Deliverance*, and the smaller, the *Patience*, set sail for Virginia, bearing with them all the castaways and as much food and equipment as they could carry. In all they had been nine months on the island, and in that time had kept themselves alive and in good health and had built, from material that was to be found there, two seaworthy vessels capable not only of making the five-hundred-mile crossing to the mainland, but also, as was almost immediately done by the tiny *Patience,* of crossing the Atlantic itself.[38] This success was due almost entirely to Gates and Somers, who inspired the settlers to construct these ships, and while doing so maintained law and order among a company of rebellious individualists by the power of personal example rather than by the use of force.

On May 20 the two ships entered Chesapeake Bay and the following morning cast anchor opposite Fort Algernon, on Point Comfort, at the mouth of the James River. A longboat was sent ashore, and the party learned for the first time of the safe arrival of the rest of the fleet and of the difficulties that had been encountered by the colonists in Virginia while they had been cast away on the Bermudas.[39]

[38] Smith, *op. cit.*, II, 639–40, tells us that after Somers' death in the Bermudas, where he went to seek food after the party had reached Virginia, his men carried his body home in "this Cedar ship"; which Strachey (Purchas, *op. cit.*, XIX, 61) identifies as the *Patience.*

[39] Many accounts have been written of the early colonization

The experiments and errors of the first colonists had culminated in a disaster far greater than had ever been feared by the company in London. The latter had foreseen that a much more definite form of government was needed and for this reason had petitioned for, and had been granted, the charter of 1609, with revised clauses concerning the government of the colony and the appointment of an absolute governor; but the delay of nine months while Gates had been in Bermuda, and the charter with him, had seen the undoing of the colony. In order to obtain a picture of the chaos Gates found waiting for him, we must briefly consider the history of the three years of settlement since the foundation of Jamestown early in 1607.

The three vessels that had left England on December 20, 1606, had carried with them sealed instructions that were not to be opened until the ships were actually off the coast of Virginia. It was only then that the settlers knew the names of the members of the Council, seven in number, among whom was Captain Newport. From this body a president was chosen, and the rest of the history of the colony until the arrival of Gates records

---

of Virginia. Of the contemporary ones relating to the period 1606–12, extracts are to be found in Purchas, *op. cit.*, XIX; considerable detail is given in Smith, *op. cit.*, and George Percy, *A trewe relatyon of the proceedings and occurrentes of momente which have happened in Virginia*, printed in *Tyler's Quarterly*, Vol. III (1921–22). Brown, *op. cit.*, provides a vast amount of material, from both manuscript and printed sources, for the period 1605–16. Narrative histories include William Stith, *The history of the first discovery and settlement of Virginia* (Williamsburg, 1747); Justin Winsor, *Narrative and critical history of America* (Cambridge, Mass., 1884), III; Andrews, *op. cit.*; and Wesley Frank Craven, *The southern colonies in the seventeenth century* (Baton Rouge, 1949). A list of bibliographies of the subject is given in Godfrey Davies (ed.), *Bibliography of British history, 1603–1714* (Oxford, 1928), and a list of contemporary printed accounts in F. W. Bateson (ed.), *The Cambridge bibliography of English literature* (Cambridge, 1940), I.

the wrangles and dissension among members of the Council. The president had no special powers beyond that of a casting vote at meetings and could be deposed by the Council at its will—a situation ripe for the emergence of factions—and, as happened in the Bermudas, the inevitable malcontents appeared, who by the strife they engendered seriously impaired the efficient running of the colony. Much of the vacillation and dilatory proceeding of the settlers stemmed directly from this divided command, and it was while Gates was in Bermuda that matters reached a head under the presidency of the famous Captain John Smith, who, antagonizing the other members of the Council, had ended up by being returned to England.

An even graver mistake had been made by the settlers, however. The faults of government could be attributed to the company in England, whose aim was that the venture should show an immediate profit and who had not at first realized the necessity for a firm and settled foundation of authority. When the time came to establish the settlement in Virginia itself, the selection of a site was left to the colonists. After a preliminary exploration of the river, they decided on a peninsula on the eastern bank formed by a meander of the stream, some fifty miles from the mouth. Ships could anchor close inshore, and the narrow isthmus and marshy hinterland made it easy to defend. Such considerations, while ideal from the standpoint of a temporarily sited military establishment, doomed the settlement. Palisades were constructed, and some fifty or sixty dwellings were erected within the perimeter—and the colonists then settled down to fight a losing battle against malaria, dysentery, and the multitude of other diseases that bred in the swamps. With one way of exit only, it was as easy for the Indians to lie in wait in ambush as it was for the defenders to man the gates to repulse them.

Divided command and lack of a settled policy had rendered it fatally easy to drift into antagonizing the natives, on whom the settlers were dependent for their supplies of grain since, because of the faulty siting, it was impossible to plant in the vicinity of Jamestown. Furthermore, the prices of commodities had steadily risen through the actions of visiting sailors whose aim was to make a quick profit out of their visit to the country.[40]

Once the impracticability of the site of the town had been realized, instead of removing in a body to a more suitable place, the colonists remained and tried to establish small settlements elsewhere; but again the dissensions among them were too great for this to be a success. Disease continued to take its toll, and the number of colonists steadily dwindled. But worse was to come. Although the other ships that had accompanied the *Sea Venture* arrived safely in 1609, bringing substantial reinforcements and considerable supplies of food, this was soon exhausted, and the settlers' attempts to obtain more from the natives were futile. Then ensued what was known to all of them as the "starving time."[41] Food supplies ran completely out, disease struck the community more fiercely than ever, and, besieged by the natives, it was impossible for the inhabitants of Jamestown to venture beyond the palisades in search of food. The death roll was prodigious, and of some nine hundred souls that had ventured to Virginia, either in the first ships or the succeeding ones, only sixty were left alive when Gates in the *Deliverance* cast anchor

---

[40] William Strachey, *For the colony in Virginea Britannia. Lawes divine, morall and martiall, &c.* (London, 1612). Articles 19 and 20 deal specifically and in considerable detail with the obligations of visiting mariners.

[41] Percy, *op. cit.,* pp. 266–67, gives the most graphic description of this time, which is also mentioned by a number of the other writers, including John Smith and Strachey.

before Jamestown. He had been joined at Fort Algernon by Captain George Percy, president of the colony,
and together they went ashore to view the scene of deso-
lation: the fortifications destroyed, gates open, empty
houses torn down for fuel, and the starving remnant of
the settlers in the last stages of hopeless despair. Summoned by the bell, the wretched band gathered in the
church, where, after a sorrowful prayer had been offered up by Bucke, the minister who had been on board
the *Sea Venture,* Strachey, by now high in the confidence of the leaders of the party, read for Gates his commission as governor, and Percy resigned his position to
him.

In the Bermudas, Gates had faced and mastered
serious difficulties, but here he encountered greater.
The party from the islands had brought with them
only such food as they needed for the voyage, and here
they found none. First the disorganization had to be
overcome, and supplies of food had to be assured.
Gates, armed with an authority the presidents had
lacked, immediately drew up and posted in the church
a set of laws containing a preface and twenty-one articles, "for Pietie, Loyaltie and Politie convenient to
the Colonie."[42] He then called together such men of
experience as were still in the colony, and between
them they tried to find a remedy for the evil state of
the settlement. Not only had the Indians reached such
a pitch of daring that they were openly assaulting boats
on the river, even within sight of the town, but there
seemed no way of supplementing the diet of herbs
and mushrooms that served merely to keep the colonists
alive.

[42] Later incorporated into *Lawes.* Strachey is credited with having assisted in compiling these laws of Gates's, but while it is
possible that due to his experience at the Inns of Court he was
able to advise the regular soldiers in command, there is nowhere
a definite statement that he did so; see p. 146.

Finally it was decided that there was nothing that they could do but board the ships again and abandon the country, making their way to Newfoundland in the hope of meeting with English vessels fishing there, which could give them food and help the small ships transport the settlers to England. Gates with some difficulty dissuaded the colonists from burning down the town, and on June 7 the whole party took to their boats and sailed down the river, leaving the scene of so many disasters behind them.

The following afternoon, as the ships lay anchored in the river awaiting the turn of the tide, a longboat was seen making its way toward them. Thomas West, Lord De la Warr, in whose place Gates was acting as governor of the colony, had arrived at Fort Algernon on June 6 with a fleet of three ships bearing "plants, seedes, and all other provisions and grayne as well to sowe and to victuale 1000 men for one yeare."[43] Learning of the desperate plight of the settlers and of Gates's decision to depart, he had hastily dispatched the longboat to intercept them, whereupon the ships were turned about and that evening the settlers found themselves again at Jamestown. Two days later De la Warr's three vessels anchored before the fort, where Gates, with a guard of honor, waited to welcome his successor. Strachey tells us:

It pleased him [Gates], that I should beare his Colours for that time: his Lordship landing, fell upon his knees, and before us all, made a long and silent Prayer to himselfe, and after, marched up into the Towne, where at the Gate, I bowed with the Colours, and let them fall at his Lordship's feete.[44]

---

[43] Brown, *op cit.*, I, 413. De la Warr later informed the settlers, however, that the supplies were sufficient for 400 men for a year (Purchas, *op. cit.*, XIX, 60).

[44] Purchas, *op. cit.*, XIX, 59.

A sermon was read to the colonists assembled in the church, and Gates formally surrendered his commission to the new governor, who then

delivered some few words unto the Company, laying many blames upon them for many vanities, and their idlenesse, earnestly wishing, that he might no more finde it so, least he should be compelled to draw the sword of Justice, to cut off such delinquents, which he had much rather, he protested, draw in their defence, to protect them from injuries.[45]

With supplies assured, an attempt could be made to reestablish the settlement on a firmer foundation. The new governor was a man of resource and experience and, having almost absolute power, could bring discipline to the colonists and order into their affairs. After choosing and swearing in his Council, his first action was to revise and expand the laws drawn up by Gates. The twenty-one articles were increased to thirty-seven, and they covered all the important aspects of life in the colony, including religious observance, theft, sexual crime, trade, sanitation, working hours, and the like. They were specifically designed to apply to any mariners who might visit the coast as well as to the settlers. Punishments, severe at first sight, ranged from whipping to death, but the laws were sufficiently simple and so vital to the survival of the colony that there was no excuse for breaking any of them.[46] In order that they might be understood and borne in mind by all the colonists, arrangements were made for them to be read in the church each Sunday.

The Council, sworn in at this first meeting, included Gates, Somers, Newport, and Percy, also Sir Ferdinando

[45] *Ibid.*, XIX, 60.

[46] See Strachey, *Lawes*, sig. Blv. Although Sir Thomas Dale is credited with having drawn up these laws, it is clear that his additions were those dealing with military matters.

Wainman, who had newly arrived with Lord De la Warr. Along with these distinguished and experienced colonists, Strachey was chosen secretary and recorder to the Council, a position of considerable importance. For the next twelve months he was to be in the closest association with the leaders of the colony, a participant in the meetings of the Council, and in constant communication with the governing body in England. He was to see the emergence of the settlement from the chaos in which Gates found it and materially assisted in its consolidation and survival. This was a far cry from Constantinople. Here he had been chosen for the ability he had shown and for his loyalty to his superiors. The indiscretions of his earlier post had not been repeated, and he had not been seduced by the specious arguments of the various malcontents while they were cast away in the Bermudas.

One of his first tasks was to compose, on behalf of the governor and council, a report on the state of the colony.[47] This was to be delivered to the company in London by Sir Thomas Gates, who sailed for England on July 10, bearing with him also Strachey's *True reportory*, the letter to an "Excellent Lady,"[48] which, after it had come to the hands of the company and been incorporated into its *True declaration*, designed to encourage faint-hearted investors, was to be used by Shakespeare and eventually to be included by Samuel Purchas in his *Pilgrimes*.

Meanwhile, although De la Warr had brought considerable supplies of grain, the colonists were severely handicapped by a complete lack of meat of any kind. Somers, in his tiny *Patience*, volunteered to sail to the

[47] Reproduced in the introduction to *The historie of travaile* (ed. Major), this letter was signed by De la Warr, Gates, Percy, Wenman, and Strachey and contains a number of passages identical with portions of *A true reportory*.

[48] See pp. 152–54.

Bermudas and there obtain a six months' supply of fish and hog meat,[49] and another ship was dispatched to fish along the northern coast. The most pressing problem, however, was the pacification of the natives, who, undeterred by the settlers' new show of strength, continued to lie in ambush in the woods without the fort, to assault boats on the river, and to send spies into Jamestown, ostensibly to trade. A message was sent to Powhatan, the paramount chief, demanding an end to the hostility. He returned an answer that not only must the English quit the country, but that they must present him with a coach and three horses so that he might travel in a manner befitting his rank; whereupon De la Warr sent parties on a number of successful punitive expeditions, sacking the larger native villages in the vicinity of Jamestown and putting to the sword such Indians as they could capture.

We know that Strachey was present at at least two of these skirmishes,[50] but apart from one further incident we have no record of his activities during the remainder of his stay in the colony. In 1611 a Spanish ship appeared off Fort Algernon, and when the captain and two of his officers came ashore they were captured by a party of English soldiers. The ship made good her escape, and the three prisoners were brought to Jamestown, where, Percy tells us:

Shortly after Sir Tho: Dale sentt my selfe Capt Newport and Mr Stracy secretary to the Collonie to examine them And so Accusing them to have come for spies

[49] He died, however, in the Bermudas, and his body was carried on to England in the *Patience* (Smith, *op. cit.*, II, 640).

[50] Purchas, *op. cit.*, XIX, 63. Smith, *op. cit.*, II, 503, mentions Mr. Stacy accompanying Percy on a larger expedition. There appears to have been no gentleman of this name among the colonists, so it almost certainly was Strachey, even though he is not mentioned by Percy (*op. cit.*, p. 272). The latter mentions only two of his officers who carried out specific orders.

they utterly denied the same butt still urginge them therewith Anto: Pereos answered that we had noe cawse att all to feare any thinge this yere butt what might happen the nexte he could nott tell.[51]

Accounts covering the life of the colony from 1610 to 1612 emphasise the emergence of order, the rise of a new spirit and enthusiasm among the colonists, the pacification of the Indians, and the increase in planting, until the venture became almost self-supporting. Jamestown, repaired and again fortified, became more of an administrative center, and forts and settlements were established on the fertile plains toward the mouth of the river and upstream from Jamestown, where a series of cataracts proved an impassable barrier to shipping. De la Warr, his work of reconstruction completed, fell victim to one of the numerous diseases still rampant and was forced to return to England, leaving the government to Percy, who after a brief charge surrendered it to Sir Thomas Dale in May 1611. In August of the same year Sir Thomas Gates returned to Virginia and resumed command, and shortly after his arrival Strachey quitted the colony and returned to London. His departure at a time when the colony was at last showing every prospect of success and when at last the investments both of the colonists and of the shareholders seemed about to show a profit would seem to indicate that his decision was made for him, regardless of his own preferences. It may have been that he was summoned home by the company or dispatched by Gates to report on his behalf, but it seems more probable that he, in turn, had breathed the noxious miasma of the swamps and, falling ill, had been forced to return to England.

He took with him a copy of the laws first framed by Gates and expanded in turn by his successors De la

[51] Percy, *op. cit.*, p. 278.

Warr and Dale, together with some notes on Virginia, later to be expanded into his *Historie of travaile*.[52] In his preface to the *Lawes*, published on his return, he tells the company:

When I went forth vpon this voyage, (Right worthy Gentlemen) true it is, I held it a seruice of dutie, (during the time of my vnprofitable seruice, and purpose of stay in the Colonie, for which way else might I adde vnto the least height of so Heroicke and pious a building) to propose vnto my self to be (though an vnable) Remembrancer of all accidents, occurrences, and vndertakings thereunto, *adventitiall*: In moste of which since the time our right famous sole Governour then, now Lieutenant Generall Sir Thomas Gates Knight, after the ensealing of his Commission, hasted to our fleete in the West, there staying for him, I haue both in the *Bermudas* and since in *Virginea* beene a sufferer and an eie witnesse, and the full storie of both in due time shall consecrate vnto your viewes.[53]

He had also received encouragement from the company to embark on a task of this nature. When Gates had returned to England in 1610 and the company received the first news of his survival and of that of the colonists with him, a letter was dispatched to Strachey by his old friend Richard Martin, now appointed secretary to the Council of the company in London, in which he requested on the company's behalf an account of the colony as it then was and praised the work Strachey had so far done:

Sir,

Although length of the voyage, & distance of the place where you are, wold require a long letter, and the busines that we have in hand touching your plantacon a large discourse, (yet must I crave pardon of you, if considering many present Impediments) I wrap vp a

---

[52] Reasons for believing that a portion of this work was composed in Virginia are given on pp. 184–89.

[53] Sig. A2r.

great desyre of advertisement and of good affection in
fewe wordes, my desire is cheefely to let you vnderstand
how well your travell in that place where you are, is
interpreted amongst all good & wise men, which having
bene still in love with longe & hazardous voyages, more
to profytt your knowledge then for any other profytt,
shewes that you have a mynde much in love with vertue,
and are a fytt *Achates* for such an *Aeneas*, as is our
Noble & worthie Generall the lord *Delawarre*. Yf you
know good Mr Strachey, the care that I have of this
Plantacon, the travell that I have taken therein, (bothe
before & since it pleased them to call me into the
counsell) and the Fire that doth not onlie burn in mee,
but flames out to the view of every one, for the fur-
therance of this honorable enterprise, you wolde thinke
that my speeche hath neither fashion nor purpose of a
complement. Yf the wysest man that ever spake or
wrytt (except him that was both God & man) summed
vp all the reckoninge of worldly felicitie in these two
words *Laetari et benefacere*, implying a cheerefull
Mirthe accompanied with well doinge, (from which
it cannot be severed,) who hath more cause to be cheere-
ful & inly glad then you, that hath comfort of so greate
a well doing, to which no other may be compared,
for what welldoing can be greater, then to be the
stocks and authors of a people, and of a people that
shall serve & glorifie God, which is the ende of all our
Creation, and to redeeme them from Ignorance & in-
fidelitie, to the true knowledg & worshippe of God,
whereby you are made partakers of this promisse, that
they which lead others vnto Righteousnes, shall shine as
the Starres in the firmament, wherein I envie your
happines, that I cannot (by reason of my profession)
be a partaker of that Comfort by my travell their, as
I am by my endevour here at home, I shall not need
to advise you how to carie your selfe, for your experience there hath made you outgone all vse of my ad-
monition, which my affection wold willingly afforde you,
if there were cause, and I know, that the difficulties
& straitenes of the place, and the hardnes of these
people with whom you have to doe, with those other
difficulties (of which we are even sensible here for
your sake) will make you carefull to please God, who

must blesse all that you vndertake, and walke in a Noble example of Justice & truthe, which onely doth enforce a reputation & respect from other men. And in vaine it is in such a place to pretend to be vertuous, except a man be vertuous indeede, and that vertue extend it self vnto example.

Therefore, since I assure my self, that of this advise you have no neede, I will conclude with an earnest request, that you wold be pleased by the return of this shippe to let me vnderstand from you the nature & qualitie of the soyle, & how it is like to serue you without helpe from hence, the manners of the people, how the Barbarians are content with your being there, but especially how our owne people doe brooke their obedience how they endure labor, whether willingly or vpon constraint, how they live in the exercise of Religion, whether out of conscience or for fashion, And generally what ease you have in the government there, & what hope of the successe, wherein I desire you & coniure you, by our auncient acquaintance & good intentions, to deale Clearely with me, as I wold do with you in the like case, that thereby I may be truly able to satisfie others, & to direct my counsells & endevors for prevention of evill, if there be any; In requitall whereof, you shall commaund me both there, & els where, wheresoever it shall please God to direct our fortunes to meete, to assist you in any course for your good, And so recommending my service & affection to your self & your high honorable Lord, I recommend you & your endevors in my prayers to the direction & protection of Gods divine providence.

Resting./
Your ever loving friend to commaund
RICH. MARTIN.
M. temple. 14 December. 1610.

The letter itself[54] was addressed "To the worthy my very loving frend. William Strachey Esquire in Virginia." It was to travel "By the hercules whom God preserve."

Such accounts as Strachey may have sent to the Coun-

[54] Folger MS 420, 423, ff. 62–62b.

cil in London are no longer preserved, but the details that Martin asks for—the nature and fertility of the soil and in particular the reaction of the English settlers to their new home—are not those that give the subsequently written *Historie of travaile* its value. Strachey's interest seems rather to have been in the Indians themselves, and it is in the chapters dealing with their way of life and their religion that we find him drawing from his own experience and giving evidence of a power of detailed observation.[55]

He probably returned to England in the *Prosperous*, which, leaving Virginia in September 1611, arrived back in London either in late October or early November of that year.[56] The *Lawes* was entered for publication on December 13.[57] Strachey, who in his prefatory letter states that he is writing "from my lodging in the blacke Friers," tells the Council: "I assure me, that by you I shall bee encouraged to go on in the discharge of greater offices by examining and fauouring my good intentions in this, and in what else my poore knowledge or faithfulnesse may enable me to be a servant in so beloved and sacred a businesse"; and asks that he may be allowed to return to Virginia or to help in some way from England.[58]

He had, of course, Martin's promise that he would help him in any way he could, and it is probable that through his cousins in Kent he had access to the treasurer and most important man in the Council of the Virginia Company, Sir Thomas Smith.[59] When, in January 1612, the *Lawes* was printed, Strachey presented one copy to William Crashaw, preacher to the Middle Temple, who, partly as a result of a sermon he had delivered before the assembled adventurers to

[55] See Chapter 7.   [56] Brown, *op cit.*, I, 497, 523.
[57] Pollard and Redgrave, *op. cit.*, s.v. "Strachey."
[58] Sig. A3v.   [59] See p. 153.

Virginia in 1609[60] and also because of his enthusiasm and interest in the venture, was highly regarded by the company.

To the Reuerend; and right worthy the Title of a Devine, who in so sacred an Expedition as is the reduction of Heathen to the knowledg of the euer-liuing true God, stands vp, the only vnsatisfyed and firme Freinde of all that possess & sit in so holy a Place Wm Crashawe Minister in the Midle-Temple William Strachey sometyme a Personall servaunt, and now a Beadsman, for that Christian Colonie setling in Virginea-Britania; wisheth full accomplishment of all Goodnes; & to that Plantation all happines, and reall, (and if it may be, Royall) Freindes.[61]

Other copies were presented to Sir William Wade, a member of the Council,[62] and to Sir Anthony Aucher, who, though at this time merely a shareholder in the company, was later to become a member of the council.[63]

[60] See *D.N.B.*, "Crashaw," and Brown, *op. cit.* Of the sermon, printed the next year, it has been said that "there is no nobler sermon than this of the period."

[61] This dedication in Strachey's own hand is found on the flyleaf of the British Museum copy of the *Lawes*, press mark *c.33.c.30.* Another copy of the *Lawes*, now apparently in America and referred to in J. St. Loe Strachey, *The adventure of living*, (London, 1922), pp. 58–59, contains an autograph inscription to Thomas Lawson, Esq., described by Strachey as "his right truly honoured, and best beloved friend" and dated January 21. Lawson, who arrived in Virginia with De la Warr in 1610, was one of the minor members of the Council and in command of a troop of soldiers.

[62] Sotheby & Co., *Catalogue of exceedingly rare and valuable Americana* (London, 1928), p. 70. Wade's copy had a printed unsigned sub-title page inserted, "To the Right Worthy, and one of the chiefe Fautors of this Christian expedition, Sir William Wade Knight &c."

[63] Strachey, *Lawes*, British Museum copy, press mark *G.7126.* This also consists of a printed insert following the title page: "To the ever heartie and happie Advancer of all his deare Countries honoured Services, the right Noble Sr. Anthonie Anger Knight, &c." Strachey has corrected "n" to "u" in "Anger" and added, in his own hand, "Ever to honnor, your free and noble

Strachey clearly hoped that his service with the company would not pass unrewarded and that through their good offices he might obtain some post where he could hope to relieve his now all too pressing embarrassments. Meanwhile he had begun work on *The historie of travaile*, but found that "many impediments, as yet must detaine such my observations in the shadow of darknesse, vntill I shall be able to deliver them perfect vnto your iudgements."[64]

The impediments were very present, and had appeared almost as soon as Strachey stepped off the ship that had brought him back to England. Even as the *Lawes* was coming off the press, his attorney was appearing in the Court of Common Pleas on his behalf to answer a writ of praecipe issued by Jasper Tien, from whom Strachey had borrowed thirty pounds four years before, and to request an adjournment of the case until the next term.[65]

Constantinople, Ireland, and Virginia—and his fortune had not yet been repaired; the possibility of 1606 had become the fact of 1612. His credit gone, he could not hope to pay his creditor by borrowing from another moneylender, but could only rely on the assistance of his friends, not only to help pay his debts, but also to find him a post where he might be assured of some income, however small, to keep him from the "place of dead men" he had already envisaged.

---

disposition William Strachej." This unusual spelling of his name appears also in the Percy copy of *The historie*, but apparently nowhere else. Details of Aucher's part in the affairs of the company are given in Brown, *op. cit.*, II, 818–19.

[64] *Lawes*, sig. A2.

[65] P.R.O. C.P.40/1881, f. 918, *Tien* v. *Strachey*, Hilary 1611–12. The record of the case does not show when the writ was issued, but it was probably applied for during the Michaelmas Term, 1611, within a month or so of Strachey's return.

6.   Closing Years

STRACHEY was later to observe somewhat bitterly that "the fashion of the world is to deal with us a Pilate did with Christ, put a goodly superscribtion upon us, first entreating us with honnor, & much ostentation of glory, as Pylat upon Christ Jesus King of the Jewes, and afterward he caused him to be crucifyd"; and that "the worlds promises, are only fayre, nothing so in performance. it is as Sabans words to Jacob, a promise of the beautiful Rachael if wee will serve it, but performes unto us bleerd Eyd Leah."[1]

As the young country country gentleman come to London he had seen before him the brightest prospects of advancement and success; he had been on a friendly footing with those who had made their names in the world of literature or the law; and, reasonably wealthy and well-connected, he had every hope that he might succeed in his turn. Even though, seduced by the delights of city life, he had wasted his earlier years, his post in Turkey had offered a good chance of retrieving his position; and when he had been forced to leave Constantinople, he had shown in Virginia that he possessed considerable ability and was capable of positive and effective action. Now, having returned to England

[1] In his manuscript commonplace book, f. 279, in the Alderman Library, University of Virginia.

and knowing that the Virginia Company thought well of his work in the colony, Strachey found the world's promises again fair.

Again he was to be disappointed. Although he remained friendly with members of the Virginia Company, and was a shareholder until his death, he did not serve the company again, and the remaining years of his life were to be spent in obscurity and, if not in poverty, at least in reduced circumstances.

During 1612 he continued to work on *The historie of travaile*, but despite his hopes from the company it would appear that the Council had little encouragement to offer him. He had been forestalled by the publication of John Smith's *Map of Virginia*, and Samuel Purchas, in possession of Hakluyt's manuscripts, was at work on a collection of voyages which would inevitably cover much of the same ground as Strachey proposed to treat. He was thus forced to turn elsewhere for assistance. In June 1612 his friend George Percy, late of the Council of the colony in Virginia, for a time acting governor there, and one of the most energetic of the early settlers, returned to England,[2] and it was probably at his suggestion that Strachey dedicated and presented to his elder brother Henry Percy, Earl of Northumberland

the first Catagraph or Draught, as I haue had tyme to digest into forme and Method, out of my Iournall or diary bookes: in which I haue not thought yt amisse neither to epitomise briefly somewhat of the former Colonies (though for the present discontynued) since they making all to one Story, the whole maie appeare so much the more cliere and perfect for your Lordships absolute knowledge.[3]

[2] *Va. mag. hist. biog.*, LVII (1949), 241. He left Jamestown on April 22, 1612.

[3] *Historie* (ed. Wright), p. 3.

Although the earl was at this time confined in the Tower, mainly for too outspoken criticism of the king but ostensibly because of too close a relationship to Thomas Percy, one of the Gunpowder conspirators, he was nevertheless a privileged prisoner and was permitted to gather around him men of learning, to whom he paid salaries for assisting him in his studies. A lifelong friend of Raleigh, his fellow prisoner, he had shown considerable interest in the voyages of colonization and exploration, and among his servants was Thomas Harriot, who had in 1585 been sent by Raleigh as surveyor with Sir Richard Grenville to Virginia. Harriot's *Briefe and true report* was the most detailed and accurate account of Virginia published until Smith's *Map* appeared. Furthermore, despite his imprisonment, the earl still wielded considerable power and influence, and as Prince Henry, whom he ardently supported, came to take more part in the affairs of the realm, his position became even stronger.[4]

If Strachey had hoped to be included in the circle of scholars who relieved the tedium of the earl's durance he was disappointed, and very shortly afterward he presented another copy of *The historie* to Sir Allen Apsley, purveyor to His Majesty's Navy, who, while not himself connected with the Virginia Company, was the nephew by marriage of Sir George Carew, a member of the Council. Strachey's dedicatory letter would make it appear that he was not personally acquainted with Apsley, but that, from what friends had said, he believed that Apsley would give the work a sympathetic reading. After summarizing arguments in favor of colonization, Strachey goes on:

But worthie Sir I doe forgett myself to openn a Book unto your knowledge which is full of Love and under-

[4] *D.N.B.*

standing of the true endes of this great action, yet so yt
maie be that these geathered observations thus bungled,
bound up, and to *your view alone intended* by me maie
fall into such handes as maie put some doubtes which
even this entraunce may resolve them in, and so begett
towards the further reading hereof a better opinion:
Be yt only your honour to pardonn me the appealing
of you from your more serious affaires to the perusall of
these infirme and scattered collections, since yf I have
offended, the noblenes & Bountie of your faire Disposi-
cion (expressed evenn in my knowledge to manie of
my best Freindes) makes me presume that I cannot
(in any actioun, which hath relish of virtue and goodnes) too much challenge or provoak your patience.

And so not striving to be unnecessarily troublesome
I wish unto you the iust accomplishment of your owne
vertuous desires: by him who is truly to you divoted.

William Strachey.[5]

The choice of Sir Allen Apsley seems an unusual one.
However, Strachey was at this time lodging in the
Blackfriars, and Apsley, if not resident there in 1612,
was certainly connected with the parish of St. Anne's
not very much later. The register records the marriage
on October 23, 1615, of Sir Allen Apsley and Mistress
Lucy St. John. He may have been a near neighbor of
Strachey, whose friend Francis Michell, moreover, had
been in an official position in Ireland at the time
Apsley was victualer to the forces there; and while we
have no evidence that Strachey was at this time still
friendly with Michell, it may well have been at his
suggestion that he approached this prospective patron.
Once again it would appear that Strachey received no
encouragement, and *The historie* remained unpub-
lished.

Meanwhile Tien's suit had dragged its leisurely way
through the Easter, Trinity, and Michaelmas Terms of
1612, and finally, on February 8, 1613, judgment was

⁵ Brown, *op. cit.*, II, 564–65.

given in his favor at the Guildhall for the debt of thirty pounds, and a further £5 10*s.* in costs was awarded against Strachey, who, failing to appear, was declared "at mercy." Tien could now enter Strachey's lodgings and take possession of such of his belongings as were necessary to satisfy his claim.[6]

This is the only record of any action taken against Strachey for debt, but we have from his pen a graphic description of his plight at this time:

Sir
Necessitie, not my will, sendes me vnto you a borrower of 20s. if you may: this last dismall arrest, hath taken from all my Frends something, & from me all I had: & today I am to meete with some Frends at dinner returned from Virginia, & God is witnes with me I have not to pay for my dinner, All my things be at Pawne, and I yet indebted to Ro: wife, Love me you still (if you please) I will give you no other cause, & let not N. know of my name, or beeing in my place hereafter, I am Jelious of him: if I were assured of what is very likely, I wold not be so evill intreated, and have patience: looke well unto your self: and looke well upon your self, & you shall finde he is no companion for you; but it may be I sound herein harshly to your love, yet know it comes from a true love to you;

> Vale; yours ever,
>
> W. S.[7]

The situation was one only too familiar to any Londoner of the day: the arrest for debt, the friends' assistance, the goods in pawn, and finally the unfortunate debtor keeping to his house, or remaining in hiding,

---

[6] P.R.O. CP40/1887, f. 903. The form of an action for debt is detailed under this heading in Jacob, *Law dictionary.*

[7] Folger MS 420, 423, f. 60 Although this is only a copy of the letter, the practice throughout the MS is to try to reproduce the signatures of the correspondents, and the initials given resemble Strachey's as they appear elsewhere. The friends to whom he refers cannot, unfortunately, be identified, nor can the person to whom this letter was written.

knowing that once his creditors were aware of his whereabouts he might expect the sheriff's men hard on his heels and the portals of the debtors' prison again open to welcome him.

The brewhouse property had again become a source of embarrassment. During Strachey's absence in Virginia his sister Martha had died before she was due to receive the sum of 200 marks from the rents of the property under the terms of her father's will, and his brother Howard, having taken out letters of administration on her estate, promptly sold her interest in the brewhouse, for some eighty pounds, to George Shiers. When he returned, Strachey found that the first payment of the money due to the deceased Martha had already been made to Shiers and promptly, as head of the family, repudiated Howard's authority and refused to make any further payment—an action that was later to result in a suit in Chancery.[8]

Before Shiers' action was commenced, however, Strachey's old opponent, Matthew Clayton, his ten years' annuity granted him by the Court of Requests having expired, commenced another suit, this time in Chancery, to contest the title to the property.[9] Once again he appeared *in forma pauperis,* but on this occasion the court showed less sympathy than it had ten years earlier, and the case was thrown out.[10]

Shiers allowed some seven years to elapse before he presented his bill in Chancery, on April 14, 1619, alleging collusion between William and Howard with intent to defraud him of his right to the income from the property. Strachey, who until this time had neglected to do so, promptly took out letters of administration

[8] P.R.O. C2/Jas 1/S10/51, *Shiers* v. *Strachey.*

[9] P.R.O. C2/Jas 1/C21/83, *Clayton* v. *Strachey,* November 1615.

[10] P.R.O. C33/129, ff. 227, 304. Dismissed on December 1, 1615.

himself on Martha's estate, and, the case coming to trial, Shiers' claims were thrown out by the court.[11] Howard, although at fault, made no answer to Shiers' bill of complaint, and there is no record whether Shiers succeeded in recovering his money in any other court.

A year later the brewhouse property finally passed out of Strachey's hands. In April 1619 his son William had married Eleanor, the daughter of John Read of London,[12] and on July 20, 1620, Strachey, together with his trustees John and Sir Edmund Bowyer, conveyed to him the property "in consideracion of some competent livinge to be assured to the said William Strachey the sonne & to the said Ellenor after the death of the said William Strachey the Father." During Strachey's life his son was to pay him the sum of forty pounds per year, and after his death twenty pounds annually to his other son Edmund, and the Bowyers were to continue to supervise the property.[13]

Three other property transactions are recorded in which Strachey plays a minor part. With all his lands in Saffron Walden mortgaged to the Bowyer brothers, it was necessary that Strachey's name be associated with theirs in the indentures of bargain and sale in order to provide an absolutely secure conveyance when they came in their turn to sell the property. Hence on April 14, 1613, we find Sir Edmund Bowyer of Camberwell, John Bowyer, Esquire, of Wandsworth, and William Strachey, gentleman, of London, selling two dwellings in Walden to William Palmer;[14] on October 28, 1616, Sir Edmund and John Bowyer, and William Strachey, all of Camberwell, sold three acres of land in Walden to Thomas Gyver;[15] and on May 20, 1617, Sir Edmund

---

[11] P.R O. C33/137, f. 3.   [12] Camberwell parish register.
[13] P.R.O. C54/2425, Indenture, Strachey and Bowyer.
[14] P.R.O. C54/2177, Indenture, Strachey and Palmer.
[15] Corp. Mun., III, 191.

Bowyer of Camberwell, John Bowyer of Wandsworth, and William Strachey, also of Wandsworth, sold a further twenty acres of land in Walden to Geoffrey Tanner.[16]

These transactions make it clear that Strachey was closely associated with his brothers-in-law and that he was actually living close to them, yet in the diary of Edward Alleyn, lord of the manor of Dulwich and neighbor of Sir Edmund Bowyer, who was one of the governors of Alleyn's College of God's Gift, there is no mention of Strachey. Alleyn tells us of the occasions when he met Sir Edmund,[17] of how the Bowyers came to dine with him and how he went in his turn to dine with them,[18] and of how he called at Sir Edmund's mansion one evening after dinner and saw a play produced there;[19] but of Bowyer's brother-in-law, the former shareholder in the Blackfriars Theatre and friend of dramatists whom Alleyn knew personally, he makes no mention.

It seems probable that Strachey, during this obscure period of his life, remained associated with affairs in London, rather than in the county of Surrey, but we have only one record that links him with the city and the life he lived there prior to his adventures overseas.

In 1616, after the imprisonment of the Earl and Countess of Somerset for their part in the murder of Sir Thomas Overbury, there appeared another edition of the latter's *Wife*, "With addition of many new elegies upon his untimely and much lamented death." The work, originally written to dissuade Somerset from his contemplated marriage, had first been printed after Overbury had been poisoned in the Tower in 1613

---

[16] Essex R.O. D/DGn 174. This original deed bears Strachey's signature.
[17] On November 24 and 25, 1617.
[18] September 13, 1618; November 12, 1618.
[19] January 5, 1620.

and the prefatory verses had consisted only of commendations of his character; but now, with the truth brought to light, it was safe to comment on the actual circumstances of the murder, and the additional verses all expressed their detestation both of the deed and of the principal plotters. Among these new verses appeared,

TO THE CLEANE CONTRARY WIFE.

Look here: and chide those spirits which maintaine
Their empire, with a strong command in you,
That all good eyes, which do your follies view,
Pitty, what you for them must once sustaine:
O from those evils, which free soules disdaine
To be acquainted with, and but pursue
Worst minds from them (as hatefull as untrue.)
By reading this, for Fames faire sake refraine:
Who would let feed upon her birth, the brood
Of lightnesse, indiscretion, and the shame
Of foule incontinence, when the base blood
Is carelesse onely of an honour'd name?
Be all that gentle are, more high improv'd,
For loose dames are but flatter'd, never lov'd.

W. Stra.[20]

The poems are signed only with the poets' initials, but among them are three by members of the Inns of Court —B. G. and P. B. of the Middle Temple and W. B. of the Inner Temple. Others have been attributed to Christopher Brooke, John Ford, and John Fletcher.[21] Another set of verses is signed with the initials W. S.

[20] It must be pointed out however that these verses are attributed to William Stradling by E. F. Rimbault ((ed.), *The miscellaneous works in prose and verse of Sir Thomas Overbury, Knt.* (London, 1856). Although Stradling was a common enough name, there is no record of any William Stradling connected with the Inns of Court, and we know that Strachey used the initials "W. St." in his prefatory verses to *The historie*, so the attribution appears reasonable. See also *Va. mag. Hist. Biog.*, LVII (1949), 121.

[21] Rimbault, *op. cit.*, pp. 279–81.

and not only contains a verbal parallel, but expresses much the same sentiments as Strachey's sonnet.[22]

It was natural enough that Strachey, living in London, should have retained his connections with the Inns of Court, but these verses tell us little about him. Overbury, a member of the Middle Temple and a courtier to King James, was an intimate friend of Robert Carr, Earl of Somerset, and when that nobleman set his heart on marrying Frances Howard, divorced Countess of Essex, was foolish enough to interfere, pointing out that the lady was "a strumpet and her mother and brother bawds." Coming to the ears of Frances Howard, this did nothing to endear Overbury to her, and she and the infatuated Somerset hatched a plot, with the result that Overbury was cast into the Tower, and after living for some three months on a diet of arsenic, blue vitriol, and corrosive sublimate, eventually died in September 1613. Somerset then married the lady, and two years later, when the plot came to light, they were both sentenced to imprisonment in the Tower after a trial that excited as much public interest as any event during James's reign.[23] Not only did the trial involve the principals and their accomplices, but one of Strachey's friends, Thomas Campion, found himself also under suspicion, although after interrogation he was cleared of complicity.[24] Overbury's fellow members of the Middle Temple were greatly interested in the whole affair, and the publication of *A wife* was due mainly to this interest.

[22] Attributed by Rimbault to William Shipton, who cannot be identified.

[23] Rimbault, *op. cit.*, Introduction. See also T. B. Howell, *A complete collection of state trials* (London, 1816–28), II, 911–1022.

[24] Campion's patron, Sir Thomas Monson, was himself brought to trial, having acted as an intermediary for Somerset, but was acquitted (Howell, *op. cit.*, II, 950–51; Vivian, *Campion's works*, pp. xliv–xlv).

Strachey's continued association with the Inns of Court is further suggested by the dedication of the third copy of *The historie of travaile*, in 1618, to the newly created Lord Chancellor, Sir Francis Bacon, Lord Verulam.[25]

To the Right Honourable Sir Francis Bacon, Knight, Baron of Verulam, Lord High Chancellor of England, and of His Majesties most honorable Privy Counsell.

Most worthely honor'd Lord,

Your Lordship ever approving yourself a most noble fautor of the Virginian Plantation, being from the beginning (with other lords and earles) of the principall counsell applyed to propogate and guide yt: and my poore self (bound to your observaunce, by being one of the Graies-Inne Societe) having bene there three yeares, thither imploied in place of secretarie so long there present; and setting downe with all my welmeaning abilities a true narration or historie of the countrie: to whome shoulde I submitt so aptly, and with so much dutye, the most humble present thereof, as to your most worthie and best-judging Lordship? who in all vertuous and religious endeavours have ever bene, as a supreame encourager, so an inimitable patterne and perfecter: nor shall my plaine and rude composition any thought discourage my attempt, since howsoever I should feare to appeare therein before so matchles a maister in that facultie (if any opinionate worth of mine owne worke presented me) yet as the great Composer of all things made all good with his owne goodnes, and in our only will to his imitation takes us into his act, so be his goodnes your good Lordship's in this acceptation: for which with all my poore service I shall abide ever

Your best Lordship's most humbly
WILLIAM STRACHEY.[26]

---

[25] He was created Baron Verulam on July 12, 1618, so the manuscript, although revised in 1617 (see p. 188) must have been presented after this date.

[26] *Historie* (ed. Major), Introduction.

Bacon, immersed in the affairs of his office, appears to have taken no notice of this belated appeal from a fellow member of Gray's Inn, and nothing more is heard of Strachey in connection with the Virginia venture.

On June 21, 1621, Strachey was buried in the parish church of St. Giles, at Camberwell.[27] He had seen his son William married and the birth of his first grandchild, Helen, who died only a few months old.[28] His wife Frances had died, probably before 1615,[29] and he had remarried and left an unidentified widow, Dorothy.[30] With the brewhouse made over to his son, he had little property to bequeath, and it may be for this reason that we have no record of any will or letters of administration regarding his estate.

During these closing years of his life his thoughts seem to have turned more and more to religion. Preserved among the Ashmolean manuscripts is a set of verses, described in the contemporary index as "Mr Strachie's Harke."

Harke! Twas the trump of death that blewe
          My hower is come false world adewe
          That I to death vntymely goe.
          Thy pleasures have betrayed me soe
          For Death's the punishment of sinn
          And of all creatures I have bene
          The most vngratefull wicked one
          That ere the heauens did shine vpon.

[27] Camberwell parish register.

[28] *Ibid.* The child was baptized April 25, 1620, and buried September 1, 1620.

[29] P.R.O. C2/Jas I/C21/83, *Clayton* v. *Strachey*, November 14, 1615, refers to "William Stracheye and Frauncis his then wife."

[30] P.R.O. C54/2425, Indenture, Strachey and Bowyers, July 7, 1620, contains the only reference to her as "Dorothie the nowe wife of the said William Strachey the Father." Extant London parish registers contain no record of his remarriage or Frances' death.

Harke! I have sinnd against Earth & heaven
  Early by date late in the even
  All manner sinnes all manner wayes
  I have committed in my daies
  Hell and hell fire is my due
  O but deare Christe I humbly sue
  Thy blood may wash my red sowle white
  Mercy not Iudgment is thy delight.

Harke! at which mercy gate I knocke
  Let sobbes & sighes the same vnlocke
  Prostrate I fall & begg for grace
  O doe not turne away thy face
  my cryinge sinnes beate at thy Throane
  Once bowe the heavens looke downe vpon
  A wretch more overthrowne then greefe
  That beggs for mercy not for life.
     Finis
    W: Strachie.[31]

His commonplace book, compiled during these closing years of his life, provides further evidence that his
early interest in religion had become intensified and
deepened. One is tempted to speculate that Strachey,
conscious of failure, had turned to religion for consola-
tion, but nevertheless a profound interest in religious
matters was part of the make-up of many a gentleman
of the day.

Of Strachey's circle of friends during his earlier
period in London, some had achieved fame, and others
had disappeared in poverty or obscurity. Thomas
Campion, his reputation assured by his masques, his
poems, and his songs, had died in 1620; Ben Jonson's
collected plays had appeared in folio, and by 1621 he
was enjoying the favor of the King; John Donne, his

---

[31] Ashmole MS 781, f. 135. The manuscript was compiled between 1620 and 1631, and contains also verses by John Hoskins,
Sir John Harington, and Lord Howard of Walden.

earlier troubles far behind him, was chaplain to King James and Dean of St. Pauls; and Richard Martin had become Recorder of London before his death in 1618. But Hugh Holland, in his remote vicarage in Denbighshire, "preferment not answering his expectation, . . . grumbled out the rest of his life in visible discontentment";[32] John Marston had abandoned the stage and was living quietly as rector of Christchurch in Hampshire; and Strachey had vanished from the scene.

Failure can spring from defects of character, from weakness of will, and from lack of application. And it can stem too from unfortunate combinations of events that can only be called bâd luck. However much Strachey's earlier troubles may have been due to the impetuosity of youth, his later ones arose partly from an honesty of character that can hardly be regarded as a defect but largely from ill fortune. The quarrel between the ambassadors in Turkey was something that could not have been foreseen and could not be avoided, and Strachey had little option but to make his preference clear. The arrival of Hugh Holland in Constantinople at such an inappropriate time can only be regarded also as a misfortune. So, too, on his return from Virginia, it was another coincidence of time that produced John Smith's *Map of Virginia* while Strachey was at work on his own *Historie of travaile.*

One is tempted to say "If . . . ." If Lello had left Constantinople before Glover arrived and if Hugh Holland had not been waiting on the shore at Chios, we might have found William Strachey of Saffron Walden, gentleman, eventual ambassador to the court of the Grand Signior and, returning to England, knighted and settling down to a comfortable and prosperous old age. If John Smith had not published his

---

[32] Thomas Fuller, *The history of the worthies of England,* ed. P. A. Nuttall (London, 1840), III, 503–4.

Map and if Samuel Purchas had not set out to follow in the footsteps of Hakluyt, then we might have had from Strachey's pen a complete and detailed history of the settlement of Virginia, and he might in his turn have continued honorably in the service of the Virginia Company and have eventually been found among the members of the Council.

As it is, his travels over, he vanishes from view, meditating, with the Apostle John, "The world first uttereth good wyne, & when men have wel drunke, than that which is worse," but hoping that "the sonne of Man shall send forth his Angells, & they shall gather out of his Kingdom all things that shall offend, & them which do iniquity."[33]

[33] Commonplace Book, f. 279.

7. Works

STRACHEY's reputation has depended to the present day on his writings rather than on his actions or his circle of friends. Scholars have linked Strachey and *A true reportory* with Shakespeare and *The tempest*; his various prefatory verses have been noted; and to students of early American history the name of Strachey immediately brings to mind *The historie of travaile, A true reportory,* and the *Lawes.*

It may be that, like his friend Hugh Holland, Strachey in his own time enjoyed some reputation as a poet and that his manuscript verses circulated and were received with acclaim among his friends both of the Inns of Court and the playhouses. But today, when any estimate of his poetical ability must depend on such of his verses as have survived to us, we can only regard Campion's epigram as a somewhat flattering compliment to a friend of whom he thought highly. The prefatory verses to the *Lawes, The view of Fraunce, A wife, Sejanus,* and *The historie of travaile* could have been written by any one of the many educated gentlemen to whom the composition of a set of verses was a mental exercise, a pastime to while away an idle hour, or by any poetaster, accustomed to write to order occasional verses to celebrate any event, however great or small.

Competently written, but no more, these occasional

verses of Strachey's refer solely to the work they preface and reflect only the most commonplace of contemporary ideas: that virtue is its own reward;[1] that moderation is good in all things;[2] or that the spreading of the Gospel is a noble task.[3]

The sonnets expressing the latter theme that are prefixed to the *Lawes* and addressed to the Council of the Virginia Company were written at a time when Strachey was hoping for a further post with the company, and while there there can be no doubt that he believed sincerely in the religious aspect of the settlement of Virginia, the views expressed had been set out at length by many a writer on colonization before him and were to be found also in the manifestoes published from time to time by the company itself.[4] Even the penitential verses, alone striking a personal note, read rather as a poetical exercise than the expression of a genuine and profound repentance. Once more the ideas are conventional in the extreme.

Fortunately, however, his reputation depends not on his verse, but on his works relating to the early colonization of Virginia: the *Lawes divine, morall and martiall*, *A true reportory*, and *The historie of travaile into Virginia Britannia*.

[1] Verses to *The view of Fraunce*.   [2] Verses to *Sejanus*.
[3] Verses to the *Lawes* and *The historie*.
[4] The earliest colonizers, the Spaniards, had regarded the spreading of the Gospel as one of their chief aims, and the religious argument in favor of colonization had been advanced also by Sir George Peckham, *op. cit.*; Richard Hakluyt, *Discourse on the western planting*, in *Doc. history of the state of Maine* (Portland, 1869–1909), II; William Symonds, *Virginia: a sermon preached at Whitechapel* (London, 1609); William Crashaw, *A sermon preached before the Lord Lawarre* (London, 1610). The same argument appears in Virginia Company, *A true and sincere declaration of the purpose and ends of the plantation begun in Virginia* (London, 1610), and in the company's instructions to Sir Thomas Gates when he departed for Virginia in 1609 (Kingsbury, *op. cit.*, III, 27).

The *Lawes* can be dismissed briefly. It is based on the "Preface and 21. Articles for Pietie, Loyaltie and Politie convenient to the Colonie" established by Gates on his arrival in 1610 and sent to England by Strachey,[5] which was expanded by De la Warr after his providential appearance in Virginia. The first section of the published work consists of a preface by De la Warr (in which he states that he has, "with the advise and counsell of Sir Thomas Gates Knight, Lieutenant Generall," added to those laws already in force)[6] and thirty-seven articles regulating most aspects of life in the colony.[7] The second section, "The Summarie of the Marshall Lawes," contains fifty-one clauses, all dealing with military affairs. Additions made by Sir Thomas Dale on his arrival in 1611 consisted of detailed statements of the duties of the colonel, the captain of the guard, and so on down the military ladder to the lowliest private soldier.

There is no reason to believe that Strachey had any hand in their compilation.[8] He tells us that Gates, when he first arrived at Jamestown, "published certaine Orders and Instructions, which hee enjoyned them strictly to observe, the time that hee should stay amongst them";[9] and that the laws were expanded by De la Warr and added to yet again by Dale;[10] but neither in *A true reportory* nor in his introduction to the *Lawes* are we told that Strachey himself gave any assistance or advice. The laws moreover are so simple

[5] But omitted by Purchas in his editing of *A true reportory* (see marginal note, *Pilgrimes*, XIX, 46).

[6] *Lawes*, sig. Blv.

[7] Summarized in Herbert L. Osgood, *American colonies in the seventeenth century* (New York, 1904), I, 69–72.

[8] Winsor, *op. cit.*, III, 137, states that the *Lawes* was actually compiled by Strachey; and Andrews, *op. cit.*, I, 114, says it was the work of Strachey, Gates, and Dale.

[9] Purchas, *Pilgrimes*, XIX, 45–46.

[10] Strachey, *Lawes*, sig. A3v.

and so obviously essential to the survival of the colony
that they could have been drawn up by any commander
who saw clearly the root of the settlers' troubles and
who had set out to provide the discipline necessary to
help them find their feet again. Indeed the very sim-
plicity of the laws, expressed as they are in the plainest
language, might argue that no gentleman from the Inns
of Court, whether qualified in the law or merely acquainted with lawyers, had so much as been present
when the code was being drawn up; nor is there any
reason to believe that the laws were revised, prior to
publication, by any of the eminent members of the
legal profession connected with the Virginia Company.[11]

Strachey, as secretary, would naturally have been
concerned with the laws, and would undoubtedly have
been responsible for their inditing and posting up in
the church at Jamestown.[12] But where in 1610 there
was only a small band of colonists eking out a miserable
existence within the palisades of the single settlement,
twelve months later subsidiary colonies had been established at the mouth of the river and at the falls, and
the settlers were beginning to disperse more widely
through the country. It was probably at the express
wish of the governor, Sir Thomas Dale, and with the
consent of the Council in London, that the laws were
published, so that they might be the more readily
accessible to all the colonists, and in particular to the
troops in Virginia. Strachey, having brought with him
the manuscript copy and having been present at the
various Council meetings when the laws were compiled,
was instructed by the company to prepare the manu-

[11] Brown, *op. cit.*, II, 528, suggests that they were revised by
Edward Cecil, mainly because his is one of the names entered
in the Stationers' Register, along with those of other members
of the Council.

[12] As was done with Gates's first set (Purchas, *Pilgrimes*,
XIX, 46).

script for publication and supervise its printing. His task was solely that of an editor, and although Strachey's name is connected permanently with the *Lawes*, it contains nothing, apart from his prefatory verses and his brief introduction, that is his own work.

Much the same must be said about *The historie of travaile into Virginia Britannia*, which, although it is described as "a highly authoritative work and probably the most ably written of the contemporary histories of the region,"[13] is predominantly a compilation representative of a type of work that had attained great popularity during the sixteenth century, when England was first beginning to assert herself as a maritime power and when Englishmen, aware of the prospects of wealth beyond the seas, were beginning to vie with the Spaniards in voyages of trade and discovery. Many accounts of travels and explorations had appeared on the continent, among them the exploits of Marco Polo and Peter Martyr's *Decades of the ocean*, printed in final form in 1530; and twenty-five years later Richard Eden, translating and adapting Martyr, published the first collection of voyages in the English language, *The decades of the newe worlde or West India, conteyning the navigations and conquestes of the Spanyardes*. He was followed in 1577 by John Dee, with his *Great volume of famous and rich discoveries*, and Richard Willes, who published an expanded version of Eden's work as *The history of travayle in the West and East Indies*. In 1582 Richard Hakluyt, with his *Divers voyages, touching the discoverie of America,* laid the foundation of the great work with which his name is always associated; seven years later he published in a single volume *The principall navigations, voiages and discoveries of the English nation . . . within the compasse of these 1500 yeares*; and then, after a further

[13] *D.A.B.*, "Strachey."

ten years' painstaking and detailed research, he put out his monumental *Principal navigations, voiages, traffiques and discoveries . . . these 1600 yeres* in three large folio volumes.[14]

Along with the collections of voyages had appeared accounts of the explorations of men whose names are famous to this day, among them Sir John Hawkins,[15] Sir Humphrey Gilbert,[16] Sir Francis Drake,[17] and Sir Walter Raleigh.[18] Toward the end of the century there was a spate of works dealing with the North American continent, and Virginia in particular.[19] Many of these earlier works had been gathered by Hakluyt into his *Voyages,* but after the turn of the century still more appeared, some as translations sponsored by Hakluyt and others as accounts of settlement published either privately or under the auspices of the Virginia Company.

Strachey, who, as he tells us, had set out to be a "Remembrancer of all accidents, occurrences, and undertakings" while he was in the colony, produced in *The historie of travaile,* with its description of the country and its account of explorations and settlement from Raleigh's first voyage in 1584 to an abortive attempt to settle New England in 1606, a work in every way typical of these popular collections of voyages. As a history the work is purely a compilation of material

---

[14] Published over the years 1598–1600.

[15] Sir John Hawkins, *A true declaration of the troublesome voyadge . . . to the parties of Guynea and the West Indies* (London, 1569).

[16] Sir George Peckham, *A true reporte of the late discoveries . . . of the newfound landes* (London, 1583).

[17] Walter Bigges, *A summarie and true discourse of Sir Frances Drakes West Indian voyage* (London, 1589).

[18] Sir Walter Raleigh, *The discoverie of . . . Guiana* (London, 1596).

[19] For an account of these works see Edward Geoffrey Cox, *A reference guide to the literature of travel* (Seattle, 1935–38).

to be found in Willes' *History of travayle in the West and East Indies* and Hakluyt's *Voyages,* brought more up to date by the addition of condensations of two printed accounts—John Brereton's *Briefe and true relation of the discoverie of the north part of Virginia,* published in 1602, and James Rosier's *True relation of the most prosperous voyage made . . . by Captaine George Waymouth, in the discovery of the land of Virginia,* published in 1605—and one manuscript account reproduced in full, James Davies' *Relation of a voyage unto New-England.*[20] Even his first book, in which he describes the country, its products, and its inhabitants, is based on John Smith's *Map of Virginia,* of which Strachey incorporates the greater part unchanged, but here he is able to add considerably to Smith's account from his own experience while in the colony.

He was, after all, in an exceptional position to write a detailed narrative of one of the most important periods in the history of the colony—the period when, the ill fortune and errors of the first three years overcome and disaster providentially averted, the settlers under wise and experienced governors were proceeding from success to success, pacifying the natives, expanding their plantations, establishing new settlements on the James River, and in every way laying a firm foundation for the colony's survival. This improvement and reestablishment was brought about during the period that Strachey was actually in Virginia, and the success was mainly due to the efforts of the Council, of which Strachey was one of the more important members inasmuch as through his hands passed all reports to the company in London detailing action taken, obstacles surmounted, and prospects of further achievement.

The story of the reverses of the early settlers had

[20] See Appendix.

been told in detail by John Smith,[21] but after his departure from Virginia toward the end of 1609 his account, compiled from the evidence of friends still in Virginia, is sketchy.[22] Strachey had shown in *A true reportory* his ability to write graphic and convincing narrative and had continued Smith's account of the affairs of the colony up to the events immediately following De la Warr's arrival. But where we might expect a balanced, detailed, and realistic account of the revival of the colony under Gates, De la Warr, and Dale, of policy decided at the meetings of the Council, of the part played by individual members of the Council, and of the day-to-day life of the settlers—all matters that he had already shown that he could deal with capably— we find instead in *The historie of travaile* notes and observations particularly relating to the Indians and merely supplementing Smith's account. For the chronicle of events during Strachey's sojourn in Virginia we have to rely mainly on George Percy's pedestrian *Trewe relatyon*.

Strachey's major contribution to the early history of the colonization of America is to be found in his *True reportory of the wracke, and redemption of Sir Thomas Gates Knight,* written shortly after his safe arrival in Virginia and dispatched to England as a letter to an unnamed "Excellent Lady," whom Strachey addresses in terms of considerable respect.[23] Although the letter was not published until it was included by Purchas in the 1625 edition of his *Pilgrimes,* it came into the hands

[21] John Smith, *A true relation of such occurrences . . . as hath hapned in Virginia* (London, 1608); and, attached to his *Map of Virginia, The proceedings of the English colonie in Virginia* (Oxford, 1612).

[22] The period from the arrival of De la Warr in 1610 till that of Gates in August 1611 occupies less than a page in Smith's *Proceedings of the English colonie in Virginia.*

[23] Purchas, *Pilgrimes,* XIX, 67.

of the council of the Virginia Company very soon after its arrival in England. Considerable use was made of it in the drawing up of *A true declaration of the estate of the colonie in Virginia*, published hard on the heels of the news of Gates's survival to dispel uneasiness among supporters and confound enemies of the venture.[24] It has been reasonably shown also how, through friends on the Council in London, Shakespeare came into possession of this letter that served him as the main source of *The tempest*.[25]

The "Excellent Lady" would appear to have been the wife of one of the members of the Council, and attempts have been made to identify her as Elizabeth, wife of Theophilus, Baron Howard of Walden, on whose lands the Strachey family had dwelt throughout the sixteenth century. In support of this identification it is held that

On only one occasion does he specify the previous habitat of any person connected with the voyage or with Virginia, and that is when he tells her ladyship, as a matter of interest to both of them, that one of the Bermuda mutineers, John Want, was "an Essex man of Newport by Saffronwalden."[26]

For this one reference to Essex, however, there are four to Kent, all in the northern part of the county and not far distant one from the other. Strachey mentions "one Frubbusher, borne at Graves end, and at his comming forth now dwelling at Lime House";[27] compares the James River with the Thames "betweene Queeneburrough and Lee"[28] and "betweene Green-

[24] See C. M. Gayley, *Shakespeare and the founders of liberty in America* (New York, 1917), pp. 229–30. *A true declaration* was entered for publication on November 8, 1610.

[25] Leslie Hotson, *I, William Shakespeare* (London, 1937), pp. 224–26.

[26] Gayley, *op. cit.*, p. 231.

[27] Purchas, *Pilgrimes*, XIX, 27–28.   [28] *Ibid.*, p. 43.

wich, and the Ile of Dogges";[29] and, discounting the marshy site of Jamestown, he says, "We condemne not Kent in England, for a small Towne called Plumsted, continually assaulting the dwellers there (especially new commers) with agues and fevers."[30] Strachey's own knowledge of the area is easily accounted for by the fact that his uncle's manor of Lesness lay on the Kent bank of the Thames and adjoined the marshes of Plumstead. There was also an "Excellent Lady" who, while not of Kentish birth, lived in the county, knew the Thames bank well, and was much closer to the Council than was Lady Howard.

In the 1609 charter of the Virginia Company fifty of the shareholders were named members of the Council, but any four of these councilors, with the treasurer, could form a quorum. No matter how the Council met, there was one member, the most influential, who was always present, the treasurer, Sir Thomas Smith. Many of the decisions of the company were made by Smith alone, and it was he who at a later date was accused of imposing a tyrannical government on the colonists.[31]

Not only was Sir Thomas Smith born in Kent, but at this time his country residence, received from his father, consisted of a substantial property, "Skinner's Place," in "West Greenwich, *alias* Depford."[32] From the windows of the house one could look across the Thames "betweene Greenwich, and the Ile of Dogges"; Limehouse lay on the other side of the stream, and Plumstead and the Cooke manors a mere six miles away. Sir Thomas was, moreover, in addition to his other

[29] *Ibid.*, p. 43.   [30] *Ibid.*, p. 59.
[31] Leo Francis Stock (ed.), *Proceedings and debates of the British Parliaments respecting North America* (Washington, 1924), I, 45.
[32] Henry H. Drake, *Hasted's history of Kent* (London, 1886), I, 13. A biographical account of Sir Thomas Smith is given in *Archaeologia Cantiana*, XX (1893), 82–103.

posts, one of the commissioners of the Navy and so fully conversant with the Thames from London to the sea. Dame Sara Smith, daughter of William Blount, a mercer of Cheapside, and third wife of Sir Thomas, seems a more likely recipient of the letter than the more remote Lady Howard of Walden, and Strachey could well have met her through his uncle or cousins in Kent.

Moreover, it would appear that, just as the *Lawes* was later presented to the company and included a dedicatory sonnet to Sir Thomas Smith and as *The historie of travaile*, although first presented to Henry Percy, had been intended for the view of the Council of the Virginia Company, so also *A true reportory* was meant by Strachey to come without delay into the Council's hands.

Another account of the wreck of the *Sea Venture*, Silvester Jourdan's *Discovery of the Barmudas*, was published in London at this time. A piece of hack writing by a returned survivor who intended to profit from the general interest aroused by the news of Gates's escape, it treats the storm perfunctorily, lists the products of the islands, and is generally silent on the troubles encountered by the settlers both in the Bermudas and on their arrival in Virginia. Like so many of the "True declarations" or "True reports" published by parties interested in schemes of colonization or exploration, Jourdan's *Discovery* looks only on the bright side and glosses over, or omits entirely, such relevant details as the mutinies on the islands and the desperate plight of the settlement at Jamestown. Not so Strachey, who had set out to record all "accidents and occurrences" during his time abroad and whose account, uncompromising in its honesty, could not be published at that time by a Virginia Company busily defending itself against the attacks and accusations of its enemies. We know from Richard Martin's letter that the Council members were impressed by Strachey's *True reportory*, but their *True declaration* shows how much they had to modify it.

Where many other similar accounts consist either of lists of latitudes and longitudes and detailed sailing directions[33] or, at the other extreme, descriptions only of things which impressed the narrator as strange or outlandish,[34] Strachey's *True reportory* is the work of a participant always mindful of his reader, a keen observer who is not an expert and who sets out to make his whole account as graphic as possible. In his attempt to present the whole picture he does not hesitate to assign praise or blame and is prepared to attribute many of the troubles of the settlement to the ill-advised earlier policy of the Virginia Company itself,[35] but the great value of *A true reportory* lies in Strachey's use of the humble and convincing detail. While Captain Gabriel Archer dismisses the storm in a few words,[36] noting that it was the tail of a hurricane and that several ships were disabled and the *Sea Venture* lost, Strachey gives a powerful and graphic account, describing all that had impressed him during the four days and nights of terror: how the pumps became choked with biscuit, how a leak in the gunner's room was stopped with salt beef, or how, when land was at last discovered, from the decks of the *Sea Venture* "the very trees were seen to move with the wind"[37]—details unimportant in a purely factual account but adding a convincing vividness to the narrative.

So too it is Strachey's inclusion of the unimportant

---

[33] Cf. for instance the voyage that forms Chapters Eight, Nine, and Ten of Book II of *The historie of travaile*.

[34] Jean Ribaut, *The whole and true discovery of Terra Florida*, trans. T. Hackitt (London, 1563), for instance, contains an account of the "wonderful straunge Nature and Maners of the People."

[35] Purchas, *Pilgrimes*, XIX, 46–47.   [36] *Ibid.*, pp. 2–3.

[37] *Ibid.*, p. 13.

detail that gives value to his account of events on the islands. The fertility and hospitality of the Bermudas, while essential to survival, became important only through the use made of these resources by the castaways, and the success of the venture depended not only on the leaders but on every member of the commoner sort. The quality of the individual settlers was, after all, the most important factor in the success of any attempt at colonization, and in his narrative Strachey makes plain his interest in his companions. While John Smith tells us a great deal about his quarrels with fellow members of the Council in Virginia, he makes little mention of the ordinary settlers. Strachey, on the other hand, devotes much of his time to describing the day-to-day life of the minor and unimportant members of their small community and mentions many of them by name; much of the authenticity and interest of his account derives from the fact that he places them in their surroundings and regards them as more important and of greater interest than the mere physical environment in which they found themselves. The storm gains in vividness from the incidental details of actions of members of the crew: of the sailor who sprang to catch the unmanageable tiller "and with much clamour incouraged and called upon others" to come to his aid[38] or of the "Master, Masters Mate, Boateswaine, Quarter Master, Coopers, Carpenters, and who not" creeping candle in hand amid the cargo in the holds, endeavoring to trace the leak.[39]

In like manner it is the detail of the actions of individuals that adds color to Strachey's account of the happenings on the Bermudas and at Jamestown. He does not merely mention that there were hogs on the island, but tells us that after a boar had been seen following their tame swine:

[38] *Ibid.*, p. 10.　　　[39] *Ibid.*, p. 8.

One of Sir George Summers men went and lay among the Swine, when the Boare being come and groveled by the Sowes, hee put over his hand and rubbed the side gently of the Boare, which then lay still, by which meanes hee fastned a rope with a sliding knot to the hinder legge and so tooke him.[40]

Concerning a bird native to the Bermudas, the sea owl, he says,

Our men found a prettie way to take them, which was by standing on the Rockes or Sands by the Sea side, and hollowing, laughing, and making the strangest outcry that possibly they could: with the noyse whereof the Birds would come flocking to that place, and settle upon the very armes and head of him that so cryed, and still creepe neerer and neerer, answering the noyse themselves: by which our men would weigh them with their hand, and which weighed heaviest they tooke for the best and let the others alone.[41]

When he comes to describe the palm tree, he is not content merely to note that its leaves were edible, but that

roasting the Palmito or soft top thereof, they had a taste like fried Melons, and being sod they eate like Cabbedges, but not so offensively thankefull to the stomacke. Many an ancient Burger was therefore heaved at, and fell not for his place, but for his head: for our common people, whose bellies never had eares, make it no breach of Charitie in their hot blouds and tall stomackes to murder thousands of them.[42]

So, too, when he comes to recount the mutinous outbreaks on the islands, he details the arguments used by the mutineers and gives brief sketches of their leaders: Nicholas Bennit, "who made much profession of Scripture, a mutinous and dissembling Imposter";[43] John Want, "both seditious, and a sectary in points of

---

[40] *Ibid.*, p. 23.   [41] *Ibid.*, p. 22.   [42] *Ibid.*, p. 19.
[43] *Ibid.*, p. 29.

Religion, in his own prayers both devout and frequent, but hardely drawne to the publique";[44] or Stephen Hopkins, "A fellow who had much knowledge in the Scriptures, and could reason well therein."[45]

His frequent use of parallels and illustrations gives even more color to his detailed descriptions, and in general he makes comparisons that will have meaning for his reader. From his own experience he compares the storm in the Atlantic with those he had met with in the Mediterranean[46] or likens the upper leaves of the palm tree to "an overblowne Rose, or Saffron flower not early gathered."[47] He is prepared also to enhance his descriptions with passages from his reading, either of Peter Martyr,[48] of Acosta,[49] or from the well-known stories of the classical writers. A huge wave, striking the *Sea Venture* halts her "as if shee had beene caught in a net, or then, as if the fabulous Remora had stucke to her fore-castle";[50] or the early settlers, exploring the James River, eventually chose a site for their town, "as Virgill writeth Aeneas did, arriving in the region of Italy called Latium, upon the bankes of the River Tyber."[51]

These qualities found in *A true reportory* likewise give value to the original sections in *The historie of travaile*. Here his interest in his fellow men turns from his European companions to the Indians of Virginia, and from his own observation Strachey is able to improve considerably on Smith's account of them. He describes in detail the paramount Indian chief Powhatan, and tells also of his famous daughter Pocahontas, turning cartwheels with the lads of Jamestown, "naked as she was, all the fort over." [52] To illustrate his descrip-

[44] *Ibid.*, p. 30.   [45] *Ibid.*   [46] *Ibid.*, p. 8.
[47] *Ibid.*, p. 19.   [48] See Appendix, p. 167, "Willes."
[49] See Appendix, p. 165, "Acosta."
[50] Purchas, *Pilgrimes*, XIX, 10.   [51] *Ibid.*, p. 55.
[52] *Historie,* ed. Major, p. 65; ed. Wright, p. 72.

tions he compares the Indians with two other races he had met, the Turks and the Irish. He tells us that the Indians, like the Turks, drink clear water[53] and that Indian dogs, like Turkish jackals, haunt the grave-yards.[54] Indian garments, he says, are "after the fashion of the Turkes or Irish trouses,"[55] and Indians sleep crowded together in their cabins "stark naked on the grownd, from six to twentie in a house, as doe the Irish."[56]

He does not confine his interest in the Indians merely to their way of living, to their "aeconomick or howshold affaires" or "the manner of the Virginian government," but shows considerable curiosity regarding their religion, an aspect of their lives on which the more practical Smith touches only perfunctorily. Strachey not only deals in detail with the external trappings of religion, the natives' temples, idols, and forms of worship, and the power and privileges of their priests, but turns an inquiring mind to their fundamental beliefs, gives an account of the Indian concepts of the creation of the world and of the afterlife, and concludes somewhat regretfully that they will not know "all the certaintye . . . of these their unhallowed misteries . . . untill we cann make surprize of some of their Quiyoughquisocks" (i.e., priests).[57]

His interest in the Indians appears further as that of a philologist. Along with his *Map of Virginia* John Smith had provided a short vocabulary "because many doe desire to knowe the maner of their language."[58] Strachey, however, who throughout *The historie of*

[53] *Ibid.* (M), p. 74; (W), p. 81.
[54] *Ibid.* (M), p. 124; (W), pp. 125–26.
[55] *Ibid.* (M), p. 66; (W), p. 73.
[56] *Ibid.* (M), p. 72; (W), p. 79. Although this passage is taken from Smith, the comparison with the Irish is Strachey's own.
[57] *Ibid.* (M), p. 100; (W), p. 103.
[58] Smith, *Travels and works*, I, 44–46.

travaile makes constant use of the Indian word either
along with or instead of its English equivalent—
weroance (or chief), *quiyoughquisock* (or priest),
apoke (or tobacco) —adds to his work a much longer
and more detailed "Dictionarie of the Indian Language, for the better enabling of such who shalbe
thither ymployed." He owes nothing to Smith and at
times differs from him; and it is probable that Strachey
compiled his vocabulary partly from his own observation and inquiry, but more fully from conversation with
"a boy, one Spilman, who had lyved a whole yere with
this Indian kinge, and spake his language,"[59] and with
the friendly Indians, Kemp and Machumps, who lived
with the settlers at Jamestown.

His philologist's interest in words is not, however,
confined to the Indian tongue. In an age of expanding
horizons both physical and mental, the coining of words
from Latin or Greek to express new shades of meaning
was a common practice, and Strachey in his turn does
not hesitate to make use of a classical word to serve
his purpose. Even where an already accepted word
exists, he is willing to parallel it or replace it with a
more obscure word. So we find "Chersonesus or Peninsula,"[60] "sacrifices, or catharmata,"[61] "Mnemosy-
non"[62] in preference to memorial, and the like. These
and most of the other Greek words he uses are common
in the works of the better-known classical authors, but
there is one word, "Brenthina," which is to be found
only in the Greek dictionary of Hesychius, which
remained in manuscript for some centuries until it was
first printed in 1514.[63] When Strachey comes to quote

---

[59] *Historie,* (M), p. 98; (W), p. 101.
[60] Purchas, *Pilgrimes,* XIX, 55.
[61] *Historie,* (M), p. 95; (W), p. 99.
[62] Purchas, *Pilgrimes,* XIX, 40; misprinted "Muemosynon."
[63] *Historie,* (M), p. 64; (W), p. 70.

Latin, his predilection for the more obscure word, the unusual form dear to the grammarian or philologist, is more clearly seen. He talks of cellars "called, therefore, as Plinye remembers, *favissae*";[64] of loose Indian women "like Virgill's *scrantiae*";[65] of adolescent maidens who become "*sororians virgo*";[66] or of "*postularia fulguria,* lightnings that signified religion of sacrifices."[67] These are all unusual words, and in spite of Strachey's attribution of them to well-known authors they are to be found only in the works of the grammarians who flourished long after the classical Latin period.[68]

On the other hand, when Strachey does quote from the classical authors, he shows no great level of erudition, nor any wider knowledge than might be expected of the average intelligent youth who had been thoroughly grounded at his grammar school and spent perhaps a year or two at one of the universities. He shows himself familiar with Virgil, Cicero, the *Epistles* and *Odes* of Horace, Ovid's *Metamorphoses,* and the well-known *Mostellaria* of Plautus, from which he quotes twice and which he may well have seen acted either at Cambridge or at the Inns of Court. He introduces tags from legal Latin and uses one word found only in the Codex Justinianus,[69] natural enough in a member of Gray's Inn.

This preference for the unusual word and his smattering of unnecessary Latin tags throughout *The*

---

[64] *Ibid.* (M), p. 113; (W), p. 115.

[65] *Ibid.* (M), p. 110; (W), p. 113.

[66] *Ibid.* (M), p. 109; (W), p. 112.

[67] *Ibid.* (M), p. 96; (W), p. 99.

[68] I am grateful to the Classics Department of University College, London, for assistance and advice regarding the less common words used by Strachey and for the identification of the greater number of the passages he quotes in full.

[69] *Historie,* (M), p. 109; (W), p. 112.

historie give an effect of pedantry, which is enhanced by the curious way in which he refers to works of which he has made use. At no point does he acknowledge his debt to Hakluyt, to Willes, or to Smith; but when he refers once to Thomas Cogan's obscure and unimportant *Haven of health*, he not only refers to the chapter from which he quotes but even states which edition he has used.[70] When he makes use of a work that in its turn quotes from other works, he refers to the originals, creating an impression of a much wider reading than he has actually done.[71]

These are, however, only minor faults in a pair of works, *A true reportory* and *The historie of travaile*, that present convincing, accurate, and detailed pictures of the early history of the colony of Virginia.

In spite of the obvious merits of *The historie of travaile*, Strachey's failure to achieve publication is not surprising. Not only had he been preceded by John Smith, but the final chapters of the work could never gain the approval of the Virginia Company. At a time when the settlement in Virginia had narrowly escaped disaster and when public enthusiasm for colonization had waned, the company was not likely to sponsor a work that treated in detail one of the failures of the sister Plymouth or New England Company. Moreover, although it is clear from Strachey's *Historie* that the fragment remaining in manuscript is only part of a projected work of much greater extent designed to cover the whole history of the settlement of Virginia and to provide a logical continuation to Hakluyt's accounts of the colony, he had also been anticipated here. Hakluyt's manuscripts had passed to Samuel Purchas, who, close to the Virginia Company, was, with its approval, laying the foundation of the work that was to

---

[70] *Ibid.* (M), p. 18; (W), p. 24.
[71] See for instance Appendix, p. 180, "Johann Boemus."

become his voluminous *Pilgrimes*. In 1613 his first and preliminary volume appeared, and it was clear that Hakluyt's role had descended to this other preacher. The conditions prevailing in 1612 were even more effective in 1618, when, as what must have been a last despairing effort, Strachey dedicated the other copy of his manuscript to Francis Bacon.

Had Strachey not been thus forestalled, we might have had from his pen a better, a more detailed, and a more accurate and balanced account of the early history of Virginia than has been provided either by John Smith or by that extremely bad editor, Samuel Purchas. As it was, Strachey, unlucky to the last and having given us only a hint of his ability, found no encouragement to proceed, and there remains to us only the fragment of a work that could have been of considerable merit.

Appendix: *The Historie of Travaile*

MANUSCRIPTS

THERE are no differences of any consequence between the three extant manuscripts of *The historie of travaile*. Not one is in Strachey's hand, but all contain marginal notes and minor additions made by him, all contain the same illustrations, though in slightly different order, and all are set out in the same way and written by the same scribe.

Probably the earliest, and certainly the most carefully prepared, is the Percy manuscript, a folio volume of 122 leaves, with wide margins ruled in red and proper names and dates either written or underlined in red. In addition to the text, twenty-seven engravings from De Bry's illustrations to Harriot's *Briefe and true report*, roughly colored by hand, are included, and also a copy of John Smith's map of Virginia.

Where the Percy manuscript has a lettered title page, however, the other two manuscripts have the engraved title page of Harriot's work, with the central text cut out and the title of *The historie* inserted, two extra and irrelevant illustrations from De Bry, and the "Dictionary of the Indian tongue," which is not found in the Percy manuscript. Less care has been taken in the transcribing and setting out of these two manuscripts, which, in spite of the additional matter incorporated, are considerably shorter.[1]

[1] The Sloane MS has only 105 leaves, and the Ashmole MS 102, against the 122 of the Percy MS.

In all three manuscripts, the marginal notes and the prefatory poem, "Ecclesiae et reipub," are in Strachey's own hand, but only in the Percy manuscript is the signature to the dedicatory letter his. In the other two, even the signature is in the hand of the scribe who wrote the rest of the manuscript.[2]

SOURCES

Since *The historie of travaile* is a compilation rather than an original work, Strachey's sources are of some importance. It is possible, from the evidence of *A true reportory*, to be sure that he had at least two works dealing with Virginia and the West Indies with him when he set sail from England in May 1609, and from the use he makes of these in certain portions of *The historie* it would appear that the work was compiled, at least in part, while he was in Virginia.[3] The following is an attempt to indicate the extent to which Strachey is indebted to the various writers on Virginia, and on other subjects, in his major work.

José de Acosta. *The naturall and morall historie of the East and West Indies.* London, 1604.

A description of the islands and not a history of exploration, this work was first published in Spanish in 1590 and translated into English by Edward Grimston, probably before 1601, when it was entered for publication.[4]

It is clear from one passage in *A true reportory* that Strachey had access to this work when he was writing from Virginia to the "Excellent Lady."

[2] Detailed descriptions and comparisons of the MSS are to be found in Charles M. Andrews and Frances Davenport (ed.), *Guide to the manuscript material for the history of the United States to 1783* (Washington, 1908), pp. 54, 379; Brown, *Genesis,* II, 562–68; Sotheby & Co., *Catalogue of exceedingly rare and valuable Americana* (London, 1928), pp. 63–69; and Strachey, *Historie* (ed. Wright), pp. xiii–xvii.

[3] See pp. 184–89.

[4] Cox, *A reference guide to the literature of travel,* II, 254–55.

There is another sorte of Tunalls which they esteeme much more, although it yeeldes no fruit, yet it beares an other commoditie and profit, for certayne small wormes breede in the leaves of this tree, when it is well husbanded, and are thereunto fastned, covered with a certaine small fine web, which doth compasse them in daintily; and this is that Indian Cochinille so famous and wherewith they dye. They let it drie, and being dried, carry it into Spaine, which is a great and rich merchandise.[5]

Wee oftentimes found growing to these leaves, many silkwormes involved therein, like those small wormes which Acosta writeth of, which grew in the leaves of the Tunall tree, of which being dried, the Indians make their Cochinile so precious and marchantable.[6]

In *The historie of travaile* Strachey refers to Acosta once in a marginal note added to the 1618 copy,[7] although the passage to which this note refers is actually taken from another source,[8] and three times in the text.

He mentions the chaplains of the West Indies, "in their guacas or oratories."[9] The word is used some eight times in Acosta, with various religious contexts, and spelt indifferently *guaca* and *huaca*. The phrase "Guacas, or Oratories" occurs once in Acosta,[10] and it is clear from the context that Strachey mistook the use of the word "Oratory," a religious rite, for that of a place.

Referring to child sacrifice, a subject that is dealt with at some length by Acosta,[11] he tells us "that the devill hath obteyned the use of the like offring in many other parts of

---

[5] José de Acosta, *The naturall and morall historie of the East and West Indies,* ed. C. R. Markham (London, 1879), I, 248.

[6] Purchas, *Pilgrimes,* XIX, 19.

[7] *Historie,* p. 138 (in Major's edition only).

[8] From Willes. See p. 169.

[9] *Historie,* (M), p. 90; (W), p. 95.

[10] Acosta, *op. cit.,* II, 361.   [11] *Ibid.,* pp. 323–50.

America, Acosta hath observed and related, in his morrall and naturall History of the West Indies."[12]

Finally, dealing with the emergence of life on earth, he refers the reader "to the search of Acosta, in his i. booke, cap. 20, 21, of his morrall and naturall history of the West Indies; who hath so officyously laboured herein, as he should but bring owles to Athens, who should study for more strayned or newe authority concerning the same"[13] and gives a very brief and condensed outline of the chapters in question.[14]

His debt to Acosta is not great, and apart from the irrelevant marginal reference noted above makes use of *The naturall and morall historie* only in the first book, where he describes the country of Virginia and the inhabitants. It is natural enough that he should seek his parallels from a work that describes a neighboring part of the world from the same aspect, and the chief interest of Acosta's work is that Strachey had it with him in Virginia.

Richard Willes. *The history of travayle in the West and East Indies.* London, 1577.

This is a later edition of Richard Eden's *The decades of the newe worlde or West India, conteyning the navigations and conquestes of the Spanyardes,* published in London in 1555,[15] which is "newly set in order, augmented, and finished by Richard Willes." Eden's work consists of a translation of the first three of the eight *Decades of the ocean* published by Peter Martyr in 1530 and of an abridged version of the *History of the West Indies* of Gonzalus Ferdinandus Ovideus. Willes reproduces Eden's translations unaltered, apart from the interpolation of a chapter headed "A most auncient testimonie of the West Indies, by the writing of the divine Philosopher Plato";

[12] *Historie*, (M), p. 84; (W), p. 90.
[13] *Ibid.*, (M), p. 47; (W), p. 55.   [14] Acosta, *op. cit.*, I, 57–64.
[15] Reproduced in Edward Arber (ed.), *The first three books on America* (Birmingham, England, 1885).

the addition of the Latin text and a translation of the bull
of Pope Alexander VI granting America to the king of
Spain; and a slight rearrangement of three chapters relating to Columbus, moved from the end of the earlier edition to form an introduction. His additions consist of a
series of travels in Asia and the Near East and a dedicatory
letter to preface them.

In *A true reportory* Strachey refers no less than four
times to this work. "It should seeme by the testimony of
Gonzalus Ferdinandus Ovideus, in his Booke intituled,
The Summary or Abridgement of his generall History of
the West Indies, written to the Emperor Charles the Fift"
introduces a quotation of some 150 words directly from
Willes;[16] and likewise, referring to tortoises, he prefaces a
passage of some 120 words with: "Concerning the laying
of their Egges, and hatching of their young, Peter Martyr
writeth thus in his Decades of the Ocean."[17] He mentions
that "Peter Martin [*sic*] saith, That at Alexandria in
Egypt there is a kind of Cedar, which the Jewes dwelling
there, affirme to be the Cedars of Libanus, which beare old
fruite and new all the yeere"[18] and that "the examples
whereof gives us (saith Ovideus) to understand, that in
the selfe same perill and danger doe men live in this mortall
life, wherein is no certaine security neither in high estate
nor low."[19]

These passages occur also in the earlier edition of Willes'
work, and it is only from the references in *The historie of
travaile* that we can identify the edition used. It would
appear that Willes' *History of travayle in the West and
East Indies*, with its translations of Martyr's *Decades*, suggested not only the title but also the form of Strachey's
own work, since Book II is entitled "The second book of
the first decade of the history of travaile into Virginia
Britannia." Little in Willes is relevant to the first book of
Strachey's *Historie*, which describes the country, but

[16] Purchas, *Pilgrimes*, XIX, 15; Willes, *op. cit.*, sig. Ee6v.
[17] Purchas, *Pilgrimes*, XIX, 24; Willes, *op. cit.*, sig. U1r.
[18] Purchas, *Pilgrimes*, XIX, 18; Willes, *op. cit.*, sig. J6r.
[19] Purchas, *Pilgrimes*, XIX, 21; Willes, *op. cit.*, sig. Ee6v.

Strachey's "Praemonition" and his second book, both of which mention the early exploration of America, contain a number of passages taken directly from Willes.

In the "Praemonition" Strachey quotes from Willes both the Latin and the translation of a portion of the papal bull of Donation[20] and mentions the story, referred to in Acosta,[21] of Columbus and the dying pilot who first inspired him to set out in search of America. The pilot passages from Willes and Strachey follow:

where he dwelt at suche tyme as the sayd Caravell arryved there, whose Pilot soiourned in his house, and dyed also there, bequeathing to Colon his carde of the description of suche newe landes as he had found.[22]	who, when he dwelt in the islands of Madera, arrived with a weather beaten caravelle, and dying in his house, bequeathed (as they say) to Columbus his card of the discription of such newe landes as he had found.[23]

The first chapter of Book II, dealing in more detail with the early discovery of America, draws more heavily on Willes' *History*. Strachey makes use of Willes' interpolated chapter relating to Plato's well-known theory of the sunken Atlantic islands:

Plato in his famous and divine Dialogue, named *Timaeus,* where he entreateth of the universall nature and frame of the whole worlde . . .[24]	Whether that ever famous Genoese, Christopher Columbus, were sufficiently learned, that by reading of divine allegories, named *Timaeus,* of Plato, whose subject is of the universall nature and frame of the whole world . . .[25]

[20] *Historie,* (M) , pp. 13–14; (W) , pp. 20–21; Willes, *op. cit.,* sigs. Mmm5r–Mmm7v. The passages are identical but for one word: where Willes has "confidence," Strachey prefers "assurance."

[21] Acosta, *op. cit.,* I, 54. There is however no verbal parallel between his account and Strachey's. Hakluyt makes no mention of this story.

[22] Willes, *op. cit.,* sig. A1v.

[23] *Historie,* (M) , p. 5; (W) , p. 11.

[24] Willes, *op. cit.,* sig. B1r.

[25] *Historie,* (M) , p. 137; (W) , p. 137.

and that the Sunne and starres might seeme to shewe theyr light only halfe theyr course without profite, shining only upon the sea and desolate places, destitute of man and other living creatures.[26]

running thereby half their courses without profitt and in vaine, shyning upon the solitary waters and desolate places empty and desolate of man and other living creatures.[27]

He quotes here also from the chapters on Columbus moved by Willes in the 1577 edition to form an introduction to the *Decades:*

and that he was thereby fyrst moved to seeke the lands of *Antipodes* and the rych Ilande of *Cipango,* wherof *Marcus Paulus* wryteth.[28]

by which he was therby first moved to seek the lands of antipodes and the rich island of Cipango (whereof Marcus Pawlus writeth, and Peter Martir, before his decades of the ocean, remembreth the same).[29]

From the *Decades* themselves we find:

At the length three shyppes were appoynted hym at the kinges charges: . . . Thus he departed from the costes of Spaine about the calendes of September, in the yeere of Christ, 1492. and set forwarde on his viage, being accompanied with CC.xx. Spanyardes.[30]

we find that Columbus, with three shippes and two hundred and twenty Spaniards, in the yeare of Christ [1492] sett forward on his voyage, about the kalends of September.[31]

Furthermore he quotes in full the well-known prophecy of Seneca, which appears in the *Decades;* but where each of the earlier writers had provided a translation, Eden in

---

[26] Willes, *op. cit.,* sig. B2r.
[27] *Historie,* (M), p. 137; (W), p. 137 reads "destitute of man."
[28] Willes, *op. cit.,* sig. A1v.
[29] *Historie,* (M), p. 138; (W), p. 138.
[30] Willes, *op. cit.,* sig. B4r.
[31] *Historie,* (M), p. 139; (W), p. 139.

prose and Willes in verse, Strachey, the maker of many little verses, presents his own, and better, rendering.[32] In this opening chapter of Book II also appears a mention of the discovery of Florida, adapted from Willes.[33]

Finally, in his first book, which deals with Virginia proper, he twice makes use of Willes' *History of travayle*. Referring to ancient and disproved theories of geography, he quotes directly from Willes' introduction to his additional travels in Asia:

Whiche sentence well agreeth with that olde conclusion in the scholes, *Quidquid praeter Africam et Europam est, Asia est*— Whatsoever land doeth neyther appertayne unto Africk nor to Europe is part of Asia.[34]	according to that old conclusion in the scholes: *Quicquid praeter Africam et Europam est, Asia est*— whatsoever land doth neither apperteyne unto Africk nor to Europe, is part of Asia.[35]

And he mentions the native canoes

which we may well caule *Monoxyla*, bycause they are made of one hole tree.[36]	made of one piece of timber, like the auncyent *monoxylum navigium*.[37]

While the parallel passages quoted serve to identify the work, Strachey's debt is greater than is suggested by these quotations alone. In both the "Praemonition" and the first chapter of his second book Strachey paraphrases freely the sections of Willes of which the passages form part. The importance of the book then lies in the fact that Strachey had it with him in Virginia, that it suggested the title and the form of his own work, and that he made extensive use of it in the earlier portions of *The historie of travaile*.

[32] Willes, *op. cit.,* sig. B2r; Historie, (M), pp. 138–39; (W), pp. 138–39.

[33] Willes, *op. cit.,* sig. Gg4v; *Historie,* (M), p. 140; (W), p. 139.

[34] Willes, *op. cit.,* sig. Gg8r.

[35] *Historie,* (M), p. 44; (W), p. 53.

[36] Willes, *op. cit.,* sig. M5r.

[37] *Historie,* (M), p. 68; (W), p. 75.

Richard Hakluyt. *The principal navigations, voiages, traffiques and discoveries of the English nation . . . within the compasse of these 1600 yeres.* London, 1598–1600.

We have no evidence from *A true reportory* that Strachey had Hakluyt's *Voyages* with him in Virginia and can only surmise that if he thought it worth his while to take Acosta and Willes with him he might well have taken also the greatest and most important of all the English collections of travels and explorations.

In *The historie of travaile* he makes extensive use of this work. In the "Praemonition," where Strachey mentions the early exploration of America, we find a number of parallel passages:

The most ancient Discovery of the West Indies by Madoc the sonne of Owen Guyneth Prince of North-wales, in the yeere 1170: . . .Madoc . . .left the land in contention betwixt his brethren, & prepared certaine ships, with men and munition, and sought adventures by Seas, sailing West, and leaving the coast of Ireland so farre North, that he came unto a land unknowen, where he saw many strange things.[38]

Madoc, the sonne of Owen Gwineth, Prince of Nor-Wales, in the yeare 1170 . . . leaving the land in contention betweene his two brethren . . . prepared certayne shipps with men and munition, and after many unknowne landes and straunge disdoveries made (sayling within the Atlantick sea, a sowardly course, yet still into the west) , at last setteled in the West Indies.[39]

From this Strachey and Hakluyt draw the same conclusion:

Therefore it is to be supposed that he and his people inhabited part of those countreys: for it appeareth by Francis Lopez de Gomara, that in Acuzamil and other places the

and late observations taken in these tymes may confirme the probability hereof, as first in Acuzamill (so in writing Francis Lopez de Gomera) the natives when they were first found, had

[38] Richard Hakluyt, *The principal navigations . . . these 1600 yeres* (London, 1903–5) , VII, 133–34.
[39] *Historie*, (M) , p. 5; (W) , p. 11.

people honored the crosse. Wherby it may be gathered that Christians had bene there before the coming of the Spanyards.[40]

their crosses in their chapples, and in dedicated groves, in gardens, by woodes, springes, and fowntaines, which they did honour and falle downe before, thereto saying their usuall prayers, which must mak illustration that Christians had ben there before the coming of the Spaniard.[41]

Strachey's treatment of Hakluyt is at times perfunctory, or even cavalier. He attributes the story of Madoc to "the learned and industrious antiquities of Mr. Camden,"[42] when it is clear from the *Voyages* that Camden's contribution, acknowledged by Hakluyt in a marginal note, consisted merely of a set of verses stating that Madoc had voyaged beyond the seas and that the account of his visit to the West Indies, which is referred to again in another part of *Voyages*,[43] is "taken out of the history of Wales, lately published by M. David Powel Doctor of Divinity."[44] Moreover, Strachey is not above modifying his quotations to suit his purpose even when he has no grounds for doing so. Where Hakluyt says, in the above passage, that the people "honored the crosse," Strachey expands this to "crosses in their chapples, and in dedicated groves, in gardens, by woodes, springes, and fowntaines." The only contemporary translation of López de Gómara's work, *The pleasant historie of the conquest of the Weast India,*[45] makes it clear that only one cross was referred to—"At the foote of this Temple was a plotte like a Churchyard, well walled and garnished with proper pinnacles, in the middest whereof stoode a Crosse of ten foote long, the which they

[40] Hakluyt, *op. cit.*, VII, 134.
[41] *Historie*, (M), pp. 5–6; (W), p. 12.
[42] *Ibid.*, (M), p. 5; (W), p. 11.
[43] In Peckham's *Discourse on planting*, in Hakluyt, *op. cit.*, VIII, 108.
[44] *Ibid.*, VII, 133. The work was published in 1584.
[45] Translated by T. Nicholas and published in 1598.

adored for God of the rayne"[46]—so it is clear that Strachey had no access to Gomara's work and that the expansion is drawn from his own imagination.

An instance of even more high-handed treatment is provided in Strachey's second book, where he says:

> We shall find, however, the far famous king Henry VIII . . . could not attend the seconding his royall father in his enterprize, any other then giving leave to a voluntary fryer or twoo in a shipp called the *Deus Nobiscum,* to run upon new searches.[47]

Hakluyt alone identifies the ship and mentions also the "voluntary fryer";

> And it hath bene told me by sir Martine Frobisher, and M. Richard Allen, a knight of the Sepulchre, that a Canon of St Paul in London, which was a great Mathematician, and a man indued with wealth, did much advance the action, and went therein himself in person, but what his name was I cannot learne of any. And further they told me that one of the ships was called the Dominus Vobiscum, which is a name likely to be given by a religious man of those days.[48]

In the "Praemonition" Strachey refers in two places to works which, although published separately, are also to be found in Hakluyt. Although he mentions "divers treaties, both in Lattin and English, private and publique, . . . in their particuler names and values oftentymes expressed,"[49] the only one he names is "that which hath bene published by that true lover of vertue and great learned professor of all arts and knowledges, Mr Hariots."[50] This appears in Hakluyt as *A briefe and true report of the new found land of Virginia,*[51] under which title it had been published in 1588. Strachey refers also to the *True reporte of the late discoveries of the newfound landes,* published in 1583 and incorporated by Hakluyt under a similar title into the

[46] *Op cit.,* pp. 36–37.
[47] *Historie,* (M), p. 141; (W), p. 140.
[48] Hakluyt, *op. cit.,* VIII, 2.
[49] *Historie,* (M), p. 15; (W), p. 21.
[50] *Ibid.,* (M), p. 15; (W), p. 21.
[51] Hakluyt, *op. cit.,* VIII, 348–86.

Voyages.[52] The author, Sir George Peckham, included in his *True reporte* a defense of planting in America, and Strachey makes use of his arguments in the "Praemonition," prefacing them with "Planting (saith Sir George Peckam, writing an apologye in the like cause) . . ."[53]

Other events detailed by Hakluyt and referred to in the "Praemonition" are the assault on the French in Forida by the Spaniards in 1565,[54] the letters patent granted by Henry VII to John Cabot,[55] and the early voyages of exploration by English seamen on the American coast.[56]

In the first chapter of the book describing the country Strachey quotes once from Hakluyt:

Neverthelesse to approve that there lyeth a way to Cathayo at the Northwest from out of Europe, we have experience, namely of three brethren that went that journey, as Gemma Frisius recordeth, and left a name unto that straight, whereby now it is called Fretum trium fratrum. We doe reade againe of a Portugall that passed this straight, of whom Master Frobisher speaketh, that was imprisoned therefore many yeeres in Lisbone. . . . Likewise Andrew Urdaneta a Fryer of Mexico came out of Mar del Zur this way into Germanie: his Carde . . . hath bene seene by Gentlemen of good credite.[57]

when yet againe Gemma Frisius recordeth three brethren that went this passage, and left a name unto the Streights of Anian, where the sea striketh sowth into Mar-del-zur, beyond America, whereby that streict is now called *Fretum trium fratrum*: we doe reade, likewise, of a Portugal that passed this streict, of whom Sir Martin Furbisher speaketh, that was imprisoned therefore many yeares in Lishbon, likewise Anordaneta, a frier of Mexico, came out of Mar del zur this way into Germany, whose card hath ben seene by gentlemen of good credit.[58]

[53] *Ibid.*, pp. 89–131.   [53] *Historie,* (M), p. 20; (W), p. 26.
[54] *Ibid.,* (M), p. 9; (W), p. 16; Hakluyt, *op. cit.,* IX, 90-109.
[55] *Historie,* (M), p. 6; (W), p. 12; Hakluyt, *op. cit.,* VII, 141–44.
[56] *Historie,* (M), p. 8; (W), pp. 14–15; Hakluyt, *op. cit.,* VIII, IX.
[57] Hakluyt, *op. cit.,* VII, 196.
[58] *Historie,* (M), p. 24; (W), p. 32, inserts after "Lisbon,"

It is in the second book of *The historie of travaile* when he deals with the exploration and colonization of Virginia that Strachey makes the most extensive use of Hakluyt's *Voyages.* Of the ten chapters in this book, three are condensations of accounts that appear in Hakluyt. Although certain of these voyages had been printed before, others are to be found only in Hakluyt; so it seems probable that Strachey drew of the *Voyages* for all the accounts he condenses. Moreover, he follows Hakluyt's chronological order throughout.

In the first chapter, summarizing briefly the earliest discoveries in America, he refers only twice to events detailed in Hakluyt: to the "voluntary fryer" mentioned earlier and to the granting of a commission by Edward VI to Sebastian Cabot.[59]

The second chapter, describing the voyage of Captains Amadas and Barlow, is taken entirely from Hakluyt, rearranged and condensed. One extract makes this clear:

When we first had sight of this countrey, some thought the first land wee saw to bee the continent: but after we entred into the Haven, we saw before us another mighty long sea.[60]	When they first had sight of this country, some thought the first land they saw to be the continent; but after they had entred the haven, they saw before them another mighty long sea.[61]

The whole chapter can be paralleled in this way from Hakluyt.

The third and fourth chapters dealing with the early attempts of Sir Walter Raleigh to found a colony in the southern part of Virginia, are drawn likewise from Hakluyt, where alone these accounts are to be found. In the third chapter Strachey makes one mention of his source:

" (the Spaniard at all tymes cautulous for the discovery of this Passadge) ."

[59] *Ibid.*, (M) , p. 141; (W) , p. 140; Hakluyt, *op. cit.*, VII, 156–57.

[60] Hakluyt, *op. cit.*, VIII, 308–9.

[61] *Historie,* (M) , p. 142; (W) , p. 141.

"The partycularyties of such businesses as were performed by Mr. Ralph Lane, the captaines and gentlemen, and the rest of the colony, to the nomber (as aforesaid) seene in the booke of the discoveries."[62] Ralph Lane's account appears in Hakluyt, and the whole of these two chapters can be found in the *Voyages*.[63]

Strachey's debt to Hakluyt is, as can be seen, considerable, especially in the second book of *The historie of travaile*.

John Brereton. *A briefe and true relation of the discoverie the north part of Virginia*. London, 1602.

The sixth chapter of Strachey's second book, describing the voyage of Captain Bartholomew Gosnold in 1602, is condensed directly from this work and has no other source. One quotation serves to make this clear:

it seemed by some words and signes they made, that some Basks or of S. John de Luz, have fished or traded in this place, being in the latitude of 43 degrees.[64]	and yt seemed by some wordes and signes which they made, that some barks, or of St. John de Luz, had fished and traded in this place.[65]

James Rosier. *A true relation of the most prosperous voyage made this present yeere 1605, by Captaine George Waymouth, in the discovery of the land of Virginia*. London, 1605.

A condensation of this work occupies about half of Strachey's seventh chapter in Book II.

The River it selfe as it runneth up into the main very night forty miles toward the great mountains beareth in bredth a mile, sometime	The river, likewise, ytself, as yt runneth upp into the mayne for very neere forty miles towards the high in-land mountaines, he found

---

[62] *Ibid.*, (M), p. 146; (W), p. 144, reads "the number (as aforesaid) of 100. there remayning for one whole yeare, may be further seen."

[63] Hakluyt, *op. cit.*, VIII, 310–422.

[64] Brereton, *op. cit.*, reprinted in Henry S. Burrage (ed.), *Early English and French voyages* (New York, 1906), pp. 330–31.

[65] *Historie*, (M), p. 155; (W), p. 152.

three quarters, and halfe a mile is the narrowest.[66]

to beare in breadth a myle, sometymes three quarters, and half a mile the narrowest.[67]

John Smith. *A map of Virginia: with a description of the countrey, the commodities, people, government and religion.* Oxford, 1612.

Of the 180 pages of the printed edition of *The historie of travaile,* 109 are taken up by the first book, "Expressing the Cosmographie and Comodities of the Country, togither with the Manners and Customes of the People." One third of this first book consists of extracts from John Smith's *Map,* rearranged, in a few places condensed, and in a few expanded, but in no way rewritten. Strachey borrowed about four-fifths of Smith's work and included every passage actually describing the people, the country, or its products. Smith, however, left the colony to return to England while Strachey was on his way there, and much of Strachey's additional material is derived from his experiences during his stay in Virginia.

Along with his manuscript Strachey provides a copy of the engraved map drawn by Captain Smith and forming a part of his work but gives him no credit for his wholesale borrowings. Describing the various Indian tribes he says: "Their severall habitations are more plainly described by the annexed mappe, set forth by Captain Smith, of whose paines taken herein, I leave to the censure of the reader to judge";[68] and adds a few commendatory words, which are described in the margin as "A dew remembrance of Capt. Smyth."

Two extracts from *A map of Virginia,* written by Smith in the first person, are altered and indicate the source:

for example, he caused certaine malefactors, at what tyme Captain Smith was prisoner with him, (and to the sight

[66] Rosier, *op. cit.,* reprinted in Burrage, *op. cit.,* p. 382.
[67] *Historie,* (M), p. 159; (W), p. 156.
[68] *Ibid.,* (M), p. 41; (W), p. 49.

whereof Captain Smith, for some purpose, was brought,) to be bound hand and foote.[69]

They have also divers conjurations: one they made at what tyme they had taken Captain Smyth prisoner, to know, as they reported, if any more of his countrymen would arrive there, and what they intended; the manner of yt Captain Smith observed to be as followeth.[70]

These references, however, would lead a reader to belive that Strachey was indebted to Smith only for the map and the two passages mentioned above, and that Smith was only one authority to whom he had turned, rather than that Smith's *Map of Virginia* provided the basis of the whole of Strachey's first book.

William Symonds. *Virginia: a sermon preached at Whitechapel in the presence of . . . the Adventurers and Planters for Virginia, April 25th, 1609.* London, 1609.

In the "Praemonition" Strachey, defending settlement in Virginia, makes use of arguments similar to those set out by Symonds in his sermon and refers to him once:

our obiecter would not whip a child to teach him learning and vertue, for feare of doing wrong.[71]	Let me remember what Mr. Simondes, preacher of St. Saviours, saith in this behalf: It is as much, saith he, as if a father should be said to offer violence to his child, when he beats him to bring him to goodness.[72]

Strachey was undoubtedly among the assembled adventurers who heard Symonds preach at Whitechapel not long before the *Sea Venture* set sail, and it would appear from his reference that he is not making use of the printed

---

[69] *Ibid.,* (M), p. 52; (W), p. 60. Cf. John Smith, *Travels and works,* ed. E. Arber and A. G. Bradley (Edinburgh, 1910), I, 81.

[70] *Historie,* (M), p. 92; (W), p. 96. Cf. Smith, *op. cit.,* I, 76.

[71] Symonds, *op. cit.,* p. 14.

[72] *Historie,* (M), p. 17; (W), p. 24.

copy but rather recalling an apt illustration that had impressed him when he heard the sermon.

Thomas Cogan. *The haven of health.* London, 1589.

First printed in 1584 and reissued in 1589, this work is a medical textbook in English and, as the author says in his preface, intended for the use of students.

In the "Praemonition" Strachey cites this somewhat unusual authority in support of a statement that cannibalism was once practiced in Scotland, prefacing a passage of some seventy words with:

as reciteth Tho. Cogan, bachellor of phisick, in his booke, De Sanitate, ch. 137, printed 1189 [*sic*], and dedicated to the Earle of Hertford; in which place he bringeth in St. Hierome himself, by way of Prosopopaeia, affirming so much uppon his knowledg. His wordes, there alleged, are these.[73]

It is conceivable that this book was actually the property of Dr. Bohun, who was at Jamestown with Strachey and with whom Strachey, from references in *The historie of travaile,* appears to have been on good terms.

Johann Boemus. *The manners, lawes, and customes of all nations.* London, 1611.

The subtitle of this work tells us that it was "Collected out of the best writers by Joannes Boemus Aubanus, a Dutchman. Written in Latin, and now newly translated into English by Ed. Aston." There had been an earlier and bad translation with the title *The fardle of facions,* published in 1555, but it is clear from a comparison of the editions that it is this edition of 1611 of which Strachey made use.

Strachey reworded theories expressed in this work in one section of his first book:

And Noah, because all parts of the earth might be re-	in the scattering of Noah, his children, and nephewes,

[73] *Ibid.,* (M), p. 18; (W), pp. 24–25; Cogan, *op. cit.,* p. 123. The passage "What shall I say . . . delicate meat;" is transcribed directly from Cogan.

peopled, sent his sonnes, nephews, and kinsfolke, with their companies to dwell, some into one country, some into an other. Into Aegipt (according to the opinion of *Berosus*) he sent Esennius with the Colonies of Cham: *Tritamen* into Lybia and Cyrene, and Iaphet Priscus Attolaa, to inioy the rest of Affrick. Into East Asia hee sent *Canges*, with some of the sonnes of *Gomen Gallus*: *Sabus*, surnamed *Thurifer* went into Arabia foelix: *Arabus* ruled in the deserts of Arabia. . . . *Chanaan* hee placed in Damascus in the confines of Palestine.[74]

with their families (as little colonies), some to one, some to other borders of the earth, to dwell; as in Egypt (so writing Berosus), Esenius and his household tooke up their inhabitation; in Libia and Cyrene, Tritanes; and in all the rest of Africa, Jupetus Priscus; Attalaas in the east Asia: Ganges, with some of Comerus Gallus' childrene, in Arabia Felix, within the confines of Sabea, called the frankincense-bearer; Canaan in Damascus, unto the utmost bounds of Palestine.[75]

In this case he gives credit to his source;

so great was that destruction which the untimely banishment of one man brought to all mankinde.[76]

so great a misery (saieth Boem of Auba) brought to mankind the unsatisfied wandering of that one man.[77]

George Percy. *Discourse of the plantation of the southerne colonie in Virginia by the English, 1606.* First printed in Purchas, *Pilgrimes* (London, 1625).

From the extract given in Purchas it appears that this *Discourse* was written not long after Percy arrived in the colony and that it remained in manuscript, possibly among the collections either of the Virginia Company or of Hakluyt, until it came into Purchas' hands.

Strachey quotes from it only once, in his first book,

---

[74] Boemus, *op. cit.*, sigs. B1v–B2r.
[75] *Historie,* (M), p. 45; (W), pp. 53–54.
[76] Boemus, *op. cit.*, sig. B2v.
[77] *Historie,* (M), p. 46; (W), p. 54.

when, sandwiched between extracts from Smith, appears one from Smith's mortal enemy:

There is notice to be taken to know married women from Maids, the Maids you shall alwayes see the fore part of their head and sides shaven close, the hinder part very long, which they tie in a pleate hanging downe to hips. The married women weares their haire all of a length.[78]

There are notes to be taken by which may be discerned a marryed woman from a mayd: the maydes have the forepart of their heads and sides shaven close, the hinder part very long, which they wind very prettely and ymbroyder in playtes, letting yt hang so to the full length: the marryed women weare their haire all of a length.[79]

This single quotation nevertheless indicates that when Strachey returned to England and was writing the first book of *The historie*, he was not forced to rely only on printed material but had access to certain of the manuscript material relating to the colony.

James Davies. *The relation of a voyage unto New-England.*

This manuscript account, of doubtful authorship, was first discovered and printed in 1880.[80] The title page of the printed version states that the MS was found among the papers of Sir Ferdinando Gorges, a member of the Council of the Virginia Company, and it is referred to both by Purchas and *A briefe relation of the discovery and plantation of New England,* the official account sponsored by the New England Company and published in 1622.

Strachey says, "I have not thought it amisse to epithomize a fewe things (and which have not yet by any one bene published, or written of)"[81] concerning the abortive attempt in 1607 to settle in the northern part of Virginia, and he reproduces this account almost in full, merely

---

[78] Purchas, *Pilgrimes,* XVIII, 416.
[79] *Historie,* (M), p. 112; (W), p. 114.
[80] *Proc. Mass. Hist. Soc.,* XVIII (1880–81), 82–117.
[81] *Historie,* (M), p. 162; (W), p. 158.

changing it from the first to the third person. *The relation* takes up half of Chapter Eight and all of Chapters Nine and Ten of the second book of *The historie.*

St. Augustine. *De concensu evangelicarum.*

Strachey refers once to this work in the "Praemonition."

The glorious St. Augustine, in his firste booke, "De Concord. Evang.", cap. 32, goeth so far concerning the spredding abroad and teaching of our Saviour crucified, not only to the right, but to the leaft hand, as it is in the 54 of Esau, as he there amply discourseth how the ghospell should be published abroad.[82]

The reference to Isaiah 54 is found in the thirty-first chapter of this work, which had apparently not been published in England up to the date of *The historie of travaile;* but the thirty-second chapter deals with the matters touched on by Strachey. The fact that he was unable to reproduce the title correctly would suggest that he drew his reference from an entry in a commonplace book or some list of like nature.

Guicciardini.

Strachey refers to him once in the "Praemonition." "And compassion, saith Guicciardine, debates not causes and reasons, but proceedes to relief, for which the duty of a good man is said to be compounded of these two things, the glory of his Creator, and the love of his neighbor."[83] This quotation does not occur in either of the better-known translations of the brothers Guicciardini, where one might expect to find it: Ludovico's *Houres of recreation* (1576) or Francesco's *Aphorismes,* translated by Sir Robert Dallington in 1613. It may however be in one or the other of their *Histories,* in which case this would appear again to be a reference culled from a commonplace book.

Strachey, however, makes one remark, in *A true repor-*

[82] *Ibid.,* (M) , p. 14; (W), p. 21.
[83] *Ibid.,* (M) , p. 12; (W) , p. 9.

tory, which, while a commonplace, closely resembles two proverbs to be found in the *Houres of recreation.* Strachey tells us that "Truth is the daughter of time,"[84] and Guicciardini that

Truth is tymes daughter, and over all hath might,
Wherefore she still shineth as doth the sunnes light,[85]

and that

Time is the father of truth,
And experience is the mother of things.[86]

DATE OF COMPOSITION

ALTHOUGH it is perfectly clear that *The historie of travaile* was completed and the manuscript presented to Henry Percy after the publication of John Smith's *Map of Virginia* in 1612, it would appear nevertheless that the work was commenced while Strachey was actually in Virginia, and that when he returned to England in 1611 he brought with him the "Praemonition" and the first four chapters of what became his second book.

In his preface to the *Lawes* he tells the company that from the moment he embarked on his voyage to Virginia he had set out to be a "remembrancer of all accidents, occurrences, and undertakings thereunto adventitiall"; and he makes it clear, moreover, in this work that was entered for publication on December 13, 1611, some two months after his arrival in England, that he was already at work on a detailed account of events during his stay in Virginia, but that since there were certain impediments to be overcome before the work could see the light of day, he was in the meantime publishing the *Lawes.*[87]

He gives no indication that he intended the major portion of *The historie* to be taken up by a description of the country, but rather makes it appear that he was proposing a detailed "True relation" of the type that was already well

[84] Purchas, *Pilgrimes,* XIX, 14.
[85] Ludovico Guicciardini, *Houres,* sig. B8v.
[86] *Ibid.,* sig. H4v.   [87] *Lawes,* preface.

known and popular. He probably decided to revise his plan and incorporate the first descriptive book only after Smith's *Map* came to his notice. Original material resulting from his sojourn in the colony would, in due course, have found its place in what was initially designed to be a chronicle of the settlement of Virginia.

Both the "Praemonition" and these opening chapters of the second book are purely prefatory, providing a historical background to the events that had occurred since the foundation of the colony, and particularly during his stay there. In the "Praemonition," moreover, there are passages which may have slipped by unnoticed during the revision of the manuscript before the transcription of the final copies and which suggest that the work may have been started even while Strachey was cast away on the Bermudas.

He mentions that an attack on the French by the Spaniards in 1565 took place "44 yeares since,"[88] and that Madoc sailed from Wales in 1170, "which may be four hundred and thirty-nine years since."[89] However he could refer only to Virginia when he mentions "the idolls of the salvadges here,"[90] and that "Vesputius Americus, . . . five years after Columbus, arrived here."[91] In the course of a revision that required an alteration of dates and the changing of "here" to "there" it would be comparatively easy to overlook an occasional detail.

The educated gentleman, proceeding beyond the seas, might be expected to take with him some literature dealing with the country he was to visit, and in this, as we have seen, Strachey was no exception. *A true reportory* provides evidence that he had with him Acosta's *Naturall and morall historie of the East and West Indies* and Willes' *History of travayle in the West and East Indies*; and since he was sufficiently interested to take these works, it would seem natural that among his books there should also be the

[88] *Historie*, (M), p. 9; (W), p. 16.
[89] *Ibid.*, (M), p. 5; (W), p. 11.
[90] *Ibid.*, (M), p. 19; (W), p. 25.
[91] *Ibid.*, (M), p. 13; (W), p. 20.

most comprehensive and most important of all the English collections of travels, Hakluyt's *Voyages*.

The "Praemonition," "wherein (as the fowndation to all the succeeding busines) is derived downe to our tymes, the auntyent right and clayme which we make to this part of America," while stating in Strachey's own words well-known arguments in favor of planting, draws on Willes and Hakluyt alone for historical material to bolster up these arguments. Moreover, the unusual authorities cited in illustration of various points suggest that Strachey was forced to draw on whatever was at hand: Cogan's textbook of medicine; an aphorism attributed to Guicciardini and a reference to St. Augustine, possibly culled from a common-place book; and memory of a point raised in Symonds' sermon.

Furthermore, although Strachey refers to Symonds as the preacher of St. Saviour's, there seems reason to believe that by 1612, when the final draft of *The historie* was completed, Symonds was more closely connected with Oxford and may even by this date have relinquished his post at St. Saviour's.[92] However, when Strachey heard him preach in 1609, this was the designation by which he was best known and the one Strachey would recall when writing of him in Virginia, out of touch with affairs in England.

Of the first four chapters of the second book, the first, a general account of the early exploration of America, is based entirely on Willes and Hakluyt, and the succeeding three on Hakluyt alone. Although in this second book Strachey incorporates also the accounts of Rosier and Brereton, both of which had been published before he set sail for Virginia, he makes no use of them in the "Praemonition." These works carried the story of the colonization and exploration of Virginia up to 1603, but Strachey in his introduction, mentioning briefly the early

[92] See *D.N.B.*, "Symonds." "Surrey Wills" in the *Surrey arch. coll.*, XXIII and XXIV, mention him as Preacher of St. Saviour's only as late as January 1610. See also introduction to Smith, *op. cit.*, where it is suggested that *A map of Virginia* was published at Oxford in 1612 because Symonds was at that date resident there.

English explorations,[93] goes no further than the attempts of Sir Walter Raleigh, detailed in Hakluyt; and it is these attempts that occupy the opening chapters of the second book.

From the first book, written after his return to England, we can get some idea of the material that he had collected while he was in Virginia. As secretary to the Council he was of course in close touch with the affairs of the settlers, and it is particularly matters relating to trade, to military reprisals against the Indians, and to their conversion—matters that would have been reported in full to the Council in England—that Strachey's additions describe in the greatest detail.

He describes the trading expeditions of Captain Argall in 1610[94] and deals at length with the products of the country that might be expected to show a profit on the company's behalf.[95] One chapter, with no parallel in Smith, surveys the military resources of the Indians, village by village, and is obviously drawn from information gathered before Gates and De la Warr embarked on their series of punitive expeditions of 1610 and 1611.[96] There is considerable speculation on a matter vital to the colonists: whether any of the neighboring tribes might be induced to turn against their paramount chief, Powhatan, whose enmity was a constant source of trouble.[97] Parallel with this Strachey deals at considerable length with Powhatan himself and his famous daughter Pocahontas.[98] Likewise he greatly expands Smith's account of the religion of the Indians, and from his treatment it is apparent that Strachey had thought on the subject deeply.[99] He refers once to a report submitted by Dale to the Council in London[100]

[93] *Historie*, (M), pp. 8–9; (W), pp. 14–15.
[94] *Ibid.*, (M), pp. 38, 42–43, 98–99; (W), pp. 46, 50–51, 101–2.
[95] *Ibid.*, (M), pp. 31, 121, 123–32; (W), pp. 38, 122, 125–133.
[96] *Ibid.*, (M), pp. 55–63; (W), pp. 63–69.
[97] *Ibid.*, (M), pp. 86–7; (W), pp. 91–93.
[98] *Ibid.*, (M), pp. 49–51, 65, 101–4, 111; (W), pp. 57–59, 72, 105–7, 113–14.
[99] *Ibid.*, (M), pp. 83–89, 98–100; (W), pp. 89–94, 101–3.
[100] *Ibid.*, (M), p. 120; (W), p. 121.

and quotes once from his own *True reportory*,[101] the letter written to the "Excellent Lady."

From this it is clear that Strachey as secretary kept copies of some of the reports sent home by the Council in Virginia, reports moreover which would have been indited by Strachey himself. Along with these he had his own notes, compiled from his own observation or embodying information given him by the two friendly Indians who had returned to Virginia with Gates's party.[102] These would, in course of time, have found their place in a chronological narrative of events during his stay in the colony.

As it was, Strachey found his hand forced by the publication of John Smith's *Map* in 1612, and, as he had adapted the form and title of Willes' *History of travayle* to his own work, so now he borrowed not only the material but also the general layout from Smith's account of the country. We do not know in what month in 1612 *A map of Virginia* was published, but it must have been early in the year, since the fair copy of *The historie of travaile* was completed before November 6 of that year, when Prince Henry died and his younger brother Charles became Prince of Wales.

Strachey, quoting Smith, tells us, "The cape of this bay, on the south side, we call Cape Henry, in honour of our most royall Prince. . . . The north foreland of this bay, which the Indians terme Accowmack, we call Cape Charles, in honour of our princely Duke of York."[103] This is altered in the copy presented to Bacon in 1618 by the insertion of "deceased" before "Prince" and the changing of "our princely Duke of York" to "our now prince, at that time Duke of York." These additions appear to have been made in 1617;[104] hence all three copies of the manuscript must have been completed before the death of Henry.

---

[101] *Ibid.*, (M), p. 44; (W), p. 51; Purchas, *Pilgrimes*, XIX, 43.

[102] *Historie*, (M), pp. 79–80; (W), pp. 85–87.

[103] *Ibid.*, (M), p. 28; (W), p. 36.

[104] They are not in Strachey's handwriting and appear to be in the same ink as the alteration of "six" to "11" mentioned in note 107.

Lest it may be thought that an event of the magnitude of the death of the heir to the throne might have slipped by unnoticed during the revision or transcription of Strachey's manuscript, other evidence can be found to confirm the year 1612 for the completion of *The historie of travaile* as it now stands. In the "Praemonition" we find "1492, which is now since one hundred and twenty years";[105] and in the first book, written after the publication of *A Map,* there is a reference to an attempt to find the northwest passage "this presente yeare";[106] that Jamestown has been settled "well neere six yeares";[107] that he was at the falls with Sir Thomas Dale "this last yeare."[108]

However, when he states that he brought home from Virginia a falcon to be presented to Prince Henry, "this yeare myself,"[109] he must have been writing earlier than March 23, 1612.[110]

From the foregoing evidence it would appear that *The historie of travaile* was conceived and begun while Strachey was in Virginia, and that he returned bringing with him the "Praemonition" and the first four chapters of his second book. While he was working on his material and adding the later chapters to his second book from manuscript and printed material available in England, John Smith's *Map of Virginia* appeared, whereupon Strachey revised the plan of the work and in the course of 1612 wrote what became his first book, describing the country, and presented the completed manuscript to Henry Percy before the death of Prince Henry on November 6, 1612.

[105] *Historie,* (M), p. 5; (W), p. 11.
[106] *Ibid.,* (M), p. 23; (W), p. 31. The expedition sailed on April 14, 1612, and returned late in 1613. See Miller Christy (ed.), *The voyages of Captain Luke Fox of Hull, and Captain Thomas James of Bristol, in search of a north-west passage* (London, 1894), I, 164 and 200.
[107] *Historie,* (M), p. 29; (W), p. 37. In the 1617 MS "six" has been struck out and "11" substituted. Jamestown was established in April 1607.
[108] *Ibid.,* (M), p. 124; (W), p. 125.
[109] *Ibid.,* (M), p. 125; (W), p. 126.
[110] When the Old Style year ended.

Bibliography

Some manuscript material included in this bibliography is not referred to in the present text, but in the omitted genealogical appendixes. It has been retained as an indication of source material throwing further light on the Strachey family and their connections.

I Strachey's Works

A true reportory of the wracke, and redemption of Sir Thomas Gates Knight.

First published in Purchas, *Pilgrimes* (1625). It appears in subsequent editions of Purchas, and, with Jourdan's account, in *A voyage to Virginia in 1609*, edited by Louis B. Wright (Charlottesville, Va., 1964). Discussions of Shakespeare's debt to Strachey are to be found in the New Variorum edition of *The tempest*, in Gayley (*q.v.*), and most minutely in Cawley (*q.v.*).

For the colony in Virginea Britannia. Lawes divine, morall and martiall, &c. London, 1612.

Republished only once in its entirety, in Force (*q.v.*). A summary of the contents is to be found in the works of most writers on the early history of America.

The historie of travaile into Virginia Britannia.

Exists in three manuscripts: Percy MS, in the Princeton University Library: Ashmole MS 1758; and Sloane MS 1622.

A description and comparison of the Sloane and Ashmole MSS are given in Brown, *Genesis* (*q.v.*) ; a further description of the Ashmole MS (but only a notice of the Sloane MS) is given in Andrews, *Materials* (*q.v.*) ; a very detailed description, with illustrations, of the Percy MS appears in Sotheby, *Americana* (*q.v.*) ; and a description and comparison of all three MSS are in Wright's edition of *The historie.*

The Sloane MS was printed in 1849 by the Hakluyt Society and edited by R. H. Major and the Percy MS in 1953 by the Hakluyt Society again and edited by Louis B. Wright and Virginia Freund.

Penitential Verses.

Ashmole MS 781, f. 135. A portion has been printed in Sanders, *William Strachey* (*q.v.*) .

II Manuscript Materials

These are listed (with the exception of parish registers) according to the repositories where the documents are kept.

BRITISH MUSEUM

Add. MS 19,819—Miscellaneous pedigrees compiled during the eighteenth century, including, at ff. 1–2, that of Michell, of Old Windsor.

Add. MS 34,110—Account book of the overseers of Paris Garden Liberty, in the parish of St. Saviour, Southwark, from 1608. (Sir Edmund Bowyer was one of the overseers.)

Add. MS 34,730—West Papers. Miscellaneous seventeenth-century correspondence, including, at f. 1, a letter by John Strachey (brother to the secretary) .

Cotton MS Nero B.XI—Miscellaneous papers relating to the Russian and Levant trade, including, at ff. 140–155, "A continuation of the series of Henry Lello's [draft] letters to the Levant company, being 20 in number, and of the years 1603, 4, 5, 6, and 7."

Egerton MS 1967—Rentals, customaries, abstracts of titles, etc., of manors in Surrey and Sussex; with, at ff. 200–220, a survey of the manor of Chellows.

Egerton MS 2410—Letters and papers addressed to Sir Lionel Tollemache and his son Lionel, 1502–1713. Ff. 20, 22 contain letters from John Strachey.

Harleian MS 1441—"An heraldical book in fol. written, tricked, & painted by divers hands"; including, at f. 8b, a copy of the grant of arms to William Strachey of Saffron Walden.

Harleian MS 1541—Miscellaneous pedigrees, with, at f. 198, the only copy of the pedigree of the Stracheys of Saffron Walden.

Harleian MS 1912—Miscellaneous material, compiled in 1680, relating to the membership of the Inns of Court.

ESSEX RECORD OFFICE

In addition to the general records of the county, this repository has the complete records of the manor of Walden. A guide is in process of publication; F. G. Emmison, *Guide to the Essex record office* (2 vols., Chelmsford, 1946–48).

DBB/767—Deed of 1588 referring to land held by the Strachey family in Saffron Walden.

DDB/770—Deed of 1594 also mentioning lands of the Strachey family in the town.

DDB/771—Indenture made December 12, 1599, between William Adam and Thomas Rowley to declare the uses of a fine made with William Strachey the secretary.

DDB/772—Deed of January 1, 1600, between William Strachey and Thomas Adam. (Bears the original signatures of William, Thomas, and Howard Strachey.)

D/DGn/174—Deed of May 20, 1617, between William Strachey and Jeffrey Tanner. (Signatures of Sir Edmund and John Bowyer and William Strachey.)

Abstract of Court Rolls—Compiled c.1590, with summaries of land transfers carried out by members of the Strachey family between 1458 and 1560.

D/DBy/M26—Abstract of Court Rolls, 1548–1614. (Different in treatment from the preceding abstract, this records only the major land transfers resulting from the death of a holder. The Strachey family are represented by William Strachey and his widow Elizabeth.)

D/DBy/M32—Rental of the manor of Walden, 1524. (Lists the freehold land of Thomas Strachey.)

Sessions Records—In addition to the original rolls, there is an indexed calendar in typescript.

FOLGER SHAKESPEARE LIBRARY

MS 420, 423—The Jonson-Chapman Letter Book. (Contains three letters to or by Strachey, reproduced in full, from microfilm, in the text.)

PARISH REGISTERS

Use has been made of the registers of the following churches, and full reference is given in the text. In each case the register is in good condition and is available at the church.

St. Mary, Bexley.
St. Mary, Bury St. Edmunds.
St. Giles, Camberwell.
St. George, Crowhurst.
St. Mary, Lambeth.
St. Mary the Virgin, Saffron Walden.

PRINCIPAL PROBATE REGISTRY, SOMERSET HOUSE

The parish of Saffron Walden came under the jurisdiction of the Archdeaconry Court of Colchester, and it is among the records of this court that the wills of the earlier Stracheys are to be found.

I ARCHDEACONRY COURT OF COLCHESTER

Roberts 172—Agnes Strachye of Walden. 1561.
Puckell 91—Thomas Strachey thelder of Walden, yeoman. 1558.
Puckell 178.b.—William Strachie thelder of Walden. 1564.
Hore 179.b.—Katherin Stratchie, of Walden, singlewoman. 1570.
Roote 14—Richard Strachye of Walden, yeoman. 1575.
Roote 101—Thomas Strachye of Walden, yeoman. 1578.
Roote 317.b.—Amiable Strachie of Walden, widow. 1585.

II PREROGATIVE COURT OF CANTERBURY

Administration Act Books, 1587–1589. (Contain the administration of the estate of William Strachey.)
32 Bucke—Henry Cooke of London and Lesness. 1551.
16 Tasshe—George Richardson of London and East Greenwich. 1553.
25 Ketchyn—Henry Goodere of London. 1556.
13 Loftes—Ralph Bickerdicke, alderman of Cambridge. 1561.
34 Lyon—John Bowyer Esq., of Camberwell. 1570.
33 Daughtrey—Matthew Draper gent., of Camberwell. 1577.
63 Leicester—John Strachey of Saffron Walden. 1589.
9 Kidd—William Strachey, gent., of Saffron Walden. 1599.
58 Kidd—Humphrey Michell, Esq., of Old Windsor, Berkshire. 1599.
36 Stafforde—Humphrey Michell. Sentence after dispute of his will, 58 Kidd. 1606.
43 Stafforde—Hugh Lancaster, gent., of Westacre in Norfolk. 1606.
89 Dorset—Robert Cox, citizen and tallow chandler of London. 1609.
13 Hele—John Strachey, clothworker, of London. 1626.
26 Skynner—Sir Edmund Bowyer, Knt., of Camberwell. 1627.

DISTRICT PROBATE REGISTRY, MAIDSTONE

Among the records of the Consistory Court of Rochester kept at this repository is the original signed will of Edmund Cooke, gent., of North Cray. 1619.

PUBLIC RECORD OFFICE

I CHANCERY

1 *Proceedings.* These consist of the bills and answers presented to the court in the opening stages of a suit. The period dealt with in the text is covered by two series of proceedings, Series I (C2), and Series II (C3), which are further divided according to the reigning monarch when the suit took place.

C2 Eliz/F2/49—Peter Ferryman v. Edmund Peshall. Action for debt in 1589. (Casts some light on Ferryman.)

C2 Eliz/S2/28—John Strachey v. William Kellam. 1582–83. (Financial affairs of John Strachey.)

C2 Jas I/C21/83—Matthew Clayton v. William Strachey and Sir Edmund Bowyer. 1615. (Claim to brewhouse property; provides some genealogical and biographical information.)

C2 Jas I/P24/30—Edmund Peshall v. John Strachey. 1611. (One of a long series of suits contested between John Strachey and a business rival, concerning only John Strachey and his immediate family and associates and throwing no light on the affairs of his cousin, William Strachey.)

C2 Jas I/S6/16—John Strachey v. Edmund Peshall. 1612.

C2 Jas I/S10/51—George Shiers v. William and Howard Strachey. 1619. (Concerns the rent of the brewhouse property and Howard's actions during his brother's absence.)

C2 Jas I/S21/18—John Strachey v. Thomas Symondes. 1605. (Business affairs in the Levant of John Strachey.)

C2 Jas I/T2/67—Edward Topsell v. Sir William Forster. 1615. (Strachey's father-in-law and the rectory at Crowhurst.)

C2 Chas I/S25/36—Abigail Strachey v. Sir Daniel Norton and Edward Tucker. 1631. (Genealogical interest.)

C2 Chas I/S73/6—Abigail Strachey v. Dame Mary Cowper, 1631. (Genealogical interest.)

C3/162/65—Amiable Strachey v. John Strachey. c. 1570. (Quarrel over property in Walden. Early family history.)

C3/163/82—Thomas Strachey v. Owen Wilson. c.1570. (Property in Cambridge. Genealogical interest.)

C3/289/13—William Strachey v. Anthony Penistone. 1601. (Summarized in the text. Of biographical interest.)

C3/324/8—Sir Edward Sackville v. John Strachey. 1619. (Light on the affairs of John Strachey, brother to William Strachey the secretary.)

2 *Depositions* (C24). Not all proceedings reached the stage when parties appeared to give evidence on behalf of plaintiffs or defendants. When depositions exist, they generally contain much more detail than the bills or answers and cast light on the deponents themselves. Depositions are bundled according to the legal term when they were taken, and the reference denotes the bundle, from which the case must be abstracted.

C24/327—Kendall and others v. Evans and Hawkins. July, 1606. (Strachey deposed in this suit and indicated his connection with the Blackfriars Theatre.)

C24/390—John Strachey v. Edmund Peshall. Trinity term, 1613.

C24/638—Edward Baber v. Howard Strachey. Easter term, 1639. (Light on the affairs of Howard Strachey, who was executor of the estate of his nephew William.)

3 *Affidavits* (C31). Only three have been found with any bearing on the affairs of the Strachey family, all relating to the series of suits between John Strachey and Edmund Peshall.

C31/4/393—Strachey v. Peshall. Michaelmas, 1618.

C31/6/92, C31/6/93—Strachey v. Peshall. Easter, 1620.

4 *Entry Books of Decrees and Orders* (C33). Substantial volumes in two parallel series, with contemporary in-

dexes, these record the progress of suits in Chancery from the presentation of the bill of complaint to the end of the action. The following entries refer to suits already mentioned in Section 1, *Proceedings*, or 2, *Depositions*.

C33/102, f. 707—Strachey v. Penistone. June 21, 1602.

C33/107, ff. 597.v., 600—Kendall v. Evans. April, 1605.

C33/109, f. 385.v.—Kendall v. Evans. February, 1606.

C33/111, ff. 483.v., 542—Kendall v. Evans. May, 1607.

C33/113, f. 79—Kendall v. Evans. October, 1607.

C33/129, ff. 227, 304—Clayton v. Strachey. December, 1615.

C33/137, f. 3.—Shiers v. Strachey. May, 1619.

5 *Indentures* (C54). Deeds enrolled for safety in the close rolls in the custody of the Lord Chancelor. Contemporary indexes are available at the P.R.O., in two series, under the names of the grantor and of the grantee. The reference indicates the entire roll.

C54/797—William Strachey and Edward Taylor. 1569. (Original acquisition of brewhouse property.)

C54/1127—John Strachey and John Cage. 1582 (Light on the affairs of John Strachey.)

C54/1205—John Strachey and Geoffrey Thorowgood. 1585. (Financial affairs of John Strachey.)

C54/1665—William Strachey and Thomas Adam. 1600. (William Strachey sells land in Walden.)

C54/1818—William Strachey and Sir Edmund Bowyer. 1605. (Strachey sells land in Walden to his brother-in-law prior to leaving for the Levant.)

C54/2130—John Strachey and John Snelling. 1611. (John Strachey sells all his land in Walden.)

C54/2177—Bowyer brothers, Strachey, and William Palmer. 1613. (Sale of lands in Walden by William Strachey.)

C54/2425—Sir Edmund Bowyer and William Strachey, and William Strachey junior and his wife Eleanor. 1620. (Transfer of the brewhouse property to Strachey's son. Of biographical and genealogical interest.)

6 *Inquisitions Post Mortem* (C142). Held when a tenant of the Crown died in order to ascertain his heir and the amount of land held. Duplicate copies are also sometimes

found among the records of the Exchequer or the Court of Wards. Of genealogical and biographical interest.

C142/93/112—Henry Cooke, citizen and merchant tailor of London. 1551.

C142/214/211—William Strachey of Walden. 1587.

II COMMON PLEAS

In addition to the business of administering the common law, this court concerned itself with property transfers, either by fines or recoveries.

1 *Feet of Fines* (CP25 (2)). Parties to a sale of land signed three copies of a set form, which was then cut up and one section deposited with the court, the other two sections being retained by the parties.

C.P.25 (2) /124—Feet of Fines, Essex. Michaelmas, 35–6 Eliz. (William Strachey and Thomas and John Pamfling.)

C.P.25 (2) /124—Feet of Fines, Essex. Trinity, 38 Eliz. (William Strachey and William Woodhall.)

C.P.25 (2) /125—Feet of Fines, Essex. Michaelmas, 41–2 Eliz. (William Strachey, William Adam, and Thomas Rowley.)

C.P.25 (2) /125—Feet of Fines, Essex. Michaelmas, 42–3 Eliz. (William Strachey and Thomas Adam.)

2 *Plea Rolls* (CP40). Records of judicial proceedings, with contemporary indexes.

C.P.40/1881, f. 918—Tien v. Strachey. Hilary term, 1611–12.

C.P.40/1887, f. 903—Tien v. Strachey. Eastern term, 1612. (Action for debt; of biographical interest.)

3 *Recovery Rolls* (CP43). A method of avoiding the entail on property, in order to sell it, by staging a fictitious case for possession in the Court of Common Pleas.

C.P.43/96—Recovery, Clarke v. Draper, to bar the tail of the brewhouse property. Hilary, 1606.

III DUCHY OF LANCASTER

The manor of Walden fell within the jurisdiction of

the Duchy of Lancaster, and many cases involving the residents of the town that might otherwise have been heard in Chancery appeared before the court of the Duchy. Several cases on record concern the earlier members of the Strachey family.

DL2/8/S3—William Strachey and Thomas Byrde v. Thomas Smythe. 1530. (Early Saffron Walden.)

DL1/13/S3—The King v. William Strachey and Margaret his wife. 1533. (Genealogical interest.)

DL1/18/R14—The King v. William Strachey and Thomas Byrde. Undated. (Early Saffron Walden.)

DL1/19/W3—The Guild of the Holy Trinity v. Nicholas Smith. Undated. (Early Saffron Walden.)

DL1/22/R28—The King v. Thomas Strachey and Joan Strachey. Undated. (Genealogical interest.)

IV EXCHEQUER

1 *Muster Rolls* (E101). These provide a list of all able-bodied men in each parish and indicate their obligations should they be called on for military service. The only extant roll applicable to Walden during the period is E101/549/8—June 5, 1535.

2 *Certificates of Residence* (E115). People were generally assessed for taxation according to the district or parish in which they lived. Certificates of residence, indicating a change of address, were submitted to the Exchequer by the assessors for the new district in order to avoid double taxation. They are generally of considerable genealogical and biographical interest.

E115/35/99—Robert Ballard of Bexley, 1557.

E115/71/119—Robert Ballard of Bexley, 1558.

E115/71/120—Robert Ballard of Bexley, 1558.

E115/151/123—Sir William Forster of South Lambeth, 1609.

E115/158/42—Peter Ferryman of Childrey, in Berkshire, 1595.

E115/380/76—William Strachey of Crowhurst in Surrey, 1602. (Of biographical interest. Shows that he had moved from Saffron Walden by this date.)

3 *Subsidy Assessments* (E179). When a subsidy was granted to the crown by Parliament, the residents of each district were assessed for taxation by commissioners living there. A large class of documents, generally in a good state of preservation, these assessment rolls provide a list of the residents of each district and give an indication of their financial status. Unless otherwise indicated, the assessments listed are those for Uttlesford, Freshwell, and Clavering Hundreds in Essex, the district in which Saffron Walden fell.

E179/108/155—15 Henry VIII. (16 MS pages of names, in fairly good condition.)

E179/108/171—16 Henry VIII. (15 MS pages in good condition.)

E179/109/281—35 Henry VIII. (32 MS pages but partly damaged.)

E179/110/342—3 Edward VI. (4 MS pages in good condition.)

E179/110/417—9 Elizabeth. (6 MS pages in good condition.)

E179/111/441–14 Elizabeth. (6 MS pages in good condition.)

E179/111/500—40 Elizabeth. (4 MS pages but damaged.)

E179/111/513—41 Elizabeth. (5 MS pages in good condition.)

E179/111/519—42 Elizabeth. (5 MS pages in good condition.)

E179/186/420—Brixton Hundred, 22 James I. (Strachey's son was living in Camberwell.)

v Kings Bench

1 *Plea Rolls* (K.B.27). The complete records of common law proceedings in this court are preserved in the plea rolls, with contemporary indexes. Cases of interest are

K.B.27/1412, f. 758—William Hobbes v. Peter Ferryman, 1609. (Action for debt, throwing light on Ferryman.)

K.B.28/1412, f. 470—Robert Turner v. Clement Turner, 1609. (Action for debt involving Strachey's brother-in-law.)

vi Lord Chancellor

1 *Recognizances* (LC4). A debt could be acknowledged not only by the signing of a bond but also by the appearance of both parties in the office of the Lord Chancelor, where a recognizance would be duly entered on their behalf.

LC4/194/369—Howard Strachey and William Strachey, £200. 1601.

LC4/194/407—William Strachey and Josias Bull, £100. 1601.

LC4/195/224—William Strachey and John Lancaster, £200. 1603.

vii Court of Requests

The proceedings of this court have been calendared for the reign of Elizabeth, but only a few of the bundles for the reign of James I have been done. The finding of bills and answers for cases known to have taken place during this reign is thus virtually impossible, but the progress of a case can be followed from the Entry Books of Decrees and Orders and other miscellaneous books of the court.

1 *Miscellaneous Books* (Req 1).

Req 1/22—Appearance and Order Book, 2–3 James I, f. 662, Clayton v. Strachey.

Req 1/26, ff. 522, 598, 638, 721, 845—Entry Book of Decrees and Orders, Strachey v. Peshall. 1612.

Req 1/27, ff. 517, 519, 523—Draft Order Book, Strachey v. Peshall. 1612.

Req 1/50—Draft Order Book, 3 James I, Clayton v. Strachey. (First recorded suit regarding the brewhouse property.)

Req 1/199—Witness Book. (Covers the period of the reigns of Elizabeth and James I and gives the names of witnesses who appeared to give evidence in any suit. It was through this book that the Bellott-Mountjoy suit was discovered.) Mentions Clayton v. Strachey.

2 *Judicial Proceedings* (Req 2). This class includes bills and answers, affidavits, and the like.

Req 2/391/188—Clement Turner and Howard Strachey. Undated. (Affidavit; of genealogical interest.)

Req 2/393/12—John Strachey v. Edmund Peshall. Undated.

VIII STAR CHAMBER

1 *Proceedings* (St.Ch.8, for the reign of James I).

St.Ch.8/272/2—John Strachey v. Bartholomew Haggott. 1612. (Light on the affairs in the Levant of John Strachey.)

IX STATE PAPERS

The following State Papers relate to events in the Levant during Strachey's stay there.

S.P.97/5—State Papers, Turkey, Vol. V. (Contain letters from the ambassadors to the Secretary of State, giving both sides of their quarrel.)

S.P.105/109, S.P.105/110—Letter Books of the Levant Company. (Contain copies of their letters to their ambassadors and agents in the Mediterranean.)

S.P.105/143—Register Book of the Levant Company, 1605–48. (Copies of instructions to ambassadors and agents, charter parties, and the like.)

SAFFRON WALDEN

The early municipal records are kept at the Town Hall, are in a good state of repair, and are readily available.

Almshouse Ordinances—A vellum book, originally the property of the Abbey, containing the original ordinances of 1400, in Latin and English, which are of considerable interest. It also has details of subsequent endowments, casting light on the early Stracheys of Walden and the early history of the town.

Corporation Ordinances—Also in a vellum book, previously belonging to the Abbey (the first few pages are those of an illuminated book of hours), the ordinances date from the establishment of the corporation in 1549 and contain reference to members of the Strachey family within the town. They also reflect the general social background of sixteenth-century Walden.

Corporation Muniments—The original deeds relating to municipal and almshouse property are kept in a chest over the church porch, but they have been transcribed and indexed. A manuscript transcription is kept at the Town Hall and a typescript copy at the Saffron Walden Museum. It is the latter copy that has been referred to throughout. Of all the Saffron Walden records, these are of the greatest genealogical interest and abound in references to the Strachey family.

Memorandum of Accounts—An abstract of the earlier pages of the Treasurer's Account Book, compiled toward the end of the seventeenth century, it makes reference to one memorandum now missing, but contains nothing else that is not found in the other records. Kept at the Museum.

Treasurer's Account Book—A record of the annual statement of accounts presented by the retiring treasurer, it adds detail to the picture of early Walden. Dating from 1546, it gives the annual receipts and expenditures, first of the Guild of the Holy Trinity and then of the corporation. Kept at the Town Hall.

III Calendared Manuscripts and Printed Records

Other printed and edited records will be found in Section IV. Here an attempt has been made to list only records directly transcribed with a minimum of comment and editing.

1 *Calendared Manuscripts*

Acts of the Privy Council of England.

Calendar of the Carew Manuscripts, preserved in the Archepiscopal Library at Lambeth. (These deal with Irish affairs.)

Calendar of the Close Rolls preserved in the Public Record Office.

Calendar of the Patent Rolls preserved in the Public Record Office.

Calendar of the Patent and Close Rolls of Chancery in Ireland, of the reigns of Henry VIII, Edward VI, Mary and Elizabeth. Ed. J. Morrin. 2 vols. Dublin, 1861.

Calendar of the State Papers, relating to Ireland . . . preserved in the Public Record Office.

Calendar of State Papers, Domestic Series, . . . preserved in the State Paper Department of the Public Record Office.

Calendar of State Papers and Manuscripts, relating to English affairs, existing in the archives and collections of Venice, and in other libraries of Northern Italy.

Letters and Papers, Foreign and Domestic, of the Reign of Henry VIII, 1509–1547.

2 *Printed Records*

BENHAM, W. Gurney (ed.). The oath book or red parchment book of Colchester. Colchester, 1907.

BOWLER, Hugh (ed.). London sessions records, 1605–1685. (Catholic Record Society Publications.) London, 1934.

BURKE, A. M. (ed.). Memorials of St. Margaret's Church, Westminster; comprising the parish registers, 1539–1660, and the churchwardens' accounts, 1460–1603. London, 1914.

DREW, Charles (ed.). Lambeth churchwardens' accounts, 1504–1645, and vestry book, 1610. (Surrey Record Society, Vols. 40, 43, 44.) London, 1940–43.

FLETCHER, R. J. (ed.). The pension book of Gray's Inn, 1569–1800. 2 vols. London, 1901–10.

FOSTER, Joseph (ed.). The register of admission to Gray's Inn, 1521–1889. London, 1889.

GLENCROSS, Reginald M. Administrations in the Prerogative Court of Canterbury, 1559–1571. Exeter, 1912.

GOMME, G. L. (ed.). Court minutes of the Surrey and Kent Sewer Commission, 1569–79. London, 1909.

HARLEIAN SOCIETY, VISITATION SECTION

I: The visitation of London in the year 1568, taken by Robert Cooke, Clarenceux king of arms. Ed. J. J. Howard and G. J. Armytage. London, 1869.

V: The visitations of the county of Oxford, taken in the years 1566, 1574, and in 1634. Ed. W. H. Turner. London, 1871.

VIII: Le Neve's Pedigrees of the knights. Ed. G. W. Marshall. London, 1873.

XIII, XIV: The visitations of Essex, 1552, 1558, 1570, 1612 and 1634. London, 1878–9.

XV, XVII: The visitation of London, anno domini 1633, 1634, and 1635. Ed. J. J. Howard and J. L. Chester. London, 1880, 1883.

XXVIII, XXIX: The visitation of Shropshire, taken in the year 1623. Ed. G. Grazebrook and J. P. Rylands. London, 1889.

XLII: The visitation of Kent, taken in the years 1619–1621. Ed. R. Hovenden. London, 1898.

XLIII: The visitations of the county of Surrey, made and taken in the years 1530, . . . 1572, . . . and 1623. Ed. W. B. Bannerman. London, 1899.

LVI, LVII: The four visitations of Berkshire, made and taken 1532, 1566, 1623, and 1665–6. Ed. W. H. Rylands. London, 1907–8.

LXV: Middlesex pedigrees, as collected by Richard Mundy in Harleian MS no. 1551. Ed. G. J. Armitage. London, 1914.

HARLEIAN SOCIETY, REGISTER SECTION

I, IV: A register of all the christninges burialls, & Weddinges within the Parish of Saint Peeters vpon Cornhill. Ed. G. W. Leveson Gower. London, 1877, 1879.

XXXI: The registers of St. Helen's, Bishopsgate, London. Ed. W. B. Bannerman. London, 1904.

XLIII: The registers of All Hallows, Bread Street, and of St. John the Evangelist, Friday Street, London. Ed. W. B. Bannerman. London, 1913.

LXXV: The registers of St. Katharine by the Tower, London. Part I, 1584–1625. Ed. A. W. H. Clarke. London, 1945.

KINGSBURY, Susan Myra (ed.). The records of the Virginia Company of London. 4 vols. Washington, 1906–35.

LE HARDY, William (ed.). County of Middlesex; calendar to the sessions records. New Ser. 3 vols. London, 1935–37.

LINCOLN'S INN. The records of the Honorable Society of Lincoln's Inn. Admissions. 2 vols. London, 189C.

——. ——. The black books. 4 vols. London, 1897–1902.

MARTIN, C. T. (ed.). Middle Temple records; minutes of Parliament, 1501–1703. 4 vols. London, 1904–5.

METCALFE, Walter C. (ed.). The visitations of Suffolk, 1561, 1577, and 1612. Exeter, 1882.

MOULTON, H. R. Palaeography, genealogy and topography. London, 1930. (Sale catalogue).

NOBLE, T. C. (ed.). The names of those persons who subscribed towards the defence of this country at the time of the Spanish Armada, 1588, and the amounts each contributed. London, 1886.

REPORTS OF THE ROYAL COMMISSION ON HISTORICAL MANUSCRIPTS

VENN, John. Biographical history of Gonville and Caius College, 1349–1897. Vol. I, 1349–1713. Cambridge, 1897.

—— (ed.). The register of baptisms, marriages and burials in St. Michael's Parish, Cambridge, 1538–1837. Cambridge, 1891.

—— and VENN, J. A. Alumni Cantabrigieneses, a biographical list of all known students, graduates and holders of office at the University of Cambridge. Part I. From the earliest times to 1751. 4 vols. Cambridge, 1922–27.

IV Secondary Works

ABBOTT, G. F. Turkey, Greece and the great powers. London, 1916.

ACOSTA, José de. The naturall and morall historie of the East and West Indies. Trans. E[dward] G[rimston]. London, 1604.

——. ——. Ed. C. R. Markham. (Hakluyt Soc., Ser. I, Vols. 60–61.) London, 1879.

ANDREWS, Charles M. The colonial period of American history. 4 vols. New Haven, 1934–38.

ARBER, Edward (ed.). The first three books on America, being chiefly translations and compilations by Richard Eden, from the writings, maps, etc., of Pietro Martire, Sebastian Munster, and Sebastian Cabot. Birmingham, 1885.

Archaeologia; or, miscellaneous tracts relating to antiquity (Oxford) Published by the Society of Antiquaries of London. In progress.

Archaeologia Cantiana: transactions of the Kent Archaeological Society (London). In progress.

Atlantic monthly: a magazine of literature, science, art and politics (Boston). In progress.

AUGUSTINE, Saint, Bishop of Hippo. The works of Aurelius Augustine, Bishop of Hippo: a new translation. Ed .M. Dods. 15 vols. Edinburgh, 1872–1934.

BEAVEN, Alfred B. The aldermen of the city of London; temp. Henry III—1908. 2 vols. London, 1908–13.

BETHAM, William. The baronetage of England. 5 vols. London, 1801–5.

BIDDULPH, William. The travels of certaine Englishmen into Africa, Asia, . . . and sundry other places. Ed. Theoph. Lavender, B. L. London, 1609.

BIGGES, Walter. A summarie and true discourse of Sir Francis Drakes West Indian voyage. London, 1589.

BLANCH, William Harnett. Ye Parish of Camerwell, a brief account of the Parish of Camberwell, its history and antiquities. London, 1877.

Boemus, Johann. The fardle of facions. Conteining the aunciente maners, customes, and lawes, of the peoples enhabiting the two partes of the earth, called Affrike and Asie. Trans. William Watreman. London, 1555.

——. The manners, lawes, and customes of all nations. Collected out of the best writers by Joannes Boemus Aubanus, a Dutchman. Trans. Ed. Aston. London, 1611.

Boyd, Percival. Roll of the Drapers' Company of London. Croydon, 1934.

Braybrooke, Lord (Richard Griffin). The history of Audley End. To which are appended notices of the town and parish of Saffron Walden, in the county of Essex. London, 1836. (Contains transcripts of some of the town documents and an account of the Guild of the Holy Trinity.)

Brereton, John. A briefe and true relation of the discoverie of the north part of Virginia. London, 1602. (Reprinted in Burrage, *q.v.*)

Brown, Alexander. The genesis of the United States . . . 1605–1616 . . . set forth through a series of historical manuscripts now first printed, together with a reissue of rare contemporaneous tracts, accompanied by bibliographical memoranda, notes, and brief biographies. 2 vols. London, 1890. (Later works have supplemented this, but nothing has superseded it, nor is anything likely to.)

Burke, Sir Bernard, and Burke, Ashworth P. A genealogical and heraldic history of the peerage and baronetage, the Privy Council and knightage. London, 1931.

Burrage, Henry S. (ed.). Early English and French voyages, chiefly from Hakluyt, 1534–1608. (Original Narratives of Early American History Series.) New York, 1906. (Contains the accounts of Brereton, Rosier, and Davies, *q.v.*)

Camden, William. Britannia: or, a chorographical description of the flourishing kingdoms of England, Scotland, and Ireland. Trans. from the edition of 1607, and enlarged by Richard Gough. 4 vols. London, 1806.

CAMPBELL, Mildred. The English yeoman under Elizabeth and the early Stuarts. New Haven, 1942.

CASS, Frederick Charles. Monken Hadley. Westminster, 1880.

CAWLEY, Robert Ralston. "Shakspere's use of the voyagers in *The tempest*," *P.M.L.A.*, *XLI* (1926), 688–726.

CHAMBERS, E. K. The Elizabethan stage. 4 vols. Oxford, 1923.

——. William Shakespeare: a study of facts and problems. 2 vols. Oxford, 1930.

CHRISTY, Miller (ed.) The voyages of Captain Luke Foxe of Hull, and Captain Thomas James of Bristol, in search of a north-west passage. (Hakluyt Society, Ser. I, Vols. 88, 89.) London, 1894.

CLODE, Charles M. Memorials of the Guild of Merchant Taylors of the Fraternity of St. John the Baptist in the city of London; and of its associated charities and institutions. London, 1875.

——. The early history of the Guild of Merchant Taylors of the Fraternity of St. John the Baptist, with notices of the lives of some of its eminent members. 2 vols. London, 1888.

COGAN, Thomas. The haven of health, chiefly made for the comfort of students. London, 1589.

COKAYNE, G. E. Some account of the lord mayors and sheriffs of the city of London during the first quarter of the seventeenth century, 1601 to 1625. London, 1897.

COOKE, John. Greenes Tu-quoque; or, the city gallant. London, 1614. (Tudor Facsimile Texts; London, 1913.)

CORYATE, Thomas. Coryat's Crudities; reprinted from the edition of 1611, to which are now added his letters from India. 3 vols. London, 1776.

CRASHAW, William. A sermon preached before the Lord Lawarre, lord governour and captaine generall of Virginea and others of his maiesties counsell for that kingdome, and the rest of the adventurers in that plantation . . . Febr. 21. 1609. London, 1610.

CRAVEN, Wesley Frank. The southern colonies in the

seventeenth century, 1607-1689. Baton Rouge, 1949.

DALLAM, Thomas. The diary of Master Thomas Dallam, 1599–1600. Ed. J. T. Bent. (Hakluyt Society, Ser. I, Vol. 87, Early Voyages and Travels in the Levant.) London, 1893.

DALLINGTON, Sir Robert. The view of Fraunce. London, 1604. (Shakespeare Association Facsimile, No. 13; London, 1936.) See also MICHELL.

——. A method for travell. Shewed by taking the view of France. As it stoode in the yeare of our Lord 1598. London, 1605.

DAVIES, James. The relation of a voyage unto New-England. (MS in Lambeth Palace. Reprinted in Strachey; in *Proceedings* of the Massachusetts Historical Society, Vol. XVIII; and in Burrage.)

DAY, John. The ile of guls. (Shakespeare Association Facsimile, No. 12.) London, 1936.

DEE, John. The great volume of famous and rich discoveries. London, 1577.

DERING, Edward. XXVII lectures, or readings, upon part of the Epistle to the Hebrues. London, 1576.

DEVON, Frederick. Issues of the Exchequer; being payments made out of His Majesty's revenue during the reign of King James I. London, 1836.

Dictionary of American Biography. Ed. Allen Johnson. 21 vols. New York, 1928–37.

Dictionary of national biography. Ed. Sidney Lee. 22 vols. (Reprint.) London, 1908–9.

DRAKE, Henry H. Hasted's History of Kent, corrected, enlarged, and continued to the present time. Part I. The hundred of Blackheath. London, 1886. (Only one volume of this work was published.)

DRAYTON, Michael. The works of Michael Drayton. Ed. J. W. Hebel. 4 vols. Oxford, 1931–33.

——. ——. Ed. Kathleen Tillotson and B. H. Newdigate. Oxford, 1941.

EDEN, Richard. A treatyse of the newe India. London, 1553.

——. The decades of the newe worlde or West India,

conteyning the navigations and conquestes of the Span-
yardes. . . . Wrytten in the Latine toungue by Peter
Martyr of Angleria, and translated into Englysshe by
Rycharde Eden. London, 1555.

EPSTEIN, Mordecai. The English Levant Company: its
foundation and its history to 1640. London, 1908.

FENNOR, William. The counters commonwealth, or a voyage made to an infernal island. London, 1617. (Reprinted in Judges, *q.v.*)

FLEAY, Frederick Gard. A chronicle history of the London
stage, 1559–1642. London, 1890.

FORCE, Peter (ed.). Tracts and other papers relating
principally to the origin, settlement and progress of the
colonies in North America, from the discovery of the
country to the year 1776. 4 vols. Washington, 1836.

FOSTER, Joseph. Some feudal coats of arms from heraldic
rolls, 1298–1418. London, 1902.

FULLER, Thomas. The history of the worthies of England.
Ed. P. A. Nuttall. 3 vols. London, 1840.

GAYLEY, C. M. Shakespeare and the founders of liberty
in America. New York, 1917.

GÓMARA, Francisco López de. The pleasant historie of
the conquest of the Weast India. Trans. Thomas Nicholas. London, 1578.

GUICCIARDINI, Francesco. Aphorismes civil and militarie
. . . exemplified with historie, out of . . . Fr. Guicciardin.
Trans. Sir R. Dallington. London, 1613.

GUICCIARDINI, Lodovico. The garden of pleasure: . . .
done out of Italian into English by J. Sanforde. London, 1573.

———. Houres of recreation, or afterdinners . . . newly . . .
enlarged. Trans. J. Sanforde. London, 1576.

HAKLUYT, Richard. Divers voyages, touching the discoverie of America. London, 1582.

———. The principall navigations, voiages and discoveries
of the English nation . . . these 1500. yeeres. London,
1589.

———. The principal navigations, voiages, traffiques and
discoveries of the English nation . . . these 1600 yeres.

3 vols. London, 1598–1600. (Reprinted in 12 vols., MacLehose edition, Glasgow, 1903–5. This edition has been used and is referred to throughout.)

HARRIOT, Thomas. A briefe and true report of the new found land of Virginia: of the commodities there found and to be raysed, as well marchantable, as others for victuall, building and other necessary vses. London, 1588. (Reprinted in Hakluyt, 1589 and 1600 editions.)

HASTED, Edward. The history and topographical survey of the county of Kent . . . collected from public records and other authorities. 2d ed. 12 vols. Canterbury, 1797–1801.

HAWKINS, Sir John. A true declaration of the troublesome voyage of Mr John Hawkins to the partes of Guynea and the West Indies. London, 1569.

HOLDSWORTH, W. S. A history of English law. 3d ed. 12 vols. London, 1922–38.

HOLINSHED, Raphael. Holinshed's Chronicles of England, Scotland, and Ireland. 6 vols. London, 1807–8.

HOTSON, Leslie. I, William Shakespeare, do appoint Thomas Russell esquire. . . . London, 1937.

———. Shakespeare's sonnets dated and other essays. London, 1949.

HOWELL, T. B. A complete collection of state trials . . . from the earliest period to the year 1783. 21 vols. London, 1816. (Vol. II, published in London, 1816, covers the period 1603–27.)

JACOB, Giles. A new law-dictionary, containing the interpretation and definition of words and terms used in the law. 9th ed. London, 1772.

JAMES, Thomas. Catalogus librorum bibliothecae publicae quam . . . Thomas Bodleius Eques nuper instituit. Oxford, 1605.

———. Catalogus universalis librorum in Bibliotheca Bodleiana. Oxford, 1620.

JOHNSON, A. H. The history of the Worshipful Company of the Drapers of London. 5 vols. Oxford, 1914–22.

JONSON, Ben. Works. Ed. C. H. Herford and P. Simpson. 8 vols. Oxford, 1925–47.

———. Sejanus his fall. London, 1605. (Facsimile, ed. de Vocht; Louvain, 1935.)

JOURDAN, Silvester. A discovery of the Barmudas, otherwise called the Ile of Divels. London, 1610. (Scholars Facsimiles and Reprints; New York, 1940.)

JUDGE, Cyril Bathurst. Elizabethan book pirates. Cambridge, Mass., 1934.

JUDGES, A. V. The Elizabethan underworld. London, 1930.

KIRK, R. E. G., and KIRK, E. F. (ed.) Returns of aliens dwelling in the city and suburbs of London from the reign of Henry VIII to that of James I. (Huguenot Society Publications.) Aberdeen, Scotland, 1908.

LEACH, A. F. The schools of mediaeval England. London, 1915.

LYNAM, Edward (ed.). Richard Hakluyt and his successors. (Hakluyt Society, Ser. II, Vol. 93; London, 1946.)

MACHYN, Henry. The diary of Henry Machyn, citizen and merchant-taylor of London, from A.D. 1550 to A.D. 1563. Ed. J. G. Nichols for the Camden Society. London, 1848.

MCKERROW, R. B. (ed.). A dictionary of printers and booksellers in England, Scotland and Ireland, and of foreign printers of English books, 1557–1640. London, 1910.

MANNING, Owen, and BRAY, William. The history and antiquities of the county of Surrey. 3 vols. London, 1804–14.

MASSACHUSETTS HISTORICAL SOCIETY. Proceedings (Boston). In progress.

MERES, Francis. Palladis Tamia. London, 1598. (Scholars Facsimiles and Reprints, New York, 1938.)

MICHELL, Francis. The view of Fraunce. London, 1604. (Unique copy in the Cambridge University Library). See also DALLINGTON.

MIDDLETON, Thomas. Works. Ed. A. H. Bullen. 8 vols. London, 1885–86.

Modern language review (Cambridge). In progress.

MORANT, Philip. The history and antiquities of Essex. London, 1768.

NEALE, J. E. The Elizabethan House of Commons. London, 1949.

Notes and queries, for readers and writers, collectors and librarians (Oxford). In progress.

NOTESTEIN, W., RELF, F. H., and SIMPSON, H. (eds). Commons debates, 1621. 7 vols. New Haven, 1935.

Nouvelle biographie universelle depuis les temps les plus réculés jusqu'à nos jours. Ed. Hoeffer. 46 vols. Paris, 1852–77.

OSGOOD, Herbert L. The American colonies in the seventeenth century. 2 vols. New York, 1904.

OVERBURY, Sir Thomas. The miscellaneous works in prose and verse of Sir Thomas Overbury, Knt. Ed. E. F. Rimbault. London, 1856.

PARKS, George Brumer. Richard Hakluyt and the English voyages. New York, 1928.

PAULE, Sir George. The life of the most reverend and religious prelate, J. Whitgift, Lord Archbishop of Canterbury. London, 1612.

PECK, Francis. Desiderata curiosa; or, a collection of divers scarce and curious pieces relating chiefly to matters of English history. London, 1732–35.

PECKHAM, Sir George. A true reporte of the late discoveries . . . of the newfound landes. London, 1583.

PERCY, George. A trewe relatyon of the proceedings and occurrentes of momente which have happened in Virginia, from the tyme Sr. Thomas Gates was shippwrackte upon the Bermudes, ano. 1609, untill my departure outt of the country which was in ano. dni. 1612. (MS described in Sotheby, *q.v.*, and printed in *Tyler's Quarterly*, Vol. III [1921–22].)

P.M.L.A.: publications of the Modern Language Association of America (Menasha, Wis.). In progress.

PURCHAS, Samuel. Purchas his pilgrimage; or, relations of the world and the religions observed in all ages and places discovered, from the Creation unto this present. London, 1613.

———. Hakluytus posthumus; or, Purchas his pilgrimes. In five bookes. 4 vols. London, 1625. (Reprinted, in 20 vols., MacLehose edition, Glasgow, 1905–7. This edition has been used and referred to throughout.)

RALEIGH, Sir Walter. The discoverie of the large, rich and bewtiful empyre of Guiana. London, 1596.

Return of members of parliament. Part I: Parliaments of England, 1213–1702. 2 vols. London, 1888.

RIBAUT, Jean. The whole and true discovery of Terra Florida (englished the florishing lande . . .). Trans. T. Hackitt. London, 1563.

RICH, Robert. Newes from Virginia. The lost flocke triumphant. With the happy arriual of that famous and worthy knight, Sir Thomas Gates. London, 1610. (Scholars Facsimiles and Reprints; New York, 1936.)

ROSIER, James. A true relation of the most prosperous voyage made this present yeere 1605, by Captaine George Waymouth, in the discovery of the land of Virginia. London, 1605. (Reprinted in Burrage.)

ROYAL COMMISSION ON HISTORICAL MONUMENTS. An inventory of the historical monuments in Essex. Vol. I. North-west Essex. London, 1916.

SANDERS, Charles Richard. "William Strachey, the Virginia colony, and Shakespeare," *Va. Mag. Hist. Biog.*, LVII (1949), 115–32. (Treats the subject in superficial fashion and contains a number of errors of fact.)

SANDERSON, John. The travels of John Sanderson in the Levant, 1584–1602. Ed. Sir William Foster. (Hakluyt Society, Ser. II, Vol. 67; London, 1931.)

SCOTT, William Robert. The constitution and finance of English, Scottish and Irish joint-stock companies to 1720. 3 vols. Cambridge, 1910–12.

SHAKESPEARE, William. The plays and poems of William Shakspeare, with the corrections and illustrations of various commentators . . . by E. Malone. 21 vols. London, 1821.

———. The tempest. Ed. H. H. Furness. (A New Variorum Edition of Shakespeare.) London, 1892.

———. Twelfth night. Ed. H. H. Furness. (A New Variorum Edition of Shakespeare.) London, 1902.

SHAW, William A. The knights of England. 2 vols. London, 1906.

SIMPSON, Evelyn M. A study of the prose works of John Donne. Oxford, 1924.

SMITH, John. Travels and works of Captain John Smith, president of Virginia, and admiral of New England, 1580–1631. Ed. E. Arber and A. G. Bradley. 2 vols. Edinburgh, 1910. (This edition has been used and referred to throughout.)

SMITH, Logan Pearsall. The life and letters of Sir Henry Wotton. 2 vols. Oxford, 1907.

SMITH, Toulmin (ed.). English gilds. (Early English Text Society.) London, 1892.

SOTHEBY & Co. Catalogue of exceedingly rare and valuable Americana . . . largely from the library of Henry Percy, 9th Earl of Northumberland. April 23–24, 1928. [London, 1928.] (Sale catalogue; contains descriptions of the Percy MS of *The historie of travaile* and of Percy's *Trewe relatyon*.)

Statutes of the realm from original records and authentic manuscripts, The. 10 vols. London, 1810–28.

STITH, William. The history of the first discovery and settlement of Virginia. Williamsburg, 1747.

STOCK, Leo Francis (ed.). Proceedings and debates of the British Parliaments respecting North America. Vol. I, 1542–1688. Washington, 1924.

STRACHEY, John St. Loe. The adventure of living, a subjective autobiography. London, 1922.

STRYPE, John. The life of the learned Sir Thomas Smith, Kt., D.C.L. Oxford, 1820.

SUGDEN, Edward Holdsworth. A topographical dictionary to the works of Shakespeare and his fellow dramatists. Manchester, 1925.

Surrey archaeological collections, relating to the history and antiquities of the county (Guildford). In progress.

Sussex archaeological collections, relating to the history and antiquities of the county (Cambridge). In progress.

SYMONDS, William. Virginia: a sermon preached at Whitechapel in the presence of . . . the adventurers and planters for Virginia, April 25th, 1609. London, 1609.

Times literary supplement (London). In progress.

Transactions of the Essex Archaeological Society (Colchester, Eng.). In progress.

Tyler's quarterly historical and genealogical magazine (Richmond, Va.).

Victoria history of the county of Essex, The. Ed. W. Page and J. H. Round. 2 vols. London, 1907— .

Victoria history of the county of Surrey, The. 4 vols. London, 1902–14.

VIRGINIA COMPANY. A true and sincere declaration of the purpose and ends of the plantation begun in Virginia. London, 1610.

———. A true declaration of the estate of the colonie in Virginia. London, 1610.

Virginia magazine of history and biography (Richmond, Va.). In progress.

VIVIAN, Percival (ed.). Campion's works. Oxford, 1909.

WALLACE, Charles William. The Children of the Chapel at Blackfriars, 1597–1603. Lincoln, Neb., 1908.

———. The evolution of the English drama up to Shakespeare, with a history of the first Blackfriars theatre. Berlin, 1912.

WARNER, George F. Catalogue of the manuscripts and muniments of Alleyn's College of God's Gift at Dulwich. London, 1881.

WILLES, Richard. The history of travayle in the West and East Indies, and other countreys lying eyther way, towardes the fruitfull and rych Moluccaes. London, 1577.

William and Mary quarterly: a magazine of early American history (Williamsburg, Va.). In progress.

WINSOR, Justin (ed.). Narrative and critical history of America. Vol. III. English exploration and settlement in North America, 1497–1689. Cambridge, Mass., 1884.

WOOD, Alfred C. A history of the Levant Company. Oxford, 1935.

WRIGHT, Louis B. Middle-class culture in Elizabethan England. Chapel Hill, 1935.

YOUNG, W. The history of Dulwich College. 2 vols. London, 1889.

Index

WILLIAM STRACHEY, 1572–1621

was composed, printed, and bound by
Kingsport Press, Inc., Kingsport, Tennessee.
The paper is Warren's Olde Style,
and the type is Baskerville.
Design is by Edward Foss.

DATE DUE

12/1/06			